Parallel Programming in MPI and OpenMP

Victor Eijkhout

1st edition 2017

This book will be open source under CC-BY license.

Two of the most common software systems for parallel programming in scientific computing are MPI and OpenMP. They target different types of parallelism, and use very different constructs. Thus, by covering both of them in one book we can offer a treatment of parallelism that spans a large range of possible applications.

Contents

Contents

Contents

Contents

PART I

MPI

Chapter 1

Getting started with MPI

In this chapter you will learn the use of the main tool for distributed memory programming: the Message Passing Interface (MPI) library. The MPI library has about 250 routines, many of which you may never need. Since this is a textbook, not a reference manual, we will focus on the important concepts and give the important routines for each concept. What you learn here should be enough for most common purposes. You are advised to keep a reference document handy, in case there is a specialized routine, or to look up subtleties about the routines you use.

1.1   Distributed memory and message passing

In its simplest form, a distributed memory machine is a collection of single computers hooked up with network cables. In fact, this has a name: a *Beowulf cluster*. As you recognize from that setup, each processor can run an independent program, and has its own memory without direct access to other processors' memory. MPI is the magic that makes multiple instantiations of the same executable run so that they know about each other and can exchange data through the network.

One of the reasons that MPI is so successful as a tool for high performance on clusters is that it is very explicit: the programmer controls many details of the data motion between the processors. Consequently, a capable programmer can write very efficient code with MPI. Unfortunately, that programmer will have to spell things out in considerable detail. For this reason, people sometimes call MPI 'the assembly language of parallel programming'. If that sounds scary, be assured that things are not that bad. You can get started fairly quickly with MPI, using just the basics, and coming to the more sophisticated tools only when necessary.

Another reason that MPI was a big hit with programmers is that it does not ask you to learn a new language: it is a library that can be interface to C/C++ or Fortran; there are even bindings to Python. A related point is that it is easy to install: there are free implementations that you can download and install on any computer that has a Unix-like operating system, even if that is not a parallel machine.

1.2   History

Before the MPI standard was developed in 1993-4, there were many libraries for distributed memory computing, often proprietary to a vendor platform. MPI standardized the inter-process communication mechanisms. Other features, such as process management in *PVM*, or parallel I/O were omitted. Later versions of the standard have included many of these features.

Since MPI was designed by a large number of academic and commercial participants, it quickly became a standard. A few packages from the pre-MPI era, such as *Charmpp* [ ], are still in use since they support mechanisms that do not exist in MPI.

1.3 Basic model

Here we sketch the two most common scenarios for using MPI. In the first, the user is working on an interactive machine, which has network access to a number of hosts, typically a network of workstations; see figure 1.1. The user types the command `mpiexec`[1] and supplies

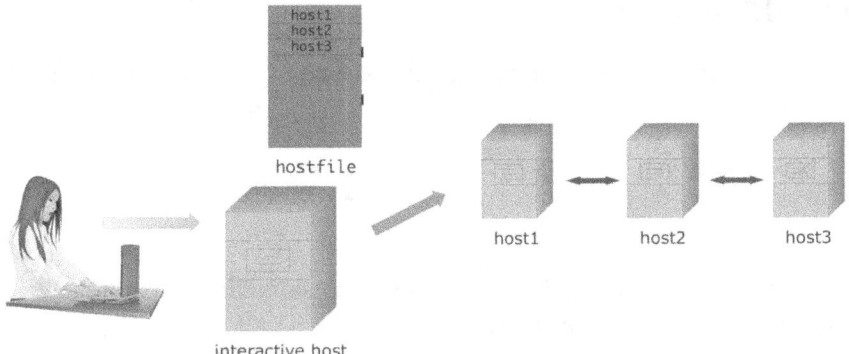

Figure 1.1: Interactive MPI setup

- The number of hosts involved,
- their names, possibly in a hostfile,
- and other parameters, such as whether to include the interactive host; followed by
- the name of the program and its parameters.

The `mpirun` program then makes an `ssh` connection to each of the hosts, giving them sufficient information that they can find each other. All the output of the processors is piped through the `mpirun` program, and appears on the interactive console.

In the second scenario (figure 1.2) the user prepares a *batch job* script with commands, and these will be run when the *batch scheduler* gives a number of hosts to the job. Now the batch script contains the `mpirun` command, and the hostfile is dynamically generated when the job starts. Since the job now runs at a time when the user may not be logged in, any screen output goes into an output file.

You see that in both scenarios the parallel program is started by the `mpirun` command using an Single Program Multiple Data (SPMD) mode of execution: all hosts execute the same program. It is possible for different hosts to execute different programs, but we will not consider that in this book.

---

1. A command variant is `mpirun`; your local cluster may have a different mechanism.

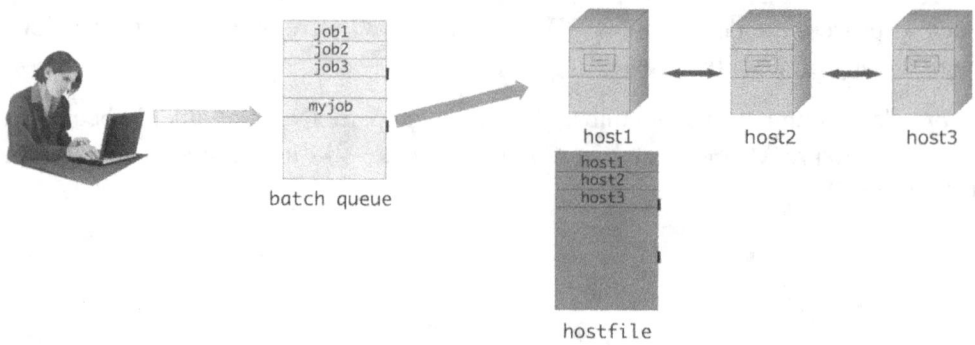

Figure 1.2: Batch MPI setup

1.4 Making and running an MPI program

MPI is a library, called from programs in ordinary programming languages such as C/C++ or Fortran. To compile such a program you use your regular compiler:

```
gcc -c my_mpi_prog.c -I/path/to/mpi.h
gcc -o my_mpi_prog my_mpi_prog.o -L/path/to/mpi -lmpich
```

However, MPI libraries may have different names between different architectures, making it hard to have a portable makefile. Therefore, MPI typically has shell scripts around your compiler call:

```
mpicc -c my_mpi_prog.c
mpicc -o my_mpi_prog my_mpi_prog.o
```

MPI programs can be run on many different architectures. Obviously it is your ambition (or at least your dream) to run your code on a cluster with a hundred thousand processors and a fast network. But maybe you only have a small cluster with plain *ethernet*. Or maybe you're sitting in a plane, with just your laptop. An MPI program can be run in all these circumstances – within the limits of your available memory of course.

The way this works is that you do not start your executable directly, but you use a program, typically called mpirun or something similar, which makes a connection to all available processors and starts a run of your executable there. So if you have a thousand nodes in your cluster, mpirun can start your program once on each, and if you only have your laptop it can start a few instances there. In the latter case you will of course not get great performance, but at least you can test your code for correctness.

> *Python note* Load the TACC-provided python:
> ```
> module load python
> ```
>
> and run it as:
> ```
> ibrun python-mpi yourprogram.py
> ```

1.5 Language bindings

1.5.1 C/C++

The MPI library is written in C. Thus, its bindings are the most natural for that language.

C++ bindings existed at one point, but they were declared deprecated, and have been officially removed in the *MPI 3* The *boost* library has its own version of MPI, but it seems not to be under further development. A recent effort at idiomatic C++ support is *MPL* `http://numbercrunch.de/blog/2015/08/ mpl-a-message-passing-library/`.

1.5.2 Fortran

The *Fortran bindings* for MPI look very much like the C ones, except that each routine has a final *error return* parameter.

> *Fortran note* Other Fortran-specific differences will be indicated with a note like this.

In the *MPI 3* standard, an MPI implementation providing a Fortran interface must provide a module named `mpi_f08` that can be used in a Fortran program. This defines MPI functions that return an integer result, rather than having a final parameter. It also defines proper interfaces, making type checking possible. For details see `http://mpi-forum.org/docs/mpi-3.1/mpi31-report/node409.htm`.

1.5.3 Python

The `mpi4py` package of *python bindings* is not defined by the MPI standards committee. Instead, it is the work of an individual, *Lisandro Dalcin*.

Notable about the Python bindings is that many communication routines exist in two variants:

- a version that can send native Python objects. These routines have lowercase names such as `bcast`; and
- a version that sends *numpy* objects; these routines have names such as `Bcast`. Their syntax can be slightly different.

The first version looks more 'pythonic', is easier to write, and can do things like sending python objects, but it is also decidedly less efficient since data is packed and unpacked with `pickle`. As a common sense guideline, use the `numpy` interface in the performance-critical parts of your code, and the native interface only for complicated actions in a setup phase.

Codes with `mpi4py` can be interfaced to other languages through Swig or conversion routines.

Data in `numpy` can be specified as a simple object, or `[data, (count,displ), datatype]`.

1.5.4 How to read routine prototypes

Throughout the MPI part of this book we will give the reference syntax of the routines. This typically comprises:

- The semantics: routine name and list of parameters and what they mean.

- C synxtax: the routine definition as it appears in the `mpi.h` file.
- Fortran syntax: routine definition with parameters, giving in/out specification.
- Python syntax: routine name, indicating to what class it applies, and parameter, indicating which ones are optional.

These 'routine prototypes' look like code but they are not! Here is how you translate them.

1.5.4.1   C

The typically C routine specification in MPI looks like:

```
int MPI_Comm_size(MPI_Comm comm,int *nprocs)
```

This means that

- The routine returns an `int` parameter. Strictly speaking you would use the routine as

  ```
  MPI_Comm comm = MPI_COMM_WORLD;
  int nprocs;
  int errorcode;
  errorcode = MPI_Comm_world( MPI_COMM_WORLD,&nprocs
  if (errorcode!=0) {
    printf("Routine MPI_Comm_world failed! code=%d\n",errorcode);
    return 1;
  }
  ```

  However, the error codes are hardly ever useful, and there is not much your program can do to recover from an error. Most people call the routine as

  ```
  MPI_Comm_world( /* parameter ... */ );
  ```

- The first argument is of type `MPI_Comm`. This is not a C built-in datatype, but it behaves like one. There are many of these `MPI_something` datatypes in MPI. So you can write:

  ```
  MPI_Comm my_comm = MPI_COMM_WORLD; // using a predefined value
  MPI_Comm_size( comm, /* remaining parameters */ );
  ```

- Finally, there is a 'star' parameter. This means that the routine wants an address, rather than a value. You would typically write:

  ```
  MPI_Comm my_comm = MPI_COMM_WORLD; // using a predefined value
  int nprocs;
  MPI_Comm_size( comm, &nprocs );
  ```

  Seeing a 'star' parameter usually means either: the routine has an array argument, or: the routine internally sets the value of a variable. The latter is the case here.

1.5.4.2   Fortran

The Fortran specification looks like:

```
MPI_Comm_size(comm, size, ierror)
INTEGER, INTENT(IN) :: comm
INTEGER, INTENT(OUT) :: size
INTEGER, OPTIONAL, INTENT(OUT) :: ierror
```

The syntax of using this routine is close to this specification: you write

```
integer :: comm = MPI_COMM_WORLD
integer :: size
CALL MPI_Comm_size( comm, size, ierr )
```

- Most Fortran routines have the same parameters as the corresponding C routine, except that they all have the error code as final parameter, instead of as a function result. As with C, you can ignore the value of that parameter. Just don't forget it.
- The types of the parameters are given in the specification.
- Where C routines have MPI_Comm and MPI_Request and such parameters, Fortran has INTEGER parameters, or sometimes arrays of integers.

1.5.4.2.1 **Python** The Python interface to MPI uses classes and objects. Thus, a specification like:

```
MPI.Comm.Send(self, buf, int dest, int tag=0)
```

should be parsed as follows.

- First of all, you need the MPI class:

  ```
  from mpi4py import MPI
  ```

- Next, you need a Comm object. Often you will use the predefined communicator

  ```
  comm = MPI.COMM_WORLD
  ```

- The keyword self indicates that the actual routine Send is a method of the Comm object, so you call:

  ```
  comm.Send( .... )
  ```

- Parameters that are listed by themselves, such as buf, as positional. Parameters that are listed with a type, such as int dest are keyword parameters. Keyword parameters that have a value specified, such as int tag=0 are optional, with the default value indicated. Thus, the typicall call for this routine is:

  ```
  comm.Send(sendbuf,dest=other)
  ```

  specifying the send buffer as positional parameter, the destination as keyword parameter, and using the default value for the optional tag.

Some python routines are 'class methods', and their specification lacks the self keyword. For instance:

```
MPI.Request.Waitall(type cls, requests, statuses=None)
```

would be used as

```
MPI.Request.Waitall(requests)
```

Chapter 2

MPI topic: Functional parallelism

2.1   The SPMD model

MPI programs conform[1] to the Single Program Multiple Data (SPMD) model, where each processor runs the same executable. This running executable we call a *process*.

When MPI was first written, 20 years ago, it was clear what a processor was: it was what was in a computer on someone's desk, or in a rack. If this computer was part of a networked cluster, you called it a *node*. So if you ran an MPI program, each node would have one MPI process; figure 2.1.

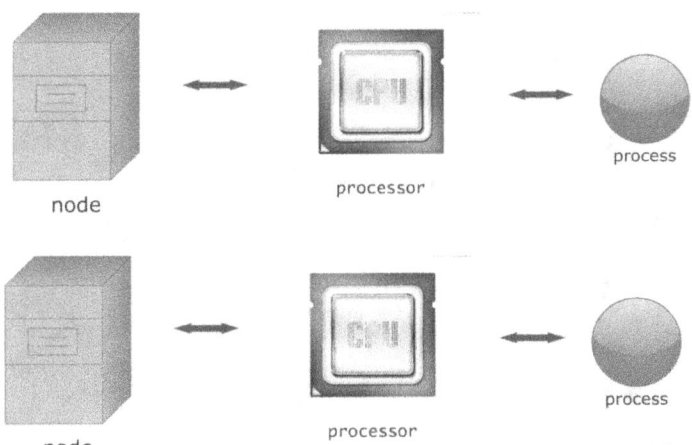

Figure 2.1: Cluster structure as of the mid 1990s

These days the situation is more complicated. You can still talk about a node in a cluster, but now a node can contain more than one processor chip (sometimes called a *socket*), and each processor chip probably has multiple *cores*. Figure 2.2 shows how you could explore this using a mix of MPI between the nodes, and a shared memory programming system on the nodes.

---

1.   Usually, but not necessarily.

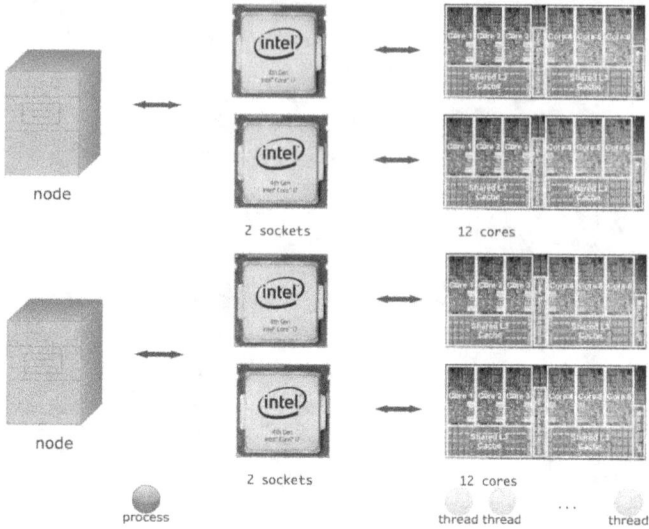

Figure 2.2: Hybrid cluster structure

However, since each core can act like an independent processor, you can also have multiple MPI processes per node. To MPI the cores look like the old completely separate processors. This is the 'pure MPI' model of figure 2.3 which we will use in most of this part of the book.

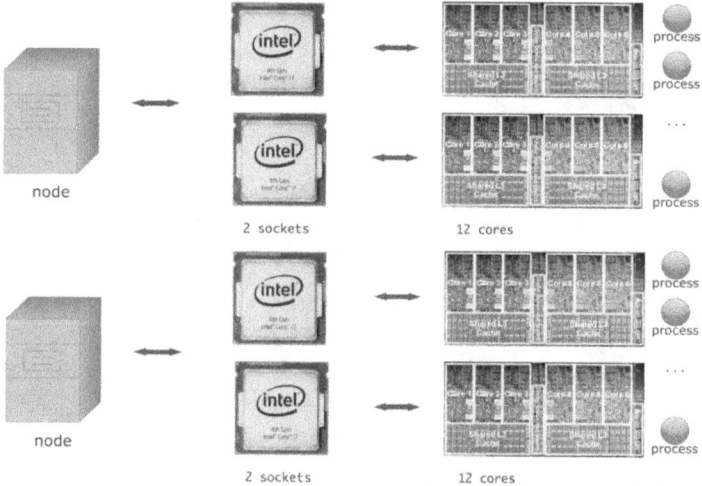

Figure 2.3: MPI-only cluster structure

This is somewhat confusing: the old processors needed MPI programming, because they were physically separated. The cores on a modern processor, on the other hand, share the same memory, and even some caches. In its basic mode MPI seems to ignore all of this: each core receives an MPI process and the programmer writes the same send/receive call no matter where the other process is located. In fact, you can't immediately see whether two cores are on the same node or different nodes. (Of course, on the implementation level MPI uses a different communication mechanism depending on whether cores are on the same socket, or on different nodes.)

2.2 Starting and running MPI processes

The SPMD model may be initially confusing. Even though there is only a single source, compiled into a single executable, the parallel run comprises a number of independently started MPI processes (see section 1.3 for the mechanism).

The following exercises are designed to give you an intuition for this one-source-many-processes setup. In the first exercise you will see that the mechanism for starting MPI programs starts up independent copies. There is nothing in the source that says 'and now you become parallel'.

The following exercise shows you that

Exercise 2.1.   Write a 'hello world' program, without any MPI in it, and run it in parallel with
`mpiexec` or your local equivalent.
Explain the output.

To get a useful MPI program you need at least the calls `MPI_Init` and `MPI_Finalize` surrounding your code. See section 2.2.2 for their syntax.

> *Python note* There are no initialize and finalize calls: the `import` statement performs the initialization.

This may look a bit like declaring 'this is the parallel part of a program', but that's not true: again, the whole code is executed multiple times in parallel.

Exercise 2.2.   Add the commands `MPI_Init` and `MPI_Finalize` to your code. Put three
different print statements in your code: one before the init, one between init and
finalize, and one after the finalize. Again explain the output.

In the following exercise you will print out the hostname of each MPI process; see section **??** for the syntax.

Exercise 2.3.   Now use the command `MPI_Get_processor_name` in between the init
and finalize statement, and print out on what processor your process runs. Confirm
that you are able to run a program that uses two different nodes.
(The character buffer needs to be allocated by you, it is not created by MPI, with size
at least `MPI_MAX_PROCESSOR_NAME`.)

2.2.1   Headers

If you use MPI commands in a program file, be sure to include the proper header file, *mpi.h* or *mpif.h*.

```
#include "mpi.h" // for C
#include "mpif.h" ! for Fortran
```

For *Fortran90*, many MPI installations also have an MPI module, so you can write

```
use mpi
```

The internals of these files can be different between MPI installations, so you can not compile one file against one `mpi.h` file and another file, even with the same compiler on the same machine, against a different MPI.

2.2.2   Initialization / finalization

Every MPI program has to start with *MPI initialization*:

```
C:
int MPI_Init(int *argc, char ***argv)

Fortran:
MPI_Init(ierror)
INTEGER, OPTIONAL, INTENT(OUT) :: ierror
```

How to read routine prototypes: 1.5.4.

where `argc` and `argv` are the arguments of a C language main program:

```
int main(int argc,char **argv) {
    ....
    return 0;
}
```

(It is allowed to pass `NULL` for these arguments.)

The commandline arguments `argc` and `argv` are only guaranteed to be passed to process zero, so the best way to pass commandline information is by a broadcast (section 3.2).

Note that the `MPI_Init` call is one of the few that differs between C and Fortran: the C routine takes the commandline arguments, which Fortran lacks.

If MPI is used in a library, MPI can have already been initialized in a main program. For this reason, one can test where `MPI_Init` has been called with

```
C:
int MPI_Initialized(int *flag)

Fortran:
MPI_Initialized(flag, ierror)
LOGICAL, INTENT(OUT) :: flag
INTEGER, OPTIONAL, INTENT(OUT) :: ierror
```

How to read routine prototypes: 1.5.4.

The regular way to conclude an MPI program is:

```
C:
int MPI_Finalize(void)
```

```
Fortran:
MPI_Finalize(ierror)
INTEGER, OPTIONAL, INTENT(OUT) :: ierror
```

How to read routine prototypes: 1.5.4.

but an abnormal end to a run can be forced by :

```
Synopsis:
int MPI_Abort(MPI_Comm comm, int errorcode)

Input Parameters
comm : communicator of tasks to abort
errorcode : error code to return to invoking environment

Python:
MPI.Comm.Abort(self, int errorcode=0)
```

How to read routine prototypes: 1.5.4.

This aborts execution on all processes associated with the communicator, but many implementations simply abort all processes. The `value` parameter is returned to the environment.

The corresponding Fortran calls are

```
call MPI_Init(ierr)
// your code
call MPI_Finalize(ierr)
```

You can test whether `MPI_Finalize` has been called with

```
C:
int MPI_Finalized( int *flag )

Fortran:
MPI_Finalized(flag, ierror)
LOGICAL, INTENT(OUT) :: flag
INTEGER, OPTIONAL, INTENT(OUT) :: ierror
```

How to read routine prototypes: 1.5.4.

2.2.3 Information about the run

Once MPI has been initialized, the `MPI_INFO_ENV` object contains:

- `command` Name of program executed.
- `argv` Space separated arguments to command.
- `maxprocs` Maximum number of MPI processes to start.
- `soft` Allowed values for number of processors.

- host Hostname.
- arch Architecture name.
- wdir Working directory of the MPI process.
- file Value is the name of a file in which additional information is specified.
- thread_level Requested level of thread support, if requested before the program started execution.

Note that these are the requested values; the running program can for instance have lower thread support.

2.2.4   Commandline arguments

The MPI_Init routines takes a reference to argc and argv for the following reason: the MPI_Init calls filters out the arguments to *mpirun* or *mpiexec*, thereby lowering the value of argc and eliminating some of the argv arguments.

On the other hand, the commandline arguments that are meant for mpiexec wind up in the MPI_INFO_ENV object as a set of key/value pairs.

2.3   Processor identification

Since all processes in an MPI job are instantiations of the same executable, you'd think that they all execute the exact same instructions, which would not be terribly useful. To distinguish between processors, MPI provides two calls

1. MPI_Comm_size reports how many processes there are in all; and
2. MPI_Comm_rank states what the number of the process is.

In other words, each process can find out 'I am process 5 out of a total of 20'.

```
Semantics:
MPI_COMM_SIZE(comm, size)
IN comm: communicator (handle)
OUT size: number of processes in the group of comm (integer)

C:
int MPI_Comm_size(MPI_Comm comm, int *size)

Fortran:
MPI_Comm_size(comm, size, ierror)
TYPE(MPI_Comm), INTENT(IN) :: comm
INTEGER, INTENT(OUT) :: size
INTEGER, OPTIONAL, INTENT(OUT) :: ierror

Python:
MPI.Comm.Get_size(self)
```

How to read routine prototypes: 1.5.4.

and

```
Semantics:
MPI_COMM_RANK(comm, rank)
IN comm: communicator (handle)
OUT rank: rank of the calling process in group of comm (integer)


C:
int MPI_Comm_rank(MPI_Comm comm, int *rank)


Fortran:
MPI_Comm_rank(comm, rank, ierror)
TYPE(MPI_Comm), INTENT(IN) :: comm
INTEGER, INTENT(OUT) :: rank
INTEGER, OPTIONAL, INTENT(OUT) :: ierror


Python:
MPI.Comm.Get_rank(self)
```

How to read routine prototypes: 1.5.4.

Exercise 2.4. Write a program where each process prints out message reporting its number, and how many processes there are.
Write a second version of this program, where each process opens a unique file and writes to it. *On some clusters this may not be advisable if you have large numbers of processors, since it can overload the file system.*

Exercise 2.5. Write a program where only the process with number zero reports on how many processes there are in total.

2.4   Functional parallelism

Being able to tell processes apart is already enough for some applications. Based on its rank, a processor can find its section of a search space. For instance, in *Monte Carlo codes* a large number of random samples is generated and some computation performed on each. (This particular example requires each MPI process to run an independent random number generator, which is not entirely trivial.)

Exercise 2.6. Is the number $N = 2,000,000,111$ prime? Let each process test a range of integers, and print out any factor they find. You don't have to test all integers $< N$: any factor is at most $\sqrt{N} \approx 45,200$.
(Hint: `i%0` probably gives a runtime error.)

As another example, in *Boolean satisfiability* problems a number of points in a search space needs to be evaluated. Knowing a process's rank is enough to let it generate its own portion of the search space. The computation of the *Mandelbrot set* can also be considered as a case of functional parallelism. However, the image that is constructed is data that needs to be kept on one processor, which breaks the symmetry of the decomposition.

Of course, at the end of a functionally parallel run you need to summarize the results, for instance printing out some total. The mechanisms for that you will learn next.

Chapter 3

MPI topic: Collectives

3.1   Working with global information

If all processes have individual data, for instance the result of a local computation, you may want to bring that information together, for instance to find the maximal computed value or the sum of all values. Conversely, sometimes one processor has information that needs to be shared with all. For this sort of operation, MPI has *collectives*.

There are various cases, illustrated in figure 3.1, which you can (sort of) motivated by considering some

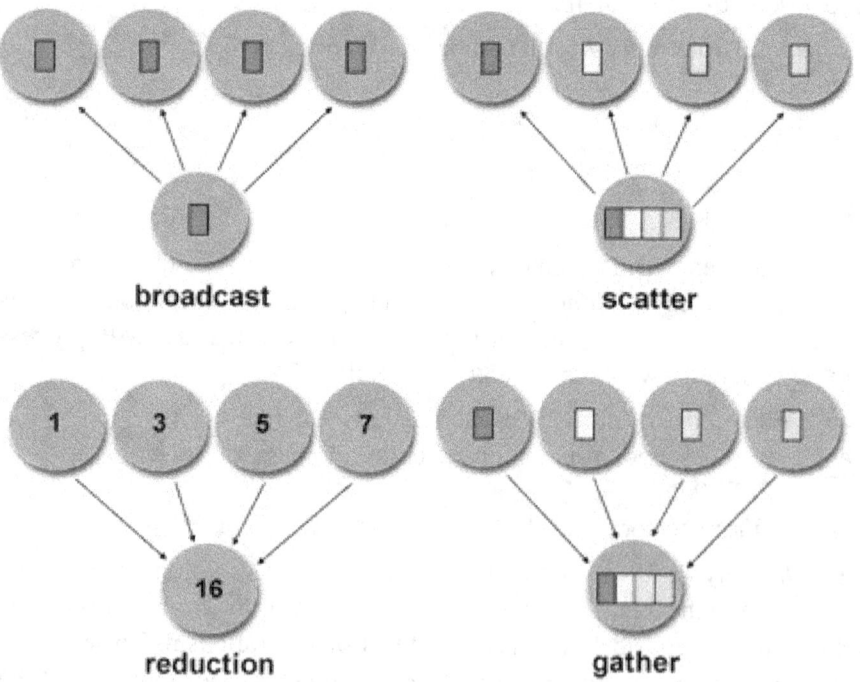

Figure 3.1: The four most common collectives

classroom activities:

- The teacher tells the class when the exam will be. This is a *broadcast*: the same item of information goes to everyone.
- After the exam, the teacher performs a *gather* operation to collect the invidivual exams.
- On the other hand, when the teacher computes the average grade, each student has an individual number, but these are now combined to compute a single number. This is a *reduction*.
- Now the teacher has a list of grades and gives each student their grade. This is a *scatter* operation, where one process has multiple data items, and gives a different one to all the other processes.

This story is a little different from what happens with MPI processes, because these are more symmetric; the process doing the reducing and broadcasting is no different from the others. Any process can function as the *root process* in such a collective.

Exercise 3.1.   How would you realize the following scenarios with MPI collectives?
- Let each process compute a random number. You want to print the maximum of these numbers to your screen.
- Each process computes a random number again. Now you want to scale these numbers by their maximum.
- Let each process compute a random number. You want to print on what processor the maximum value is computed.

3.1.1   Practical use of collectives

Collectives are quite common in scientific applications. For instance, if one process reads data from disc or the commandline, it can use a broadcast or a gather to get the information to other processes. Likewise, at the end of a program run, a gather or reduction can be used to collect summary information about the program run.

However, a more common scenario is that the result of a collective is needed on all processes.

Consider the computation of the *standard deviation*:

$$\sigma = \sqrt{\frac{1}{N}\sum_{i}^{N}(x_i - \mu)} \qquad \text{where} \qquad \mu = \frac{\sum_{i}^{N} x_i}{N}$$

and assume that every processor stores just one x_i value. The calculation of the average μ is a reduction, but then every process needs to compute $x_i - \mu$ for its value x_i. Thus μ is needed everywhere. You can compute this by doing a reduction followed by a broadcast, but it is better to use a so-called *allreduce* operation, which does the reduction and leaves the result on all processors.

For instance, if x, y are distributed vector objects, and you want to compute

$$y - (x^t y)x$$

which is part of the Gramm-Schmidt algorithm; see HPSC-12.2. Now you need the inner product value on all processors. You could do this by writing a reduction followed by a broadcast:

```
// compute local value
localvalue = innerproduct( x[ localpart], y[ localpart ] );
// compute inner product on the root
Reduce( localvalue, reducedvalue, root );
// send root value to all other from the root
Broadcast( reducedvalue, root );
```

or combine the last two steps in an allreduce, Surprisingly, an allreduce operation takes as long as a rooted reduction (see HPSC-6.1 for details), and therefore half the time of a reduction followed by a broadcast.

3.1.2   Collectives in MPI

Collectives are operations that involve all processes in a communicator. A collective is a single call, and it blocks on all processors. That does not mean that all processors exit the call at the same time: because of implementational details and network latency they need not be synchronized in their execution. However, semantically we can say that a process can not finish a collective until every other process has at least started the collective.

In addition to these collective operations, there are operations that are said to be 'collective on their communicator', but which do not involve data movement. Collective then means that all processors must call this routine; not to do so is an error that will manifest itself in 'hanging' code. One such example is MPI_Win_fence.

There are more collectives or variants on the above.

- If you want to gather or scatter information, but the contribution of each processor is of a different size, there are 'variable' collectives; they have a v in the name (section 3.5).
- Sometimes you want a reduction with partial results, where each processor computes the sum (or other operation) on the values of lower-numbered processors. For this, you use a *scan* collective (section 3.6).
- If every processor needs to broadcast to every other, you use an *all-to-all* operation (section 3.9).
- A barrier is an operation that makes all processes wait until every process has reached the barrier (section 3.9).

Thus, MPI has the following operations:

- MPI_Allreduce is equivalent to a MPI_Reduce followed by a broadcast.
- MPI_Allgather is equivalent to a MPI_Gather followed by a broadcast.
- MPI_Allgatherv is equivalent to an MPI_Gatherv followed by a broadcast.
- MPI_Alltoall, MPI_Alltoallv.

Finally, there are some advanced topics in collectives.

- Non-blocking collectives; section 3.8.
- User-defined reduction operators; section 3.3.2.

3.2   Rooted collectives: broadcast, reduce

One simple collective is the broadcast, where one process has some data that needs to be shared with all others. One scenario is that processor zero can parse the commandline arguments of the executable and send the values to all other processors. Another scenario is that you want one processor to read data from file and send it to the other processors: this is likely to be more efficient than having every process open the file.

The broadcast call has the following structure:

```
MPI_Bcast( data..., root , comm);
```

The root is the process that is sending its data. Typically, it will be the root of a broadcast tree. The `comm` argument is a communicator: for now you can use `MPI_COMM_WORLD`. Unlike with send/receive there is no message tag, because collectives are blocking, so you can have only one collective active at a time.

The data in a broadcast (or any other MPI operation for that matter) is specified as

- A buffer. In C this is the address in memory of the data. This means that you broadcast a single scalar as `MPI_Bcast( &value,  ...  )`, but an array as `MPI_Bcast( array,  ...  )`.
- The number of items and their datatype. The allowable datatypes are such things as `MPI_INT` and `MPI_FLOAT` for C, and `MPI_INTEGER` and `MPI_REAL` for Fortran, or more complicated types. See section 5 for details.

  Python note In python it is both possible to send objects, and to send more C-like buffers. The two possibilities correspond (see section 1.5.3) to different routine names; the buffers have to be created as `numpy` objects.

Example: in general we can not assume that all processes get the commandline arguments, so we broadcast them from process 0.

```
// init.c
if (procno==0) {
  if ( argc==1 || // the program is called without parameter
       ( argc>1 && !strcmp(argv[1],"-h") ) // user asked for help
       ) {
    printf("\nUsage: init [0-9]+\n");
    MPI_Abort(comm,1);
  }
  input_argument = atoi(argv[1]);
}
MPI_Bcast(&input_argument,1,MPI_INT,0,comm);

C:
int MPI_Bcast(
    void* buffer, int count, MPI_Datatype datatype,
    int root, MPI_Comm comm)

Fortran:
```

```
MPI_Bcast(buffer, count, datatype, root, comm, ierror)
TYPE(*), DIMENSION(..) :: buffer
INTEGER, INTENT(IN) :: count, root
TYPE(MPI_Datatype), INTENT(IN) :: datatype
TYPE(MPI_Comm), INTENT(IN) :: comm
INTEGER, OPTIONAL, INTENT(OUT) :: ierror

Python native:
rbuf = MPI.Comm.bcast(self, obj=None, int root=0)
Python numpy:
MPI.Comm.Bcast(self, buf, int root=0)
```

How to read routine prototypes: 1.5.4.

Exercise 3.2. If you give a commandline argument to a program, that argument is available as a character string as part of the `argv`, `argc` pair that you typically use as the arguments to your main program. You can use the function `atoi` to convert such a string to integer.

Write a program where process 0 looks for an integer on the commandline, and broadcasts it to the other processes. Initialize the buffer on all processes, and let all processes print out the broadcast number, just to check that you solved the problem correctly.

In python we illustrate the native and numpy variants. In the native variant the result is given as a function return; in the numpy variant the send buffer is reused.

```
// bcast.py
# first native
if procid==root:
    buffer = [ 5.0 ] * dsize
buffer = comm.bcast(obj=buffer,root=root)
if not reduce( lambda x,y:x and y,
               [ buffer[i]==5.0 for i in  range(len(buffer)) ] ):
    print "Something wrong on proc %d: native buffer <<%s>>" \
        % (procid,str(buffer))

# then with NumPy
buffer = np.arange(dsize, dtype=np.float64)
if procid==root:
    for i in range(dsize):
        buffer[i] = 5.0
comm.Bcast( buffer,root=root )
if not all( buffer==5.0 ):
    print "Something wrong on proc %d: numpy buffer <<%s>>" \
        % (procid,str(buffer))
```

Exercise 3.3. The *Gauss-Jordan algorithm* for solving a linear system with a matrix A (or computing its inverse) runs as follows:

for pivot $k = 1, \ldots, n$

    let the vector of scalings $\ell_i^{(k)} = A_{ik}/A_{kk}$

    for row $r \neq k$

        for column $c = 1, \ldots, n$

$$A_{rc} \leftarrow A_{rc} - \ell_r^{(k)} A_{rc}$$

where we ignore the update of the righthand side, or the formation of the inverse. Let a matrix be distributed with each process storing one column. Implement the Gauss-Jordan algorithm as a series of broadcasts: in iteration k process k computes and broadcasts the scaling vector $\{\ell_i^{(k)}\}_i$. Replicate the right-hand side on all processors.

Exercise 3.4.   Add partial pivoting to your implementation of Gauss-Jordan elimination. Change your implementation to let each processor store multiple columns, but still do one broadcast per column. Is there a way to have only one broadcast per processor?

3.3   Reduction

In the broadcast operation a single data item was communicated to all processes. Reduction operations go the other way: each process has a data item, and these are all brought together into a single item.

Here are the essential elements of a reduction operation:

```
MPI_Reduce( senddata, recvdata..., operator,
    root, comm );
```

- There is the original data, and the data resulting from the reduction. It is a design decision of MPI that it will not by default overwrite the original data. The send data and receive data are of the same size and type: if every processor has one real number, the reduced result is again one real number.
- There is a reduction operator. Popular choices are MPI_SUM, MPI_PROD and MPI_MAX, but complicated operators such as finding the location of the maximum value exist. You can also define your own operators; section **??**.
- There is a root process that receives the result of the reduction. Since the non-root processes do not receive the reduced data, they can actually leave the receive buffer undefined.

```
// reduce.c
float myrandom = (float) rand()/(float)RAND_MAX,
  result;
int target_proc = nprocs-1;
// add all the random variables together
MPI_Reduce(&myrandom,&result,1,MPI_FLOAT,MPI_SUM,
          target_proc,comm);
// the result should be approx nprocs/2:
if (procno==target_proc)
```

```
printf("Result %6.3f compared to nprocs/2=%5.2f\n",
       result,nprocs/2.);

C:
int MPI_Reduce(
    const void* sendbuf, void* recvbuf, int count, MPI_Datatype datatype,
    MPI_Op op, int root, MPI_Comm comm)

Fortran:
MPI_Reduce(sendbuf, recvbuf, count, datatype, op, root, comm, ierror)
TYPE(*), DIMENSION(..), INTENT(IN) :: sendbuf
TYPE(*), DIMENSION(..) :: recvbuf
INTEGER, INTENT(IN) :: count, root
TYPE(MPI_Datatype), INTENT(IN) :: datatype
TYPE(MPI_Op), INTENT(IN) :: op
TYPE(MPI_Comm), INTENT(IN) :: comm
INTEGER, OPTIONAL, INTENT(OUT) :: ierror

Python:
native:
comm.reduce(self, sendobj=None, recvobj=None, op=SUM, int root=0)
numpy:
comm.Reduce(self, sendbuf, recvbuf, Op op=SUM, int root=0)
```

How to read routine prototypes: 1.5.4.

Exercise 3.5. Write a program where each process computes a random number, and process 0 finds and prints the maximum generated value. Let each process print its value, just to check the correctness of your program.

Collective operations can also take an array argument, instead of just a scalar. In that case, the operation is applied pointwise to each location in the array.

Exercise 3.6. Create on each process an array of length 2 integers, and put the values 1, 2 in it on each process. Do a sum reduction on that array. Can you predict what the result should be? Code it. Was your prediction right?

3.3.1 Reduce in place

On the root, you need two buffers, which could be a significant memory demand in the case of a large array to be reduced. Therefore, you can specify `MPI_IN_PLACE` as the send buffer on the root. The reduction call then uses the value in the receive buffer as the root's contribution to the operation.

```
// reduceinplace.c
float mynumber,result,*sendbuf,*recvbuf;
mynumber = (float) procno;
int target_proc = nprocs-1;
// add all the random variables together
if (procno==target_proc) {
```

```
   sendbuf = (float*)MPI_IN_PLACE; recvbuf = &result;
   result = mynumber;
} else {
   sendbuf = &mynumber;     recvbuf = NULL;
}
MPI_Reduce(sendbuf,recvbuf,1,MPI_FLOAT,MPI_SUM,
           target_proc,comm);
// the result should be nprocs*(nprocs-1)/2:
if (procno==target_proc)
   printf("Result %6.3f compared to n(n-1)/2=%5.2f\n",
          result,nprocs*(nprocs-1)/2.);
```

In Fortran the code is less elegant because you can not do these address calculations:

```
// reduceinplace.F90
call random_number(mynumber)
target_proc = ntids-1;
! add all the random variables together
if (mytid.eq.target_proc) then
   result = mytid
   call MPI_Reduce(MPI_IN_PLACE,result,1,MPI_REAL,MPI_SUM,&
       target_proc,comm,err)
else
   mynumber = mytid
   call MPI_Reduce(mynumber,result,1,MPI_REAL,MPI_SUM,&
       target_proc,comm,err)
end if
! the result should be ntids*(ntids-1)/2:
if (mytid.eq.target_proc) then
   write(*,'("Result ",f5.2," compared to n(n-1)/2=",f5.2)') &
       result,ntids*(ntids-1)/2.
end if
```

3.3.2 Reduction operations

MPI type	meaning	applies to
MPI_MAX	maximum	integer, floating point
MPI_MIN	minimum	
MPI_SUM	sum	integer, floating point, complex, multilanguage types
MPI_PROD	product	
MPI_LAND	logical and	C integer, logical
MPI_LOR	logical or	
MPI_LXOR	logical xor	
MPI_BAND	bitwise and	integer, byte, multilanguage types
MPI_BOR	bitwise or	
MPI_BXOR	bitwise xor	
MPI_MAXLOC	max value and location	MPI_DOUBLE_INT and such
MPI_MINLOC	min value and location	

The MPI_MAXLOC operation yields both the maximum and the rank on which it occurs. However, to use it the input should be an array of real/int structs, where the int is the rank of the number.

For use in reductions and scans it is possible to define your own operator.

```
MPI_Op_create( MPI_User_function *func, int commute, MPI_Op *op);
```

3.3.3 Reduce to all

We started the explanation of reductions by giving the routine that had a root process. This makes sense if, at the end of a program run, one process needs to output some summary information. However, in many cases all processes need the result of the reduction. For example, if you want to scale a vector by its norm:

- the vector norm is the result of a reduction,
- but each process needs this value to scale its own part of the vector,
- which you could do with a broadcast operation.

This combination of reduction followed by broadcast happens often enough that there is a combined routine: MPI_Allreduce computes a reduction, but leaves the result on each process.

```
C:
int MPI_Allreduce(const void* sendbuf,
  void* recvbuf, int count, MPI_Datatype datatype,
  MPI_Op op, MPI_Comm comm)

Semantics:
IN sendbuf: starting address of send buffer (choice)
OUT recvbuf: starting address of receive buffer (choice)
IN count: number of elements in send buffer (non-negative integer)
IN datatype: data type of elements of send buffer (handle)
IN op: operation (handle)
IN comm: communicator (handle)
```

```
Fortran:
MPI_Allreduce(sendbuf, recvbuf, count, datatype, op, comm, ierror)
TYPE(*), DIMENSION(..), INTENT(IN) :: sendbuf
TYPE(*), DIMENSION(..) :: recvbuf
INTEGER, INTENT(IN) :: count
TYPE(MPI_Datatype), INTENT(IN) :: datatype
TYPE(MPI_Op), INTENT(IN) :: op
TYPE(MPI_Comm), INTENT(IN) :: comm
INTEGER, OPTIONAL, INTENT(OUT) :: ierror


Python native:
recvobj = MPI.Comm.allreduce(self, sendobj, op=SUM)
Python numpy:
MPI.Comm.Allreduce(self, sendbuf, recvbuf, Op op=SUM)
```

How to read routine prototypes: 1.5.4.

Example: we give each process a random number, and sum these numbers together. The result should be approximately $1/2$ times the number of processes.

```
// allreduce.c
float myrandom,sumrandom;
myrandom = (float) rand()/(float)RAND_MAX;
// add the random variables together
MPI_Allreduce(&myrandom,&sumrandom,
1,MPI_FLOAT,MPI_SUM,comm);
// the result should be approx nprocs/2:
if (procno==nprocs-1)
  printf("Result %6.9f compared to .5\n",sumrandom/nprocs);
```

For Python we illustrate both the native and the numpy variant. In the numpy variant we create an array for the receive buffer, even though only one element is used.

```
// allreduce.py
random_number = random.randint(1,nprocs*nprocs)
print "[%d] random=%d" % (procid,random_number)

max_random = comm.allreduce(random_number,op=MPI.MAX)
if procid==0:
    print "Python native:\n  max=%d" % max_random

myrandom = np.empty(1,dtype=np.int)
myrandom[0] = random_number
allrandom = np.empty(nprocs,dtype=np.int)

comm.Allreduce(myrandom,allrandom[:1],op=MPI.MAX)
```

Exercise 3.7. Let each process compute a random number, and compute the sum of these numbers using the MPI_Allreduce routine.
(The operator is MPI_SUM for C/Fortran, or MPI.SUM for Python.)
Each process then scales its value by this sum. Compute the sum of the scaled numbers and check that it is 1.

By default MPI will not overwrite the original data with the reduction result, but you can tell it to do so using the MPI_IN_PLACE specifier:

```
// allreduceinplace.c
int nrandoms = 500000;
float *myrandoms;
myrandoms = (float*) malloc(nrandoms*sizeof(float));
for (int irand=0; irand<nrandoms; irand++)
  myrandoms[irand] = (float) rand()/(float)RAND_MAX;
// add all the random variables together
MPI_Allreduce(MPI_IN_PLACE,myrandoms,
              nrandoms,MPI_FLOAT,MPI_SUM,comm);
// the result should be approx nprocs/2:
if (procno==nprocs-1) {
  float sum=0.;
  for (int i=0; i<nrandoms; i++) sum += myrandoms[i];
  sum /= nrandoms*nprocs;
  printf("Result %6.9f compared to .5\n",sum);
}
```

3.4   Rooted collectives: gather and scatter

In the MPI_Scatter operation, the root spreads information to all other processes. The difference with a broadcast is that it involves individual information from/to every process. Thus, the gather operation typically has an array of items, one coming from each sending process, and scatter has an array, with an individual item for each receiving process; see figure 3.2.

These gather and scatter collectives have a different parameter list from the broadcast/reduce. The broadcast/reduce involves the same amount of data on each process, so it was enough to have a buffer, datatype, and size. In the gather/scatter calls you have

- a large buffer on the root, with a datatype and size specification, and
- a smaller buffer on each process, with its own type and size specification.

Of course, since we're in SPMD mode, even non-root processes have the argument for the send buffer, but they ignore it. For instance:

```
int MPI_Scatter
    (void* sendbuf, int sendcount, MPI_Datatype sendtype,
```

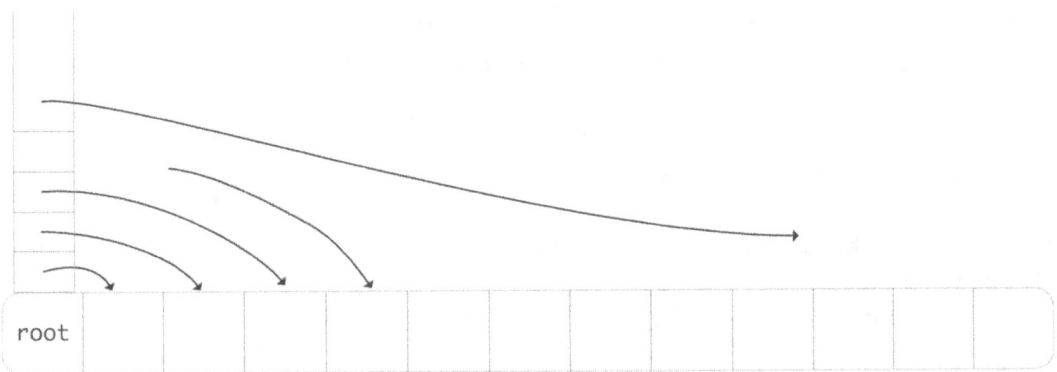

Figure 3.2: A scatter operation

```
void* recvbuf, int recvcount, MPI_Datatype recvtype,
int root, MPI_Comm comm)
```

The `sendcount` is not, as you might expect, the total length of the sendbuffer; instead, it is the amount of data sent to each process.

Exercise 3.8. Let each process compute a random number. You want to print the maximum value and on what processor it is computed. What collective(s) do you use? Write a short program.

3.4.1 Reference

In the gather and scatter calls, each processor has n elements of individual data. There is also a root processor that has an array of length np, where p is the number of processors. The gather call collects all this data from the processors to the root; the scatter call assumes that the information is initially on the root and it is spread to the individual processors.

The prototype for `MPI_Gather` has two 'count' parameters, one for the length of the individual send buffers, and one for the receive buffer. However, confusingly, the second parameter (which is only relevant on the root) does not indicate the total amount of information coming in, but rather the size of *each* contribution. Thus, the two count parameters will usually be the same (at least on the root); they can differ if you use different `MPI_Datatype` values for the sending and receiving processors.

```
int MPI_Gather(
  void *sendbuf, int sendcnt, MPI_Datatype sendtype,
  void *recvbuf, int recvcnt, MPI_Datatype recvtype,
  int root, MPI_Comm comm
);
```

Here is a small example:

```
// gather.c
```

```
// we assume that each process has a value "localsize"
// the root process collectes these values

if (procno==root)
  localsizes = (int*) malloc( (nprocs+1)*sizeof(int) );

// everyone contributes their info
MPI_Gather(&localsize,1,MPI_INT,
          localsizes,1,MPI_INT,root,comm);
```

This will also be the basis of a more elaborate example in section **??**.

The `MPI_IN_PLACE` option can be used for the send buffer on the root; the data for the root is then assumed to be already in the correct location in the receive buffer.

The `MPI_Scatter` operation is in some sense the inverse of the gather: the root process has an array of length np where p is the number of processors and n the number of elements each processor will receive.

```
int MPI_Scatter
   (void* sendbuf, int sendcount, MPI_Datatype sendtype,
    void* recvbuf, int recvcount, MPI_Datatype recvtype,
    int root, MPI_Comm comm)
```

3.4.2 Allgather

The `MPI_Allgather` routine does the same gather onto every process.

```
C:
int MPI_Allgather(const void *sendbuf, int  sendcount,
    MPI_Datatype sendtype, void *recvbuf, int recvcount,
    MPI_Datatype recvtype, MPI_Comm comm)
int MPI_Iallgather(const void *sendbuf, int  sendcount,
    MPI_Datatype sendtype, void *recvbuf, int recvcount,
    MPI_Datatype recvtype, MPI_Comm comm, MPI_Request *request)

Fortran:
MPI_ALLGATHER(SENDBUF, SENDCOUNT, SENDTYPE, RECVBUF, RECVCOUNT,
      RECVTYPE, COMM, IERROR)
   <type>    SENDBUF (*), RECVBUF (*)
   INTEGER   SENDCOUNT, SENDTYPE, RECVCOUNT, RECVTYPE, COMM,
   INTEGER   IERROR
MPI_IALLGATHER(SENDBUF, SENDCOUNT, SENDTYPE, RECVBUF, RECVCOUNT,
      RECVTYPE, COMM, REQUEST, IERROR)
   <type>    SENDBUF(*), RECVBUF (*)
   INTEGER   SENDCOUNT, SENDTYPE, RECVCOUNT, RECVTYPE, COMM
   INTEGER   REQUEST, IERROR
C++ Syntax
```

```
Parameters:
sendbuf : Starting address of send buffer (choice).
sendcount: Number of elements in send buffer (integer).
sendtype: Datatype of send buffer elements (handle).
recvbuf: Starting address of recv buffer (choice).
recvcount: Number of elements received from any process (integer).
recvtype: Datatype of receive buffer elements (handle).
comm; Communicator (handle).

recvbuf: Address of receive buffer (choice).
request: Request (handle, non-blocking only).
```

How to read routine prototypes: 1.5.4.

This routine is used in the *dense matrix-vector product* to give each processor the full input; see HPSC-6.2.2.

Some cases look like an all-gather but can be implemented more efficiently. Suppose you have two distributed vectors, and you want to create a new vector that contains those elements of the one that do not appear in the other. You could implement this by gathering the second vector on each processor, but this may be prohibitive in memory usage.

Exercise 3.9.   Can you think of another algorithm for taking the set difference of two distributed vectors. Hint: look up 'bucket-brigade algorithm' in [ ]. What is the time and space complexity of this algorithm? Can you think of other advantages beside a reduction in workspace?

3.5   Variable-size-input collectives

In the gather and scatter call above each processor received or sent an identical number of items. In many cases this is appropriate, but sometimes each processor wants or contributes an individual number of items.

Let's take the gather calls as an example. Assume that each processor does a local computation that produces a number of data elements, and this number is different for each processor (or at least not the same for all). In the regular MPI_Gather call the root processor had a buffer of size nP, where n is the number of elements produced on each processor, and P the number of processors. The contribution from processor p would go into locations $pn, \ldots, (p+1)n - 1$.

For the variable case, we first need to compute the total required buffer size. This can be done through a simple MPI_Reduce with MPI_SUM as reduction operator: the buffer size is $\sum_p n_p$ where n_p is the number of elements on processor p. But you can also postpone this calculation for a minute.

The next question is where the contributions of the processor will go into this buffer. For the contribution from processor p that is $\sum_{q<p} n_p, \ldots \sum_{q\leq p} n_p - 1$. To compute this, the root processor needs to have all the n_p numbers, and it can collect them with an MPI_Gather call.

We now have all the ingredients. All the processors specify a send buffer just as with MPI_Gather. However, the receive buffer specification on the root is more complicated. It now consists of:

```
outbuffer, array-of-outcounts, array-of-displacements, outtype
```

and you have just seen how to construct that information.

3.5.1   Reference

There are various calls where processors can have buffers of differing sizes.

- In `MPI_Scatterv` the root process has a different amount of data for each recipient.
- In `MPI_Gatherv`, conversely, each process contributes a different sized send buffer to the received result; `MPI_Allgatherv` does the same, but leaves its result on all processes; `MPI_Alltoallv` does a different variable-sized gather on each process.

```
int MPI_Scatterv
  (void* sendbuf, int *sendcounts, int *displs, MPI_Datatype sendtype,
   void* recvbuf, int recvcount, MPI_Datatype recvtype,
   int root, MPI_Comm comm)


C:
int MPI_Gatherv(
  const void* sendbuf, int sendcount, MPI_Datatype sendtype,
  void* recvbuf, const int recvcounts[], const int displs[],
  MPI_Datatype recvtype, int root, MPI_Comm comm)

Semantics:
IN sendbuf: starting address of send buffer (choice)
IN sendcount: number of elements in send buffer (non-negative integer)
IN sendtype: data type of send buffer elements (handle)
OUT recvbuf: address of receive buffer (choice, significant only at root)
IN recvcounts: non-negative integer array (of length group size) containing the
IN displs: integer array (of length group size). Entry i specifies the displace
IN recvtype: data type of recv buffer elements (significant only at root) (hand
IN root: rank of receiving process (integer)
IN comm: communicator (handle)

Fortran:
MPI_Gatherv(sendbuf, sendcount, sendtype, recvbuf, recvcounts, displs, recvtype
TYPE(*), DIMENSION(..), INTENT(IN) :: sendbuf
TYPE(*), DIMENSION(..) :: recvbuf
INTEGER, INTENT(IN) :: sendcount, recvcounts(*), displs(*), root
TYPE(MPI_Datatype), INTENT(IN) :: sendtype, recvtype
TYPE(MPI_Comm), INTENT(IN) :: comm
INTEGER, OPTIONAL, INTENT(OUT) :: ierror

Python:
Gatherv(self, sendbuf, [recvbuf,counts], int root=0)
```

How to read routine prototypes: 1.5.4.

```
int MPI_Allgatherv
   (void *sendbuf, int sendcount, MPI_Datatype sendtype,
    void *recvbuf, int *recvcounts, int *displs,
    MPI_Datatype recvtype, MPI_Comm comm)
```

MPI_Alltoallv.

```
int MPI_Alltoallv
   (void *sendbuf, int *sendcnts, int *sdispls, MPI_Datatype sendtype,
    void *recvbuf, int *recvcnts, int *rdispls, MPI_Datatype recvtype,
    MPI_Comm comm)
```

For example, in an MPI_Gatherv call each process has an individual number of items to contribute. To gather this, the root process needs to find these individual amounts with an MPI_Gather call, and locally construct the offsets array. Note how the offsets array has size ntids+1: the final offset value is automatically the total size of all incoming data.

```
// gatherv.c
// we assume that each process has an array "localdata"
// of size "localsize"

// the root process decides how much data will be coming:
// allocate arrays to contain size and offset information
if (procno==root) {
  localsizes = (int*) malloc( (nprocs+1)*sizeof(int) );
  offsets = (int*) malloc( nprocs*sizeof(int) );
}
// everyone contributes their info
MPI_Gather(&localsize,1,MPI_INT,
      localsizes,1,MPI_INT,root,comm);
// the root constructs the offsets array
if (procno==root) {
  offsets[0] = 0;
  for (int i=0; i<nprocs; i++)
    offsets[i+1] = offsets[i]+localsizes[i];
  alldata = (int*) malloc( offsets[nprocs]*sizeof(int) );
}
// everyone contributes their data
MPI_Gatherv(localdata,localsize,MPI_INT,
      alldata,localsizes,offsets,MPI_INT,root,comm);
```

3.5.2   Examples

3.5.2.1   `MPI_Gatherv`

`MPI_Gatherv`

Gather irregularly sized data onto a root. We first need an `MPI_Gather` to determine offsets.

```
// gatherv.c
// we assume that each process has an array "localdata"
// of size "localsize"

// the root process decides how much data will be coming:
// allocate arrays to contain size and offset information
if (procno==root) {
  localsizes = (int*) malloc( (nprocs+1)*sizeof(int) );
  offsets = (int*) malloc( nprocs*sizeof(int) );
}
// everyone contributes their info
MPI_Gather(&localsize,1,MPI_INT,
      localsizes,1,MPI_INT,root,comm);
// the root constructs the offsets array
if (procno==root) {
  offsets[0] = 0;
  for (int i=0; i<nprocs; i++)
    offsets[i+1] = offsets[i]+localsizes[i];
  alldata = (int*) malloc( offsets[nprocs]*sizeof(int) );
}
// everyone contributes their data
MPI_Gatherv(localdata,localsize,MPI_INT,
      alldata,localsizes,offsets,MPI_INT,root,comm);
```

```
// gatherv.py
# implicitly using root=0
globalsize = comm.reduce(localsize)
if procid==0:
    print "Global size=%d" % globalsize
collecteddata = np.empty(globalsize,dtype=np.int)
counts = comm.gather(localsize)
comm.Gatherv(localdata, [collecteddata, counts])
```

3.5.2.2   `MPI_Allgatherv`

`MPI_Allgatherv`

Prior to the actual gatherv call, we need to construct the count and displacement arrays. The easiest way is to use a reduction.

```
// allgatherv.c
MPI_Allgather
  ( &my_count,1,MPI_INT,
    recv_counts,1,MPI_INT, comm );
int accumulate = 0;
for (int i=0; i<nprocs; i++) {
  recv_displs[i] = accumulate; accumulate += recv_counts[i]; }
int *global_array = (int*) malloc(accumulate*sizeof(int));
MPI_Allgatherv
  ( my_array,procno+1,MPI_INT,
    global_array,recv_counts,recv_displs,MPI_INT, comm );
```

In python the receive buffer has to contain the counts and displacements arrays.

```
// allgatherv.py
my_count = np.empty(1,dtype=np.int)
my_count[0] = mycount
comm.Allgather( my_count,recv_counts )

accumulate = 0
for p in range(nprocs):
    recv_displs[p] = accumulate; accumulate += recv_counts[p]
global_array = np.empty(accumulate,dtype=np.float64)
comm.Allgatherv( my_array, [global_array,recv_counts,recv_displs,MPI.DOUBLE
```

3.6 Scan operations

The MPI_Scan operation also performs a reduction, but it keeps the partial results. That is, if processor i contains a number x_i, and $\oplus$ is an operator, then the scan operation leaves $x_0 \oplus \cdots \oplus x_i$ on processor i. This type of operation is often called a *prefix operation*; see HPSC-18.

The MPI_Scan routine is an *inclusive scan* operation.

```
C:
int MPI_Scan(const void* sendbuf, void* recvbuf,
    int count, MPI_Datatype datatype, MPI_Op op, MPI_Comm comm)
IN sendbuf: starting address of send buffer (choice)
OUT recvbuf: starting address of receive buffer (choice)
IN count: number of elements in input buffer (non-negative integer)
IN datatype: data type of elements of input buffer (handle)
IN op: operation (handle)
IN comm: communicator (handle)
```

```
Fortran:
MPI_Scan(sendbuf, recvbuf, count, datatype, op, comm, ierror)
TYPE(*), DIMENSION(..), INTENT(IN) :: sendbuf
TYPE(*), DIMENSION(..) :: recvbuf
INTEGER, INTENT(IN) :: count
TYPE(MPI_Datatype), INTENT(IN) :: datatype
TYPE(MPI_Op), INTENT(IN) :: op
TYPE(MPI_Comm), INTENT(IN) :: comm
INTEGER, OPTIONAL, INTENT(OUT) :: ierror

Python:
res = Intracomm.scan( sendobj=None,recvobj=None,op=MPI.SUM)
res = Intracomm.exscan( sendobj=None,recvobj=None,op=MPI.SUM)
```

How to read routine prototypes: 1.5.4.

The `MPI_Op` operations do not return an error code.

In python native mode the result is a function return value.

```
// scan.py
mycontrib = 10+random.randint(1,nprocs)
myfirst = 0
mypartial = comm.scan(mycontrib)
sbuf = np.empty(1,dtype=np.int)
rbuf = np.empty(1,dtype=np.int)
sbuf[0] = mycontrib
comm.Scan(sbuf,rbuf)
```

3.6.1 Exclusive scan

Often, the more useful variant is the *exclusive scan*

```
C:
int MPI_Exscan(const void *sendbuf, void *recvbuf, int count,
    MPI_Datatype datatype, MPI_Op op, MPI_Comm comm)
int MPI_Iexscan(const void *sendbuf, void *recvbuf, int count,
    MPI_Datatype datatype, MPI_Op op, MPI_Comm comm,
    MPI_Request *request)

Fortran:

MPI_EXSCAN(SENDBUF, RECVBUF, COUNT, DATATYPE, OP, COMM, IERROR)
    <type>    SENDBUF(*), RECVBUF(*)
    INTEGER    COUNT, DATATYPE, OP, COMM, IERROR
MPI_IEXSCAN(SENDBUF, RECVBUF, COUNT, DATATYPE, OP, COMM, REQUEST, IERROR)
    <type>    SENDBUF(*), RECVBUF(*)
    INTEGER    COUNT, DATATYPE, OP, COMM, REQUEST, IERROR
```

```
Input Parameters

sendbuf: Send buffer (choice).
count: Number of elements in input buffer (integer).
datatype: Data type of elements of input buffer (handle).
op: Operation (handle).
comm: Communicator (handle).

Output Parameters

recvbuf: Receive buffer (choice).
request: Request (handle, non-blocking only).
```

How to read routine prototypes: 1.5.4.

with the same prototype.

The result of the exclusive scan is undefined on processor 0 (None in python), and on processor 1 it is a copy of the send value of processor 1. In particular, the MPI_Op need not be called on these two processors.

Exercise 3.10. The exclusive definition, which computes $x_0 \oplus x_{i-1}$ on processor i, can easily be derived from the inclusive operation for operations such as MPI_PLUS or MPI_MULT. Are there operators where that is not the case?

3.6.2 Use of scan operations

The MPI_Scan operation is often useful with indexing data. Suppose that every processor p has a local vector where the number of elements n_p is dynamically determined. In order to translate the local numbering $0 \ldots n_p - 1$ to a global numbering one does a scan with the number of local elements as input. The output is then the global number of the first local variable.

Exercise 3.11. Do you use MPI_Scan or MPI_Exscan for this operation? How would you describe the result of the other scan operation, given the same input?

Exclusive scan examples:

```
// exscan.c
int my_first=0,localsize;
// localsize = ..... result of local computation ....
// find myfirst location based on the local sizes
err = MPI_Exscan(&localsize,&my_first,
            1,MPI_INT,MPI_SUM,comm); CHK(err);


// exscan.py
localsize = 10+random.randint(1,nprocs)
myfirst = 0
mypartial = comm.exscan(localsize,0)
```

It is possible to do a *segmented scan*. Let x_i be a series of numbers that we want to sum to X_i as follows. Let y_i be a series of booleans such that

$$\begin{cases} X_i = x_i & \text{if } y_i = 0 \\ X_i = X_{i-1} + x_i & \text{if } y_i = 1 \end{cases}$$

(This is the basis for the implementation of the *sparse matrix vector product* as prefix operation; see HPSC-18.2.) This means that X_i sums the segments between locations where $y_i = 0$ and the first subsequent place where $y_i = 1$. To implement this, you need a user-defined operator

$$\begin{pmatrix} X \\ x \\ y \end{pmatrix} = \begin{pmatrix} X_1 \\ x_1 \\ y_1 \end{pmatrix} \bigoplus \begin{pmatrix} X_2 \\ x_2 \\ y_2 \end{pmatrix} : \begin{cases} X = x_1 + x_2 & \text{if } y_2 == 1 \\ X = x_2 & \text{if } y_2 == 0 \end{cases}$$

This operator is not communitative, and it needs to be declared as such with `MPI_Op_create`; see section **??**.

3.7 MPI Operators

3.7.1 Pre-defined operators

See the list in section 13.2.

3.7.2 User-defined operators

In addition to predefined operators, the user can define new operators to use in a reduction or scan operation.

```
Semantics:
MPI_OP_CREATE( function, commute, op)
[ IN function] user defined function (function)
[ IN commute] true if commutative; false otherwise.
[ OUT op] operation (handle)

C:
int MPI_Op_create(MPI_User_function *function, int commute,
    MPI_Op *op)

Fortran:
MPI_OP_CREATE( FUNCTION, COMMUTE, OP, IERROR)
EXTERNAL FUNCTION
LOGICAL COMMUTE
INTEGER OP, IERROR
```

How to read routine prototypes: 1.5.4.

The function needs to have the following prototype:

```
typedef void MPI_User_function
    ( void *invec, void *inoutvec, int *len,
      MPI_Datatype *datatype);

FUNCTION USER_FUNCTION( INVEC(*), INOUTVEC(*), LEN, TYPE)
<type> INVEC(LEN), INOUTVEC(LEN)
INTEGER LEN, TYPE
```

The function has an array length argument `len`, to allow for pointwise reduction on a a whole array at once. The `inoutvec` array contains partially reduced results, and is typically overwritten by the function.

You can query the commutativity of an operator:

```
Semantics:
MPI_Op_commutative(op, commute)
IN  op : handle
OUT commute : true/false

C:
int MPI_Op_commutative(MPI_Op op, int *commute)

Fortran:
MPI_OP_COMMUTATIVE( op, commute)
TYPE(MPI_Op), INTENT(IN) :: op
LOGICAL, INTENT(OUT) ::  commute
INTEGER, OPTIONAL, INTENT(OUT) ::  ierror
```

How to read routine prototypes: 1.5.4.

A created `MPI_Op` can be freed again:

```
int MPI_Op_free(MPI_Op *op)
```

This sets the operator to `MPI_OP_NULL`.

3.8   Non-blocking collectives

Above you have seen how the 'Isend' and 'Irecv' routines can overlap communication with computation. This is not possible with the collectives you have seen so far: they act like blocking sends or receives. However, there are also *non-blocking collectives*. These have roughly the same calling sequence as their blocking counterparts, except that they output an `MPI_Request`. You can then use an `MPI_Wait` call to make sure the collective has completed.

Such operations can be used to increase efficiency. For instance, computing

$$y \leftarrow Ax + (x^t x)y$$

involves a matrix-vector product, which is dominated by computation in the *sparse matrix* case, and an inner product which is typically dominated by the communication cost. You would code this as

```
MPI_Iallreduce( .... x ..., &request);
// compute the matrix vector product
MPI_Wait(request);
// do the addition
```

This can also be used for 3D FFT operations [ ]. Occasionally, a non-blocking collective can be used for non-obvious purposes, such as the `MPI_Ibarrier` in [ ].

The same calling sequence as the blocking counterpart, except for the addition of an `MPI_Request` parameter. For instance `MPI_Ibcast`:

```
int MPI_Ibcast(
  void *buffer, int count, MPI_Datatype datatype,
  int root, MPI_Comm comm,
  MPI_Request *request)


Semantics

int MPI_Allreduce(
    const void *sendbuf, void *recvbuf,
    int count, MPI_Datatype datatype, MPI_Op op, MPI_Comm comm,
    MPI_Request *request)


Input Parameters

sendbuf : starting address of send buffer (choice)
count : number of elements in send buffer (integer)
datatype : data type of elements of send buffer (handle)
op : operation (handle)
comm : communicator (handle)


Output Parameters

recvbuf : starting address of receive buffer (choice)
request : communication request (handle)
```

How to read routine prototypes: 1.5.4.

```
Semantics

int MPI_Allgather(
    const void *sendbuf, int sendcount, MPI_Datatype sendtype,
    void *recvbuf, int recvcount, MPI_Datatype recvtype,
    MPI_Comm comm, MPI_Request *request)


Input Parameters

sendbuf : starting address of send buffer (choice)
sendcount : number of elements in send buffer (integer)
```

```
sendtype : data type of send buffer elements (handle)
recvcount : number of elements received from any process (integer)
recvtype : data type of receive buffer elements (handle)
comm : communicator (handle)

Output Parameters

recvbuf : address of receive buffer (choice)
request : communication request (handle)
```

How to read routine prototypes: 1.5.4.

3.9   Barrier and all-to-all

There are two collectives we have not mentioned yet. A barrier is a call that blocks all processes until they have all reached the barrier call. This call's simplicity is contrasted with its usefulness, which is very limited. It is almost never necessary to synchronize processes through a barrier: for most purposes it does not matter if processors are out of sync. Conversely, collectives (except the new non-blocking ones) introduce a barrier of sorts themselves.

The all-to-all call is a generalization of a scatter and gather: every process is scattering an array of data, and every process is gathering an array of data. There is also a 'v' variant of this routine.

MPI_Alltoall

```
int MPI_Alltoall
    (void *sendbuf, int sendcount, MPI_Datatype sendtype,
     void *recvbuf, int recvcount, MPI_Datatype recvtype,
     MPI_Comm comm)
```

3.10   Reduce-scatter

There are several MPI collectives that are functionally equivalent to a combination of others. You have already seen MPI_Allreduce which is equivalent to a reduction followed by a broadcast. Often such combinations can be more efficient than using the individual calls; see HPSC-6.1.

Here is another example: MPI_Reduce_scatter is equivalent to a reduction on an array of data (meaning a pointwise reduction on each array location) followed by a scatter of this array to the individual processes.

One important example of this command is the *sparse matrix-vector product*; see HPSC-6.5.1 for background information. Each process contains one or more matrix rows, so by looking at indices the process can decide what other processes it needs data from. The problem is for a process to find out what other processes it needs to send data to.

Using MPI_Reduce_scatter the process goes as follows:

- Each process creates an array of ones and zeros, describing who it needs data from.
- The reduce part of the reduce-scatter yields an array of requester counts; after the scatter each process knows how many processes request data from it.
- Next, the sender processes need to find out what elements are requested from it. For this, each process sends out arrays of indices.
- The big trick is that each process now knows how many of these requests will be coming in, so it can post precisely that many MPI_Irecv calls, with a source of MPI_ANY_SOURCE.

The MPI_Reduce_scatter command is equivalent to a reduction on an array of data, followed by a scatter of that data to the individual processes.

To be precise, there is an array recvcounts where recvcounts[i] gives the number of elements that ultimate wind up on process i. The result is equivalent to doing a reduction with a length equal to the sum of the recvcounts[i] values, followed by a scatter where process i receives recvcounts[i] values. (Since the amount of data to be scattered depends on the process, this is in fact equivalent to MPI_Scatterv rather than a regular scatter.)

```
Semantics:
MPI_REDUCE_SCATTER( sendbuf, recvbuf, recvcounts, datatype, op, comm)
IN sendbuf: starting address of send buffer (choice)
OUT recvbuf: starting address of receive buffer (choice)
IN recvcounts: non-negative integer array (of length group size)
    specifying the number of elements of the result distributed to each
    process.
IN datatype: data type of elements of send and receive buffers (handle)
IN op: operation (handle)
IN comm: communicator (handle)

C:
int MPI_Reduce_scatter(const void* sendbuf, void* recvbuf, const int
recvcounts[], MPI_Datatype datatype, MPI_Op op, MPI_Comm comm)

F:
MPI_Reduce_scatter(sendbuf, recvbuf, recvcounts, datatype, op, comm,
ierror)
TYPE(*), DIMENSION(..), INTENT(IN) :: sendbuf
TYPE(*), DIMENSION(..) :: recvbuf
INTEGER, INTENT(IN) :: recvcounts(*)
TYPE(MPI_Datatype), INTENT(IN) :: datatype
TYPE(MPI_Op), INTENT(IN) :: op
TYPE(MPI_Comm), INTENT(IN) :: comm
INTEGER, OPTIONAL, INTENT(OUT) :: ierror

Py:
comm.Reduce_scatter(sendbuf, recvbuf, recvcounts=None, Op op=SUM)
```

How to read routine prototypes: 1.5.4.

For instance, if all recvcounts[i] values are 1, the sendbuffer has one element for each process, and the receive buffer has length 1.

3.10.1 Examples

An important application of this is establishing an irregular communication pattern. Assume that each process knows which other processes it wants to communicate with; the problem is to let the other processes know about this. The solution is to use `MPI_Reduce_scatter` to find out how many processes want to communicate with you, and then wait for precisely that many messages with a source value of `MPI_ANY_SOURCE`.

```
// reducescatter.c
// record what processes you will communicate with
int *recv_requests;
// find how many procs want to communicate with you
MPI_Reduce_scatter
   (recv_requests,&nsend_requests,counts,MPI_INT,
    MPI_SUM,comm);
// send a msg to the selected processes
for (int i=0; i<nprocs; i++)
   if (recv_requests[i]>0)
      MPI_Isend(&msg,1,MPI_INT, /*to:*/ i,0,comm,
         mpi_requests+irequest++);
// do as many receives as you know are coming in
for (int i=0; i<nsend_requests; i++)
   MPI_Irecv(&msg,1,MPI_INT,MPI_ANY_SOURCE,MPI_ANY_TAG,comm,
      mpi_requests+irequest++);
MPI_Waitall(irequest,mpi_requests,MPI_STATUSES_IGNORE);
```

Use of `MPI_Reduce_scatter` to implement the two-dimensional matrix-vector product. Set up separate row and column communicators with `MPI_Comm_split`, use `MPI_Reduce_scatter` to combine local products.

```
MPI_Allgather(&my_x,1,MPI_DOUBLE,
   local_x,1,MPI_DOUBLE,environ.col_comm);
// bli_dgemv( BLIS_NO_TRANSPOSE,
//            BLIS_NO_CONJUGATE,
//              size_y, size_x,
//          &one,
//              local_matrix, 1, size_y,
//          local_x, 1,
//          &zero,
//          local_y, 1 );
// blas_dgemv(CblasColMajor,CblasNoTrans,
//   size_y,size_x,1.e0,
//   local_matrix,size_y,
//   local_x,1,0.e0,local_y,1);
MPI_Reduce_scatter(local_y,&my_y,&ione,MPI_DOUBLE,
```

```
MPI_SUM,environ.row_comm);
```

3.11   Performance of collectives

It is easy to visualize a broadcast as in figure 3.3: see figure 3.3. the root sends all of its data directly to

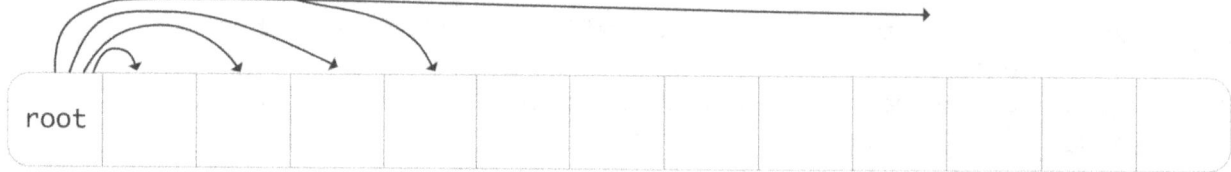

Figure 3.3: A simple broadcast

every other process. While this describes the semantics of the operation, in practice the implementation works quite differently.

The time that a message takes can simply be modeled as

$$\alpha + \beta n,$$

where α is the *latency*, a one time delay from establishing the communication between two processes, and β is the time-per-byte, or the inverse of the *bandwidth*, and n the number of bytes sent.

Under the assumption that a processor can only send one message at a time, the broadcast in figure 3.3 would take a time proportional to the number of processors. One way to ameliorate that is to structure the broadcast in a tree-like fashion. This is depicted in figure 3.4. How does the communication time now

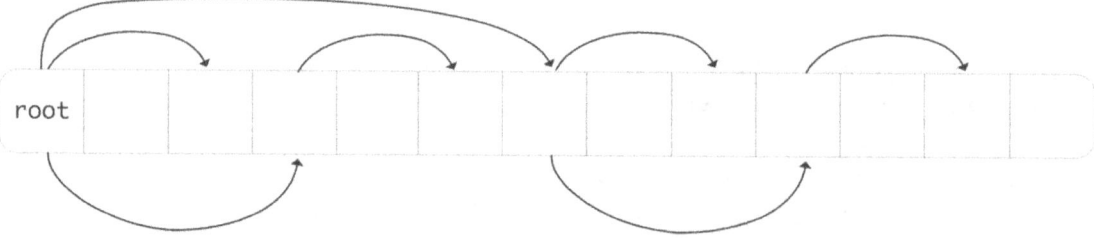

Figure 3.4: A tree-based broadcast

depend on the number of processors? The theory of the complexity of collectives is described in more detail in HPSC-6.1; see also [ ].

3.12   Collectives and synchronization

Collectives, other than a barrier, have a synchronizing effect between processors. For instance, in

```
MPI_Bcast( ....data... root);
MPI_Send(....);
```

the send operations on all processors will occur after the root executes the broadcast. Conversely, in a reduce

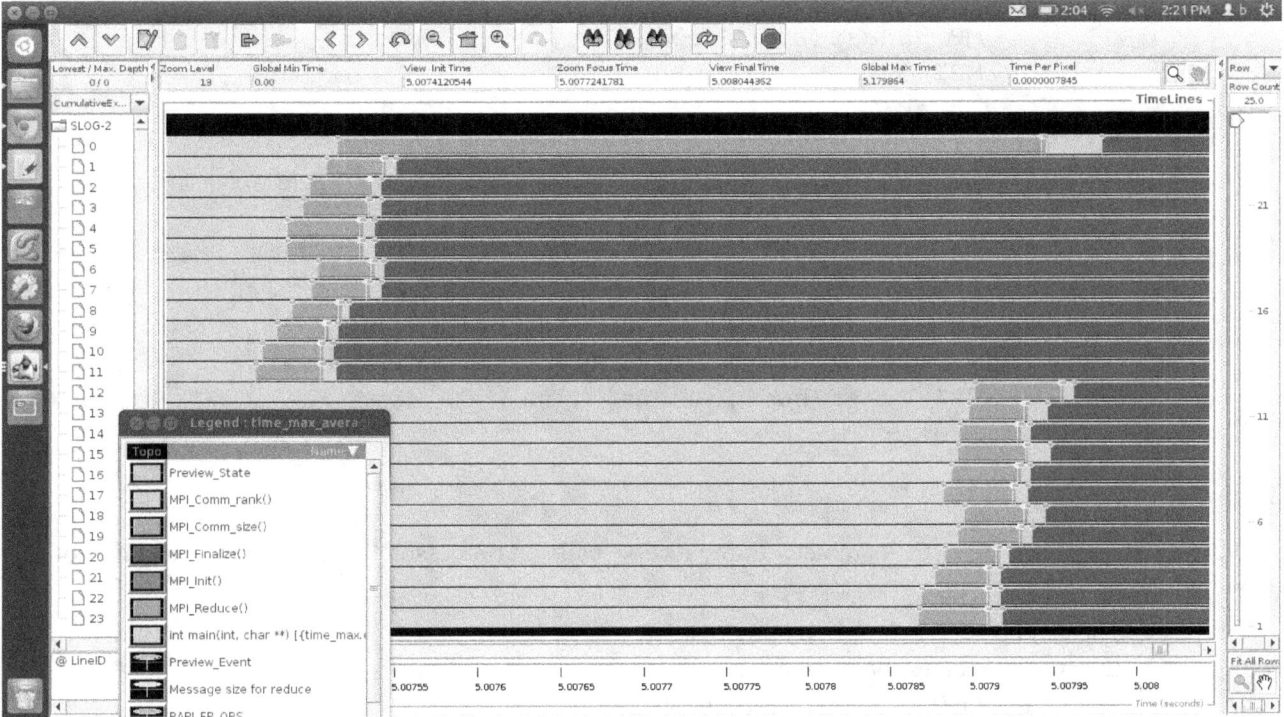

Figure 3.5: Trace of a reduction operation between two dual-socket 12-core nodes

operation the root may have to wait for other processors. This is illustrated in figure 3.5, which gives a TAU trace of a reduction operation on two nodes, with two six-core sockets (processors) each. We see that[1]:

- In each socket, the reduction is a linear accumulation;
- on each node, cores zero and six then combine their result;
- after which the final accumulation is done through the network.

We also see that the two nodes are not perfectly in sync, which is normal for MPI applications. As a result, core 0 on the first node will sit idle until it receives the partial result from core 12, which is on the second node.

While collectives synchronize in a loose sense, it is not possible to make any statements about events before and after the collectives between processors:

```
...event 1...
MPI_Bcast(....);
```

---

1.   This uses mvapich version 1.6; in version 1.9 the implementation of an on-node reduction has changed to simulate shared memory.

```
...event 2....
```

Consider a specific scenario:

```
switch(rank) {
    case 0:
        MPI_Bcast(buf1, count, type, 0, comm);
        MPI_Send(buf2, count, type, 1, tag, comm);
        break;
    case 1:
        MPI_Recv(buf2, count, type, MPI_ANY_SOURCE, tag, comm, status);
        MPI_Bcast(buf1, count, type, 0, comm);
        MPI_Recv(buf2, count, type, MPI_ANY_SOURCE, tag, comm, status);
        break;
    case 2:
        MPI_Send(buf2, count, type, 1, tag, comm);
        MPI_Bcast(buf1, count, type, 0, comm);
        break;
}
```

Note the MPI_ANY_SOURCE parameter in the receive calls on processor 1. One obvious execution of this would be:

1. The send from 2 is caught by processor 1;
2. Everyone executes the broadcast;
3. The send from 0 is caught by processor 1.

However, it is equally possible to have this execution:

1. Processor 0 starts its broadcast, then executes the send;
2. Processor 1's receive catches the data from 0, then it executes its part of the broadcast;
3. Processor 1 catches the data sent by 2, and finally processor 2 does its part of the broadcast.

Chapter 4

MPI topic: Point-to-point

4.1 Distributed computing and distributed data

One reason for using MPI is that sometimes you need to work on more data than can fit in the memory of a single processor. With distributed memory, each processor then gets a part of the whole data structure and only works on that.

So let's say we have a large array, and we want to distribute the data over the processors. That means that, with p processes and n elements per processor, we have a total of $n \cdot p$ elements.

```
int n;
double data[n];
```

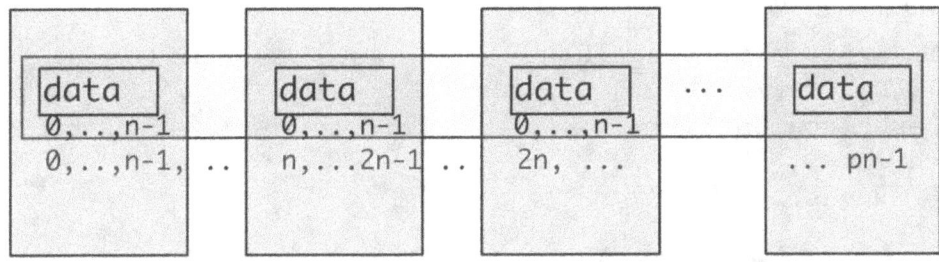

Figure 4.1: Local parts of a distributed array

We sometimes say that `data` is the local part of a *distributed array* with a total size of $n \cdot p$ elements. However, this array only exists conceptually: each processor has an array with lowest index zero, and you have to translate that yourself to an index in the global array. In other words, you have to write your code in such a way that it acts like you're working with a large array that is distributed over the processors, while actually manipulating only the local arrays on the processors.

Your typical code then looks like

```
int myfirst = .....;
for (int ilocal=0; ilocal<nlocal; ilocal++) {
    int iglobal = myfirst+ilocal;
    array[ilocal] = f(iglobal);
```

```
}
```

Exercise 4.1. We want to compute $\sum_{n=1}^{N} n^2$, and we do that as follows by filling in an array and summing the elements. (Yes, you can do it without an array, but for purposes of the exercise do it with.)

Set a variable N for the total length of the array, and compute the local number of elements. Make sure you handle the case where N does not divide perfectly by the number of processes.

- Now allocate the local parts: each processor should allocate only local elements, not the whole vector.
  (Allocate your array as real numbers. Why are integers not a good idea?)
- On each processor, initialize the local array so that the i-th location of the distributed array (for $i = 0, \ldots, N - 1$) contains $(i + 1)^2$.
- Now use a collective operation to compute the sum of the array values. The right value is $(2N^3 + 3N^2 + N)/6$. Is that what you get?

(Note that computer arithmetic is not exact: the computed sum will only be accurate up to some relative accuracy.)

Exercise 4.2. In exercise 4.1 you worked with a distributed array, computing a local quantity and combining that into a global quantity. Why is it not a good idea to gather the whole distributed array on a single processor, and do all the computation locally?

If the array size is not perfectly divisible by the number of processors, we have to come up with a division that is uneven, but not too much. You could for instance, write

```
int Nglobal, // is something large
    Nlocal = Nglobal/ntids,
    excess = Nglobal%ntids;
if (mytid==ntids-1)
  Nlocal += excess;
```

Exercise 4.3. Argue that this strategy is not optimal. Can you come up with a better distribution? Load balancing is further discussed in HPSC-2.10.1.

One of the more common applications of the reduction operation is the *inner product* computation. Typically, you have two vectors x, y that have the same distribution, that is, where all processes store equal parts of x and y. The computation is then

```
local_inprod = 0;
for (i=0; i<localsize; i++)
  local_inprod += x[i]*y[i];
MPI_Reduce( &local_inprod, &global_inprod, 1,MPI_DOUBLE ... )
```

If all processors need the result, you could then do a broadcast, but it is more efficient to use MPI_Allreduce; see section **??**.

Exercise 4.4. Implement an inner product routine: let x be a distributed vector of size N with elements $x[i] = i$, and compute $x^t x$. As before, the right value is

$(2N^3 + 3N^2 + N)/6$.

Use the inner product value to scale to vector so that it has norm 1. Check that your computation is correct.

4.2 Blocking point-to-point operations

Suppose you have an array of numbers x_i: $i = 0, \ldots, N$ and you want to compute $y_i = (x_{i-1} + x_i + x_{i+1})/3$: $i = 1, \ldots, N - 1$. As before (see figure 4.1), we give each processor a subset of the x_is and y_is. Let's define i_p as the first index of y that is computed by processor p. (What is the last index computed by processor p? How many indices are computed on that processor?)

We often talk about the *owner computes* model of parallel computing: each processor 'owns' certain data items, and it computes their value.

Now let's investigate how processor p goes about computing y_i for the i-values it owns. Let's assume that processor p also stores the values x_i for these same indices. Now, it can compute

$$y_{i_p+1} = (x_{i_p} + x_{i_p+1} + x_{i_p+2})/3$$

and likewise y_{i_p+2} and so on. However, there is a problem with

$$y_{i_p} = (x_{i_p-1} + x_{i_p} + x_{i_p+1})/3$$

since x_{i_p} is not stored on processor p: it is stored on $p - 1$.

There is a similar story with the last index that p tries to compute: that involves a value that is only present on $p + 1$.

You see that there is a need for processor-to-processor, or technically *point-to-point*, information exchange. MPI realizes this through matched send and receive calls:

- One process does a send to a specific other process;
- the other process does a specific receive from that source.

4.2.1 Send example: ping-pong

A simple scenario for information exchange between just two processes is the *ping-pong*: process A sends data to process B, which sends data back to A. This means that process A executes the code

```
MPI_Send( /* to: */ B ..... );
MPI_Recv( /* from: */ B ... );
```

while process B executes

```
MPI_Recv( /* from: */ A ... );
MPI_Send( /* to: */ A ..... );
```

Since we are programming in SPMD mode, this means our program looks like:

```
if ( /* I am process A */ ) {
  MPI_Send( /* to: */ B ..... );
  MPI_Recv( /* from: */ B ... );
} else if ( /* I am process B */ ) {
  MPI_Recv( /* from: */ A ... );
  MPI_Send( /* to: */ A ..... );
}
```

The blocking send command:

```
C:
int MPI_Send(
  const void* buf, int count, MPI_Datatype datatype,
  int dest, int tag, MPI_Comm comm)

Semantics:
IN buf: initial address of send buffer (choice)
IN count: number of elements in send buffer (non-negative integer)
IN datatype: datatype of each send buffer element (handle)
IN dest: rank of destination (integer)
IN tag: message tag (integer)
IN comm: communicator (handle)

Fortran:
MPI_Send(buf, count, datatype, dest, tag, comm, ierror)
TYPE(*), DIMENSION(..), INTENT(IN) :: buf
INTEGER, INTENT(IN) :: count, dest, tag
TYPE(MPI_Datatype), INTENT(IN) :: datatype
TYPE(MPI_Comm), INTENT(IN) :: comm
INTEGER, OPTIONAL, INTENT(OUT) :: ierror

Python native:
MPI.Comm.send(self, obj, int dest, int tag=0)
Python numpy:
MPI.Comm.Send(self, buf, int dest, int tag=0)
```

How to read routine prototypes: 1.5.4.

This routine may not blocking for small messages; to force blocking behaviour use `MPI_Ssend` with the same argument list. http://www.mcs.anl.gov/research/projects/mpi/www/www3/ MPI_Ssend.html

The basic blocking receive command:

```
C:
int MPI_Recv(
  void* buf, int count, MPI_Datatype datatype,
  int source, int tag, MPI_Comm comm, MPI_Status *status)
```

```
Semantics:
OUT buf: initial address of receive buffer (choice)
IN count: number of elements in receive buffer (non-negative integer)
IN datatype: datatype of each receive buffer element (handle)
IN source: rank of source or MPI_ANY_SOURCE (integer)
IN tag: message tag or MPI_ANY_TAG (integer)
IN comm: communicator (handle)
OUT status: status object (Status)

Fortran:
MPI_Recv(buf, count, datatype, source, tag, comm, status, ierror)
TYPE(*), DIMENSION(..) :: buf
INTEGER, INTENT(IN) :: count, source, tag
TYPE(MPI_Datatype), INTENT(IN) :: datatype
TYPE(MPI_Comm), INTENT(IN) :: comm
TYPE(MPI_Status) :: status
INTEGER, OPTIONAL, INTENT(OUT) :: ierror

Python native:
recvbuf = Comm.recv(self, buf=None, int source=ANY_SOURCE, int tag=ANY_TAG,
    Status status=None)
Python numpy:
Comm.Recv(self, buf, int source=ANY_SOURCE, int tag=ANY_TAG,
    Status status=None)
```

How to read routine prototypes: 1.5.4.

The count argument indicates the maximum length of a message; the actual length of the received message can be determined from the status object. See section **??** for more about the status object.

Exercise 4.5.   Implement the ping-pong program. Add a timer using MPI_Wtime. For the status argument of the receive call, use MPI_STATUS_IGNORE.

- Run multiple ping-pongs (say a thousand) and put the timer around the loop. The first run may take longer; try to discard it.
- Run your code with the two communicating processes first on the same node, then on different nodes. Do you see a difference?
- Then modify the program to use longer messages. How does the timing increase with message size?

For bonus points, can you do a regression to determine α, β?

Exercise 4.6.   Take your pingpong program and modify it to let half the processors be source and the other half the targets. Does the pingpong time increase?

In the syntax of the MPI_Recv command you saw one parameter that the send call lacks: the MPI_Status object. This serves the following purpose: the receive call can have a 'wildcard' behaviour, for instance specifying that the message can come from any source rather than a specific one. The status object then allows you to find out where the message actually came from.

Exercise 4.7.   The *Gauss-Jordan method* for *solving a linear system* or computing a *matrix inverse* applies the following transformations to a matrix:

for $k = 1, \ldots, n$
    find pivot:
      $p = 1/a_{kk}$
    scale current row by the pivot:
      for $r = 1, \ldots, n$
        $a_{rk} = a_{rk} \cdot p$
    sweep columns:
      for $c = 1, \ldots, n$
        $a_{rc} = a_{rc} - a_{rk} \cdot a_{kc}$

(Depending on whether the method is used for a linear system or an inverse, we use some form of *augmented matrix*.)
Explore how to parallelize this algorithm if every processor stores one column of the matrix. Use blocking send and receive calls.

4.2.2   Problems with blocking communication

The use of `MPI_Send` and `MPI_Recv` is known as *blocking communication*: when your code reaches a send or receive call, it blocks until the call is succesfully completed. For a receive call it is clear that the receiving code will wait until the data has actually come in, but for a send call this is more subtle.

You may be tempted to think that the send call puts the data somewhere in the network, and the sending code can progress, as in figure 4.2, left. But this ideal scenario is not realistic: it assumes that somewhere

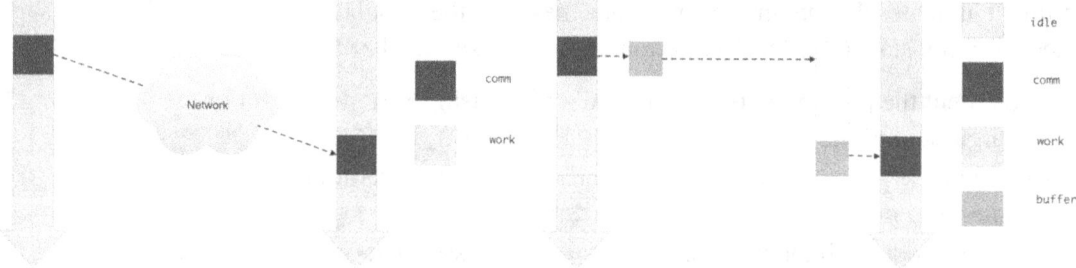

Figure 4.2: Illustration of an ideal (left) and actual (right) send-receive interaction

in the network there is buffer capacity for all messages that are in transit. This is not the case: data resides on the sender, and the sending call blocks, until the receiver has received all of it. (There is a exception for small messages, as explained in the next section.)

4.2.2.1   Deadlock

Suppose two process need to exchange data, and consider the following pseudo-code, which purports to exchange data between processes 0 and 1:

```
other = 1-mytid; /* if I am 0, other is 1; and vice versa */
receive(source=other);
send(target=other);
```

Imagine that the two processes execute this code. They both issue the send call... and then can't go on, because they are both waiting for the other to issue a receive call. This is known as *deadlock*.

(If you reverse the send and receive call, you should get deadlock, but in practice that code will often work. The reason is that MPI implementations sometimes send small messages regardless of whether the receive has been posted. This relies on the availability of some amount of available buffer space. The size under which this behaviour is used is sometimes referred to as the *eager limit*.)

The following code is guaranteed to block, since a MPI_Recv always blocks:

```
// recvblock.c
other = 1-procno;
MPI_Recv(&recvbuf,1,MPI_INT,other,0,comm,&status);
MPI_Send(&sendbuf,1,MPI_INT,other,0,comm);
printf("This statement will not be reached on %d\n",procno);
```

On the other hand, if we put the send call before the receive, code may not block for small messages that fall under the *eager limit*.

In this example we send gradually larger messages. From the screen output you can see what the largest message was that fell under the eager limit; after that the code hangs because of a deadlock.

```
// sendblock.c
other = 1-procno;
/* loop over increasingly large messages */
for (int size=1; size<2000000000; size*=10) {
  sendbuf = (int*) malloc(size*sizeof(int));
  recvbuf = (int*) malloc(size*sizeof(int));
  if (!sendbuf || !recvbuf) {
    printf("Out of memory\n"); MPI_Abort(comm,1);
  }
  MPI_Send(sendbuf,size,MPI_INT,other,0,comm);
  MPI_Recv(recvbuf,size,MPI_INT,other,0,comm,&status);
  /* If control reaches this point, the send call
     did not block. If the send call blocks,
     we do not reach this point, and the program will hang.
  */
  if (procno==0)
    printf("Send did not block for size %d\n",size);
  free(sendbuf); free(recvbuf);
}
```

```
// sendblock.F90
other = 1-mytid
size = 1
do
   allocate(sendbuf(size)); allocate(recvbuf(size))
   print *,size
   call MPI_Send(sendbuf,size,MPI_INTEGER,other,0,comm,err)
   call MPI_Recv(recvbuf,size,MPI_INTEGER,other,0,comm,status,err)
   if (mytid==0) then
      print *,"MPI_Send did not block for size",size
   end if
   deallocate(sendbuf); deallocate(recvbuf)
   size = size*10
   if (size>2000000000) goto 20
end do
20   continue
```

```
// sendblock.py
size = 1
while size<2000000000:
    sendbuf = np.empty(size, dtype=np.int)
    recvbuf = np.empty(size, dtype=np.int)
    comm.Send(sendbuf,dest=other)
    comm.Recv(sendbuf,source=other)
    if procid<other:
        print "Send did not block for",size
    size *= 10
```

If you want a code to behave the same for all message sizes, you force the send call to be blocking by using MPI_Ssend:

```
// ssendblock.c
other = 1-procno;
sendbuf = (int*) malloc(sizeof(int));
recvbuf = (int*) malloc(sizeof(int));
size = 1;
MPI_Ssend(sendbuf,size,MPI_INT,other,0,comm);
MPI_Recv(recvbuf,size,MPI_INT,other,0,comm,&status);
printf("This statement is not reached\n");
```

Formally you can describe deadlock as follows. Draw up a graph where every process is a node, and draw a directed arc from process A to B if A is waiting for B. There is deadlock if this directed graph has a loop.

The solution to the deadlock in the above example is to first do the send from 0 to 1, and then from 1 to 0 (or the other way around). So the code would look like:

```
if ( /* I am processor 0 */ ) {
  send(target=other);
  receive(source=other);
} else {
  receive(source=other);
  send(target=other);
}
```

4.2.2.2   Serialization

There is a second, even more subtle problem with blocking communication. Consider the scenario where every processor needs to pass data to its successor, that is, the processor with the next higher rank. The basic idea would be to first send to your successor, then receive from your predecessor. Since the last processor does not have a successor it skips the send, and likewise the first processor skips the receive. The pseudo-code looks like:

```
successor = mytid+1; predecessor = mytid-1;
if ( /* I am not the last processor */ )
  send(target=successor);
if ( /* I am not the first processor */ )
  receive(source=predecessor)
```

This code does not deadlock. All processors but the last one block on the send call, but the last processor executes the receive call. Thus, the processor before the last one can do its send, and subsequently continue to its receive, which enables another send, et cetera.

In one way this code does what you intended to do: it will terminate (instead of hanging forever on a deadlock) and exchange data the right way. However, the execution now suffers from unexpected *serialization*: only one processor is active at any time, so what should have been a parallel operation becomes a sequential one. This is illustrated in figure 4.3.

Exercise 4.8.   (Classroom exercise) Each student holds a piece of paper in the right hand
      – keep your left hand behind your back – and we want to execute:
      1. Give the paper to your right neighbour;
      2. Accept the paper from your left neighbour.
      Including boundary conditions for first and last process, that becomes the following
      program:
      1. If you are not the rightmost student, turn to the right and give the paper to your
         right neighbour.
      2. If you are not the leftmost student, turn to your left and accept the paper from
         your left neighbour.

Exercise 4.9.   Implement the above algorithm using MPI_Send and MPI_Receive calls.
      Run the code, and reproduce the trace output of figure 4.3. See chapter 36.2 on how

Figure 4.3: Trace of a simple send-recv code

to use the TAU utility. If you don't have TAU, can you show this serialization behaviour using timings?

It is possible to orchestrate your processes to get an efficient and deadlock-free execution, but doing so is a bit cumbersome.

Exercise 4.10. The above solution treated every processor equally. Can you come up with a solution that uses blocking sends and receives, but does not suffer from the serialization behaviour?

There are better solutions which we will explore next.

4.2.3   Pairwise exchange

Above you saw that with blocking sends the precise ordering of the send and receive calls is crucial. Use the wrong ordering and you get either deadlock, or something that is not efficient at all in parallel. MPI has a way out of this problem that is sufficient for many purposes: the combined send/recv call `MPI_Sendrecv`

```
Semantics:

MPI_SENDRECV(
     sendbuf, sendcount, sendtype, dest, sendtag,
     recvbuf, recvcount, recvtype, source, recvtag,
     comm, status)
IN sendbuf: initial address of send buffer (choice)
IN sendcount: number of elements in send buffer (non-negative integer)
IN sendtype: type of elements in send buffer (handle)
IN dest: rank of destination (integer)
IN sendtag: send tag (integer)
OUT recvbuf: initial address of receive buffer (choice)
IN recvcount: number of elements in receive buffer (non-negative integer)
```

```
IN recvtype: type of elements in receive buffer (handle)
IN source: rank of source or MPI_ANY_SOURCE (integer)
IN recvtag: receive tag or MPI_ANY_TAG (integer)
IN comm: communicator (handle)
OUT status: status object (Status)

C:
int MPI_Sendrecv(
    const void *sendbuf, int sendcount, MPI_Datatype sendtype,
    int dest, int sendtag,
    void *recvbuf, int recvcount, MPI_Datatype recvtype,
    int source, int recvtag,
    MPI_Comm comm, MPI_Status *status)

Fortran:
MPI_Sendrecv(sendbuf, sendcount, sendtype, dest, sendtag, recvbuf,
recvcount, recvtype, source, recvtag, comm, status, ierror)
TYPE(*), DIMENSION(..), INTENT(IN) :: sendbuf
TYPE(*), DIMENSION(..) :: recvbuf
INTEGER, INTENT(IN) :: sendcount, dest, sendtag, recvcount, source,
recvtag
TYPE(MPI_Datatype), INTENT(IN) :: sendtype, recvtype
TYPE(MPI_Comm), INTENT(IN) :: comm
TYPE(MPI_Status) :: status
INTEGER, OPTIONAL, INTENT(OUT) :: ierror

Python:
Sendrecv(self, sendbuf, int dest, int sendtag=0,
    recvbuf=None, int source=ANY_SOURCE, int recvtag=ANY_TAG,
    Status status=None)
```

How to read routine prototypes: 1.5.4.

The sendrecv call works great if every process is paired up. You would then write

```
sendrecv( ....from... ...to... );
```

However, in cases such as the right-shift this is true for all but the first and last. MPI allows for the following variant which makes the code slightly more homogeneous:

```
MPI_Comm_rank( .... &mytid );
if ( /* I am not the first processor */ )
  predecessor = mytid-1;
else
  predecessor = MPI_PROC_NULL;
if ( /* I am not the last processor */ )
  successor = mytid+1;
else
  successor = MPI_PROC_NULL;
```

```
sendrecv(from=predecessor,to=successor);
```

where the sendrecv call is executed by all processors.

All processors but the last one send to their neighbour; the target value of `MPI_PROC_NULL` for the last processor means a 'send to the null processor': no actual send is done.

```
C:
#include "mpi.h"
MPI_PROC_NULL

Fortran:
#include "mpif.h"
MPI_PROC_NULL

Python:
MPI.PROC_NULL = -1
```

How to read routine prototypes: 1.5.4.

The null processor value is also of use with the `MPI_Sendrecv` call; section 4.2.3

Exercise 4.11.   Implement the above three-point combination scheme using `MPI_Sendrecv`; every processor only has a single number to send to its neighbour. If you have TAU installed, make a trace. Does it look different from the serialized send/recv code? If you don't have TAU, run your code with different numbers of processes and show that the runtime is essentially constant.

This call makes it easy to exchange data between two processors: both specify the other as both target and source. However, there need not be any such relation between target and source: it is possible to receive from a predecessor in some ordering, and send to a successor in that ordering; see figure 4.4. Above you

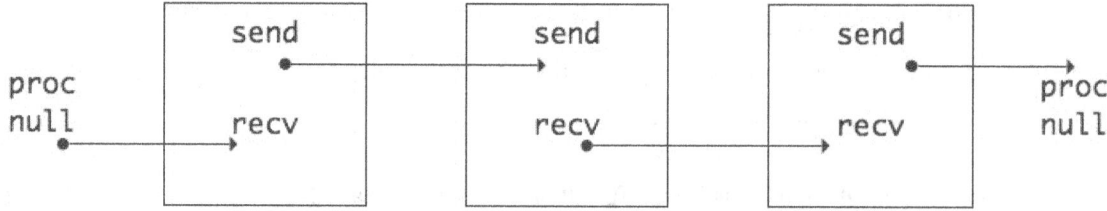

Figure 4.4: An MPI Sendrecv call

saw some examples that had most processors doing both a send and a receive, but some only a send or only a receive. You can still use `MPI_Sendrecv` in this call if you use `MPI_PROC_NULL` for the unused source or target argument.

If the send and receive buffer have the same size, the routine `MPI_Sendrecv_replace` will do an in-place replacement.

```
C:
int MPI_Sendrecv_replace(
```

```
        void *buf, int count, MPI_Datatype datatype,
        int dest, int sendtag, int source, int recvtag,
        MPI_Comm comm, MPI_Status *status)

Fortran:
MPI_SENDRECV_REPLACE(
        BUF, COUNT, DATATYPE,
        DEST, SENDTAG, SOURCE,RECVTAG,
        COMM, STATUS, IERROR)
<type>    BUF(*)
INTEGER :: COUNT, DATATYPE, DEST, SENDTAG
INTEGER :: SOURCE, RECVTAG, COMM
INTEGER    STATUS(MPI_STATUS_SIZE), IERROR

Input/output parameter:
buf : Initial address of send and receive buffer (choice).

Input parameters:
count : Number of elements in send and receive buffer (integer).
datatype : Type of elements to send and receive (handle).
dest : Rank of destination (integer).
sendtag : Send message tag (integer).
source : Rank of source (integer).
recvtag : Receive message tag (integer).
comm : Communicator (handle).

Output parameters:

status : Status object (status).
IERROR : Fortran only: Error status (integer).
```

How to read routine prototypes: 1.5.4.

The following exercise lets you implement a sorting algorithm with the send-receive call[1].

Exercise 4.12.

A very simple sorting algorithm is *exchange sort*: pairs of processors compare data, and if necessary exchange. The elementary step is called a *compare-and-swap*: in a pair of processors each sends their data to the other; one keeps the minimum values, and the other the maximum. For simplicity, in this exercise we give each processor just a single number.

The exchange sort algorithm is split in even and odd stages, where in the even stage, processors $2i$ and $2i + 1$ compare and swap data, and in the odd stage, processors $2i + 1$ and $2i + 2$ compare and swap. You need to repeat this $P/2$ times, where P is the number of processors.

Implement this algorithm using MPI_Sendrecv. (You can use MPI_PROC_NULL for the edge cases, but that is not strictly necessary.) Use a gather call to print the

---

1.   There is an MPI_Compare_and_swap call. Do not use that.

global state of the distributed array at the beginning and end of the sorting process.

4.2.4   Message status

Above, you saw that `MPI_Receive` has a 'status' argument of type `MPI_STATUS` that `MPI_Send` lacks. (The various `MPI_Wait...` routines also have a status argument; see section **??**.) The reason for this argument is as follows.

In some circumstances the recipient may not know all details of a message when you make the receive call, so MPI has a way of querying the *message status*

- If you are expecting multiple incoming messages, it may be most efficient to deal with them in the order in which they arrive. So, instead of waiting for specific message, you would specify `MPI_ANY_SOURCE` or `MPI_ANY_TAG` in the description of the receive message. Now you have to be able to ask 'who did this message come from, and what is in it'.
- Maybe you know the sender of a message, but the amount of data is unknown. In that case you can overallocate your receive buffer, and after the message is received ask how big it was, or you can 'probe' an incoming message and allocate enough data when you find out how much data is being sent.

```
C:
MPI_Status status;

Fortran:
integer :: status(MPI_STATUS_SIZE)

Python:
MPI.Status() # returns object
```

How to read routine prototypes: 1.5.4.

Using the `MPI_ANY_SOURCE` specifier. We retrieve the actual source from the `MPI_Status` object through the `MPI_SOURCE` field.

```
// anysource.c
if (procno==nprocs-1) {
  int *recv_buffer;
  MPI_Status status;

  recv_buffer = (int*) malloc((nprocs-1)*sizeof(int));

  for (int p=0; p<nprocs-1; p++) {
    err = MPI_Recv(recv_buffer+p,1,MPI_INT, MPI_ANY_SOURCE,0,comm,
        &status); CHK(err);
    int sender = status.MPI_SOURCE;
    printf("Message from sender=%d: %d\n",
```

```
      sender,recv_buffer[p]);
  }
} else {
  float randomfraction = (rand() / (double)RAND_MAX);
  int randomwait = (int) ( nprocs * randomfraction );
  printf("process %d waits for %e/%d=%d\n",
    procno,randomfraction,nprocs,randomwait);
  sleep(randomwait);
  err = MPI_Send(&randomwait,1,MPI_INT, nprocs-1,0,comm); CHK(err);
}
```

```
// anysource.py
rstatus = MPI.Status()
comm.Recv(rbuf,source=MPI.ANY_SOURCE,status=rstatus)
print "Message came from %d" % rstatus.Get_source()
```

If you are not interested in the status information, you can use the values `MPI_STATUS_IGNORE` for `MPI_Wait` and `MPI_Waitany`, or `MPI_STATUSES_IGNORE` for `MPI_Waitall` and `MPI_Waitsome`.

The `MPI_Status` object is a structure with the following freely accessible members:

```
C:
int status.MPI_SOURCE;

F:
integer :: MPI_SOURCE

Python:
status.Get_source() # returns int
```

How to read routine prototypes: 1.5.4.

```
C:
int status.MPI_TAG;

F:
integer :: MPI_TAG

Python:
status.Get_tag() # returns int
```

How to read routine prototypes: 1.5.4.

```
C:
int status.MPI_ERROR;

F:
integer :: MPI_ERROR
```

```
Python:
status.Get_error() # returns int
```

How to read routine prototypes: 1.5.4.

In section **??** we mentioned the master-worker model as one opportunity for inspecting the `MPI_SOURCE` field of the `MPI_Status` object.

There is also opaque information: the amount of data received can be retrieved by a function call to `MPI_Get_count`.

```
// C:
int MPI_Get_count(MPI_Status *status,MPI_Datatype datatype,
    int *count)

! Fortran:
MPI_Get_count(INTEGER status(MPI_STATUS_SIZE),INTEGER datatype,
    INTEGER count,INTEGER ierror)

Python:
status.Get_count( Datatype datatype=BYTE )
```

How to read routine prototypes: 1.5.4.

This may be necessary since the `count` argument to `MPI_Recv` is the buffer size, not an indication of the actually expected number of data items.

If you precisely know what is going to be sent, the status argument tells you nothing new. Therefore, there is a special value `MPI_STATUS_IGNORE` that you can supply instead of a status object, which tells MPI that the status does not have to be reported. For routines such as `MPI_Waitany` where an array of statuses is needed, you can supply `MPI_STATUSES_IGNORE`.

object describing the data that was received.

4.3 Non-blocking point-to-point operations

4.3.1 Irregular data exchange

The structure of communication is often a reflection of the structure of the operation. With some regular applications we also get a regular communication pattern. Consider again the above operation:

$$y_i = x_{i-1} + x_i + x_{i+1} : i = 1, \ldots, N - 1$$

Doing this in parallel induces communication, as pictured in figure 4.5. We note:

- The data is one-dimensional, and we have a linear ordering of the processors.
- The operation involves neighbouring data points, and we communicate with neighbouring processors.

Above you saw how you can use information exchange between pairs of processors

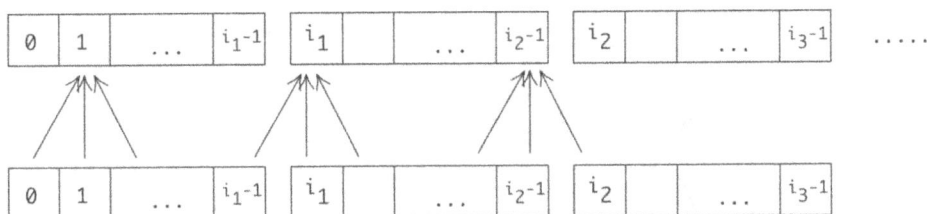

Figure 4.5: Communication in an one-dimensional operation

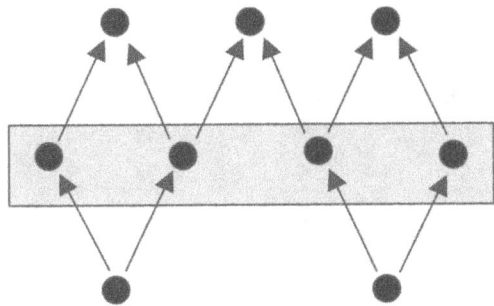

Figure 4.6: Processors with unbalanced send/receive patterns

- using `MPI_Send` and `MPI_Recv`, if you are careful; or
- using `MPI_Sendrecv`, as long as there is indeed some sort of pairing of processors.

However, there are circumstances where it is not possible, not efficient, or simply not convenient, to have such a deterministic setup of the send and receive calls. Figure 4.6 illustrates such a case, where processors are organized in a general graph pattern. Here, the numbers of sends and receive of a processor do not need to match.

In such cases, one wants a possibility to state 'these are the expected incoming messages', without having to wait for them in sequence. Likewise, one wants to declare the outgoing messages without having to do them in any particular sequence. Imposing any sequence on the sends and receives is likely to run into the serialization behaviour observed above, or at least be inefficient since processors will be waiting for messages.

4.3.2 Non-blocking communication

In the previous section you saw that blocking communication makes programming tricky if you want to avoid deadlock and performance problems. The main advantage of these routines is that you have full control about where the data is: if the send call returns the data has been successfully received, and the send buffer can be used for other purposes or de-allocated.

By contrast, the non-blocking calls `MPI_Isend` and `MPI_Irecv` do not wait for their counterpart: in effect they tell the runtime system 'here is some data and please send it as follows' or 'here is some buffer space, and expect such-and-such data to come'. This is illustrated in figure 4.7.

    C:

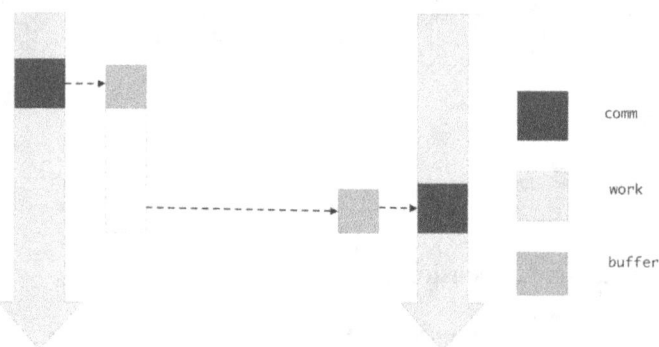

Figure 4.7: Non-blocking send

```
int MPI_Isend(void *buf,
  int count, MPI_Datatype datatype, int dest, int tag,
  MPI_Comm comm, MPI_Request *request)

Fortran:
the request parameter is an integer

Python:
request = MPI.Comm.Isend(self, buf, int dest, int tag=0)
```

How to read routine prototypes: 1.5.4.

```
C:
int MPI_Irecv(void *buf,
  int count, MPI_Datatype datatype, int source, int tag,
  MPI_Comm comm, MPI_Request *request)

Fortran:
the request parameter is an integer

Python:
request = MPI.Comm.Irecv(self,
    buf, int source=ANY_SOURCE, int tag=ANY_TAG)
```

How to read routine prototypes: 1.5.4.

While the use of non-blocking routines prevents deadlock, it introduces two new problems:

1. When the send call returns, the actual send may not have been executed, so the send buffer may not be safe to overwrite. When the recv call returns, you do not know for sure that the expected data is in it. Thus, you need a mechanism to make sure that data was actually sent or received.

2. With a blocking send call, you could repeatedly fill the send buffer and send it off.

```
double *buffer;
for ( ... p ... ) {
    buffer = // fill in the data
```

```
MPI_Send( buffer, ... /* to: */ p );
```

To send multiple messages with non-blocking calls you have to allocate multiple buffers.

```
double **buffers;
for ( ... p ... ) {
    buffers[p] = // fill in the data
    MPI_Send( buffers[p], ... /* to: */ p );
```

As you see above, a non-blocking send or receive routine yields an `MPI_Request` object. This request can then be used to query whether the operation has concluded. You may also notice that the `MPI_Irecv` routine does not yield an `MPI_Status` object. This makes sense: the status object describes the actually received data, and at the completion of the `MPI_Irecv` call there is no received data yet.

MPI has two types of routines for handling requests; we will start with the `MPI_Wait...` routines. These calls are blocking: when you issue such a call, your execution will wait until the specified requests have been completed. A typical way of using them is:

```
// start non-blocking communication
MPI_Isend( ... ); MPI_Irecv( ... );
// wait for the Isend/Irecv calls to finish in any order
MPI_Waitall( ... );
```

The `MPI_Wait...` routines have the `MPI_Status` objects as output.

```
Semantics:
MPI_WAITALL( count, array_of_requests, array_of_statuses)
IN count: lists length (non-negative integer)
INOUT array_of_requests: array of requests (array of handles)
OUT array_of_statuses: array of status objects (array of Status)

C:
int MPI_Waitall(
    int count, MPI_Request array_of_requests[],
    MPI_Status array_of_statuses[])

Fortran:
MPI_Waitall(count, array_of_requests, array_of_statuses, ierror)
INTEGER, INTENT(IN) :: count
TYPE(MPI_Request), INTENT(INOUT) :: array_of_requests(count)
TYPE(MPI_Status) :: array_of_statuses(*)
INTEGER, OPTIONAL, INTENT(OUT) :: ierror

Python:
MPI.Request.Waitall(type cls, requests, statuses=None)

Use MPI_STATUSES_IGNORE to ignore
```

How to read routine prototypes: 1.5.4.

Exercise 4.13. Now use nonblocking send/receive routines to implement the three-point averaging operation

$$y_i = (x_{i-1} + x_i + x_{i+1})/3 \colon i = 1, \ldots, N-1$$

on a distributed array. (Hint: use `MPI_PROC_NULL` at the ends.)

There is a second motivation for the `Isend`/`Irecv` calls: if your hardware supports it, the communication can progress while your program can continue to do useful work:

```
// start non-blocking communication
MPI_Isend( ... ); MPI_Irecv( ... );
// do work that does not depend on incoming data
....
// wait for the Isend/Irecv calls to finish
MPI_Wait( ... );
// now do the work that absolutely needs the incoming data
....
```

This is known as *overlapping computation and communication*, or *latency hiding*.

Unfortunately, a lot of this communication involves activity in user space, so the solution would have been to let it be handled by a separate thread. Until recently, processors were not efficient at doing such multi-threading, so true overlap stayed a promise for the future. Some network cards have support for this overlap, but it requires a non-trivial combination of hardware, firmware, and MPI implementation.

Exercise 4.14. Take your code of exercise 4.13 and modify it to use latency hiding. Operations that can be performed without needing data from neighbours should be performed in between the `Isend`/`Irecv` calls and the `Wait` call.

Remark 1 *There is nothing special about a non-blocking or synchronous message. The* `MPI_Recv` *call can match any of the send routines you have seen so far (but not* `MPI_Sendrecv`*), and conversely a message sent with* `MPI_Send` *can be received by* `MPI_Irecv`*.*

4.3.2.1 Wait and test calls

There are several wait calls.

4.3.2.1.1 Wait for one request `MPI_Wait` waits for a a single request. If you are indeed waiting for a single nonblocking communication to complete, this is the right routine. If you are waiting for multiple requests you could call this routine in a loop.

```
for (p=0; p<nrequests ; p++) // Not efficient!
  MPI_Wait(request[p],&(status[p]));
```

However, this would be inefficient if the first request is fulfilled much later than the others: your waiting process would have lots of idle time. In that case, use one of the following routines.

4.3.2.1.2 **Wait for all requests** `MPI_Waitall` allows you to wait for a number of requests, and it does not matter in what sequence they are satisfied. Using this routine is easier to code than the loop above, and it could be more efficient.

```
Semantics:
MPI_WAITALL( count, array_of_requests, array_of_statuses)
IN count: lists length (non-negative integer)
INOUT array_of_requests: array of requests (array of handles)
OUT array_of_statuses: array of status objects (array of Status)


C:
int MPI_Waitall(
    int count, MPI_Request array_of_requests[],
    MPI_Status array_of_statuses[])


Fortran:
MPI_Waitall(count, array_of_requests, array_of_statuses, ierror)
INTEGER, INTENT(IN) :: count
TYPE(MPI_Request), INTENT(INOUT) :: array_of_requests(count)
TYPE(MPI_Status) :: array_of_statuses(*)
INTEGER, OPTIONAL, INTENT(OUT) :: ierror


Python:
MPI.Request.Waitall(type cls, requests, statuses=None)


Use MPI_STATUSES_IGNORE to ignore
```

How to read routine prototypes: 1.5.4.

4.3.2.1.3 **Wait for any/some requests** The 'waitall' routine is good if you need all nonblocking communications to be finished before you can proceed with the rest of the program. However, sometimes it is possible to take action as each request is satisfied. In that case you could use `MPI_Waitany` and write:

```
for (p=0; p<nrequests; p++) {
  MPI_Waitany(nrequests,request_array,&index,&status);
  // operate on buffer[index]
}
```

Note that this routine takes a single status argument, passed by reference, and not an array of statuses!

```
Semantics:
int MPI_Waitany(
    int count, MPI_Request array_of_requests[], int *index,
    MPI_Status *status)

IN count: list length (non-negative integer)
INOUT array_of_requests: array of requests (array of handles)
OUT index: index of handle for operation that completed (integer)
OUT status: status object (Status)
```

```
C:
MPI_Waitany(count, array_of_requests, index, status, ierror)

Fortran:
INTEGER, INTENT(IN) :: count
TYPE(MPI_Request), INTENT(INOUT) :: array_of_requests(count)
INTEGER, INTENT(OUT) :: index
TYPE(MPI_Status) :: status
INTEGER, OPTIONAL, INTENT(OUT) :: ierror

Python:
MPI.Request.Waitany( requests,status=None )
class method, returns index
```

How to read routine prototypes: 1.5.4.

Finally, `MPI_Waitsome` is very much like `Waitany`, except that it returns multiple numbers, if multiple requests are satisfied. Now the status argument is an array of `MPI_Status` objects.

Figure 4.8 shows the trace of a non-blocking execution using `MPI_Waitall`.

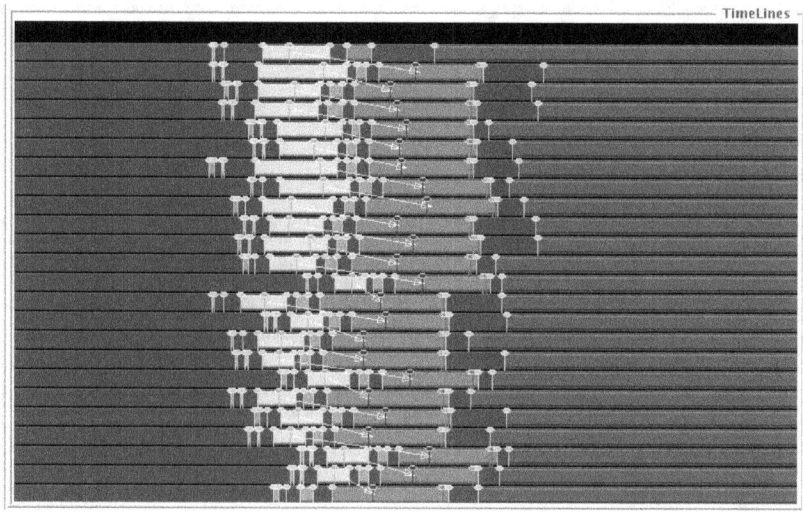

Figure 4.8: A trace of a nonblocking send between neighbouring processors

4.3.2.2 Test: non-blocking request wait

The `MPI_Wait...` routines are blocking. Thus, they are a good solution if the receiving process can not do anything until the data (or at least *some* data) is actually received. The `MPI_Test....` calls are themselves non-blocking: they test for whether one or more requests have been fullfilled, but otherwise immediately return. This can be used in the *master-worker model*: the master process creates tasks, and sends them to whichever worker process has finished its work, but while it waits for the workers it can itself do useful work. Pseudo-code:

```
while ( not done ) {
  // create new inputs for a while
  ....
  // see if anyone has finished
  MPI_Test( .... &index, &flag );
  if ( flag ) {
    // receive processed data and send new
}
```

C:
```
int MPI_Testany(
    int count, MPI_Request array_of_requests[],
    int *index, int *flag, MPI_Status *status)
```

Fortran:

```
MPI_Testany(count, array_of_requests, index, flag, status, ierror)
INTEGER, INTENT(IN) :: count
TYPE(MPI_Request), INTENT(INOUT) :: array_of_requests(count)
INTEGER, INTENT(OUT) :: index
LOGICAL, INTENT(OUT) :: flag
TYPE(MPI_Status) :: status
INTEGER, OPTIONAL, INTENT(OUT) :: ierror
```

How to read routine prototypes: 1.5.4.

```
Semantics:
MPI_TESTALL(count, array_of_requests, flag, array_of_statuses)
IN countlists length (non-negative integer)
INOUT array_of_requestsarray of requests (array of handles)
OUT flag(logical)
OUT array_of_statusesarray of status objects (array of Status)
```

C:
```
int MPI_Testall(
    int count, MPI_Request array_of_requests[],
    int *flag, MPI_Status array_of_statuses[])
```

Fortran:
```
MPI_Testall(count, array_of_requests, flag, array_of_statuses, ierror)
INTEGER, INTENT(IN) :: count
TYPE(MPI_Request), INTENT(INOUT) :: array_of_requests(count)
LOGICAL, INTENT(OUT) :: flag
TYPE(MPI_Status) :: array_of_statuses(*)
INTEGER, OPTIONAL, INTENT(OUT) :: ierror
```

How to read routine prototypes: 1.5.4.

Exercise 4.15. Read section HPSC-6.5 and give pseudo-code for the distributed sparse matrix-vector product using the above idiom for using `MPI_Test...` calls. Discuss the advantages and disadvantages of this approach. The answer is not going to be black and white: discuss when you expect which approach to be preferable.

4.3.3   Reference

Here is a simple code that does a non-blocking exchange between two processors:

```
// irecvnonblock.c
MPI_Request request[2];
MPI_Status status[2];
other = nprocs-procno;
MPI_Irecv(&recvbuf,1,MPI_INT,other,0,comm,&(request[0]));
MPI_Isend(&sendbuf,1,MPI_INT,other,0,comm,&(request[1]));
MPI_Waitall(2,request,status);
```

It is possible to omit the status array by specifying `MPI_STATUSES_IGNORE`. Other routines are `MPI_Wait` for a single request, and `MPI_Waitsome`, `MPI_Waitany`.

The above fragment is unrealistically simple. In a more general scenario we have to manage send and receive buffers: we need as many buffers as there are simultaneous non-blocking sends and receives.

```
// irecvloop.c
MPI_Request requests =
  (MPI_Request*) malloc( 2*nprocs*sizeof(MPI_Request) );
recv_buffers = (int*) malloc( nprocs*sizeof(int) );
send_buffers = (int*) malloc( nprocs*sizeof(int) );
for (int p=0; p<nprocs; p++) {
  int left_p = (p-1) % nprocs,
    right_p = (p+1) % nprocs;
  send_buffer[p] = nprocs-p;
  MPI_Isend(sendbuffer+p,1,MPI_INT, right_p,0, requests+2*p);
  MPI_Irecv(recvbuffer+p,1,MPI_INT, left_p,0, requests+2*p+1);
}
MPI_Waitall(2*nprocs,requests,MPI_STATUSES_IGNORE);
```

Instead of waiting for all messages, we can wait for any message to come with `MPI_Waitany`, and process the receive data as it comes in.

```
// irecv_source.c
if (procno==nprocs-1) {
  int *recv_buffer;
  MPI_Request *request; MPI_Status status;
  recv_buffer = (int*) malloc((nprocs-1)*sizeof(int));
```

```
request = (MPI_Request*) malloc((nprocs-1)*sizeof(MPI_Request));

for (int p=0; p<nprocs-1; p++) {
  ierr = MPI_Irecv(recv_buffer+p,1,MPI_INT, p,0,comm,
    request+p); CHK(ierr);
}
for (int p=0; p<nprocs-1; p++) {
  int index,sender;
  MPI_Waitany(nprocs-1,request,&index,&status); //MPI_STATUS_IGNORE);
  if (index!=status.MPI_SOURCE)
printf("Mismatch index %d vs source %d\n",index,status.MPI_SOURCE);
    printf("Message from %d: %d\n",index,recv_buffer[index]);
}
} else {
  ierr = MPI_Send(&procno,1,MPI_INT, nprocs-1,0,comm); CHK(ierr);
}
```

Note the `MPI_STATUS_IGNORE` parameter: we know everything about the incoming message, so we do not need to query a status object. Contrast this with the example in section **??**.

> *Fortran note* The `index` parameter is the index in the array of requests, so it uses *1-based indexing*.

```
// irecv_source.F90
if (mytid==ntids-1) then
   do p=1,ntids-1
      print *,"post"
      call MPI_Irecv(recv_buffer(p),1,MPI_INTEGER,p-1,0,comm,&
           requests(p),err)
   end do
   do p=1,ntids-1
      call MPI_Waitany(ntids-1,requests,index,MPI_STATUS_IGNORE,err)
      write(*,'("Message from",i3,":",i5)') index,recv_buffer(index)
   end do
```

4.3.4 Examples

4.3.4.1 `MPI_Waitall`

`MPI_Waitall`

Post non-blocking `MPI_Irecv` and `MPI_Isend` to/from all others, then use `MPI_Waitall` on the array of requests.

```
// irecvloop.c
MPI_Request requests =
```

```
            (MPI_Request*) malloc( 2*nprocs*sizeof(MPI_Request) );
    recv_buffers = (int*) malloc( nprocs*sizeof(int) );
    send_buffers = (int*) malloc( nprocs*sizeof(int) );
    for (int p=0; p<nprocs; p++) {
      int left_p = (p-1) % nprocs,
        right_p = (p+1) % nprocs;
      send_buffer[p] = nprocs-p;
      MPI_Isend(sendbuffer+p,1,MPI_INT, right_p,0, requests+2*p);
      MPI_Irecv(recvbuffer+p,1,MPI_INT, left_p,0, requests+2*p+1);
    }
    MPI_Waitall(2*nprocs,requests,MPI_STATUSES_IGNORE);
```

In python creating the array for the returned requests is somewhat tricky.

```
    // irecvloop.py
    requests = [ None ] * (2*nprocs)
    sendbuffer = np.empty( nprocs, dtype=np.int )
    recvbuffer = np.empty( nprocs, dtype=np.int )

    for p in range(nprocs):
        left_p = (p-1) % nprocs
        right_p = (p+1) % nprocs
        requests[2*p] = comm.Isend( sendbuffer[p:p+1],dest=left_p )
        requests[2*p+1] = comm.Irecv( sendbuffer[p:p+1],source=right_p)
    MPI.Request.Waitall(requests)
```

4.3.4.2 MPI_Waitany

MPI_Waitany

Each process except for the root does a blocking send; the root posts `MPI_Irecv` from all other processors, then loops with `MPI_Waitany` until all requests have come in. Use `MPI_SOURCE` to test the index parameter of the wait call.

```
    // irecv_source.c
    if (procno==nprocs-1) {
      int *recv_buffer;
      MPI_Request *request; MPI_Status status;
      recv_buffer = (int*) malloc((nprocs-1)*sizeof(int));
      request = (MPI_Request*) malloc((nprocs-1)*sizeof(MPI_Request));

      for (int p=0; p<nprocs-1; p++) {
        ierr = MPI_Irecv(recv_buffer+p,1,MPI_INT, p,0,comm,
          request+p); CHK(ierr);
```

```
    }
    for (int p=0; p<nprocs-1; p++) {
      int index,sender;
      MPI_Waitany(nprocs-1,request,&index,&status); //MPI_STATUS_IGNORE);
      if (index!=status.MPI_SOURCE)
    printf("Mismatch index %d vs source %d\n",index,status.MPI_SOURCE);
      printf("Message from %d: %d\n",index,recv_buffer[index]);
    }
  } else {
    ierr = MPI_Send(&procno,1,MPI_INT, nprocs-1,0,comm); CHK(ierr);
  }
```

In python creating the array for the returned requests is somewhat tricky.

```
// irecv_source.py
if procid==nprocs-1:
    receive_buffer = np.empty(nprocs-1,dtype=np.int)
    requests = [ None ] * (nprocs-1)
    for sender in range(nprocs-1):
        requests[sender] = comm.Irecv(receive_buffer[sender:sender+1],sourc
    # alternatively: requests = [ comm.Irecv(s) for s in .... ]
    status = MPI.Status()
    for sender in range(nprocs-1):
        ind = MPI.Request.Waitany(requests,status=status)
        if ind!=status.Get_source():
            print "sender mismatch: %d vs %d" % (ind,status.Get_source())
        print "received from",ind
else:
    mywait = random.randint(1,2*nprocs)
    print "[%d] wait for %d seconds" % (procid,mywait)
    time.sleep(mywait)
    mydata = np.empty(1,dtype=np.int)
    mydata[0] = procid
    comm.Send([mydata,MPI.INT],dest=nprocs-1)
```

4.4   More about point-to-point communication

4.4.1   Message probing

MPI receive calls specify a receive buffer, and its size has to be enough for any data sent. In case you really have no idea how much data is being sent, and you don't want to overallocate the receive buffer, you can use a 'probe' call.

The calls `MPI_Probe`, `MPI_Iprobe`, accept a message, but do not copy the data. Instead, when probing tells you that there is a message, you can use `MPI_Get_count` to determine its size, allocate a large enough receive buffer, and do a regular receive to have the data copied.

```
// probe.c
if (procno==receiver) {
  MPI_Status status;
  MPI_Probe(sender,0,comm,&status);
  int count;
  MPI_Get_count(&status,MPI_FLOAT,&count);
  float recv_buffer[count];
  MPI_Recv(recv_buffer,count,MPI_FLOAT, sender,0,comm,MPI_STATUS_IGNORE
} else if (procno==sender) {
  float buffer[buffer_size];
  ierr = MPI_Send(buffer,buffer_size,MPI_FLOAT, receiver,0,comm); CHK(ie
}


int MPI_Probe( int source, int tag, MPI_Comm comm,
    MPI_Status *status )

Input parameters:
source - source rank, or MPI_ANY_SOURCE (integer)
tag    - tag value or MPI_ANY_TAG (integer)
comm   - communicator (handle)

Output parameter:
status - message status
```

How to read routine prototypes: 1.5.4.

There is a problem with the `MPI_Probe` call: in a multithreaded environment the following scenario can happen.

1. A thread determines by probing that a certain message has come in.
2. It issues a blocking receive call for that message...
3. But in between the probe and the receive call another thread has already received the message.
4. ... Leaving the first thread in a blocked state with not message to receive.

This is solved by `MPI_Mprobe`, which after a successful probe removes the message from the *matching queue*: the list of messages that can be matched by a receive call. The thread that matched the probe now issues an `MPI_Mrecv` call on that message through an object of type `MPI_Message`.

```
int MPI_Mprobe(int source, int tag, MPI_Comm comm,
    MPI_Message *message, MPI_Status *status)

Input Parameters:
source - rank of source or MPI_ANY_SOURCE (integer)
tag    - message tag or MPI_ANY_TAG (integer)
comm   - communicator (handle)
```

```
Output Parameters:

message - returned message (handle)
status  - status object (status)
```

How to read routine prototypes: 1.5.4.

```
int MPI_Mrecv(void *buf, int count, MPI_Datatype type,
    MPI_Message *message, MPI_Status *status)
```

```
Input Parameters:
count    - Number of elements to receive (nonnegative integer).
datatype - Datatype of each send buffer element (handle).
message  - Message (handle).

Output Parameters:
buf    - Initial address of receive buffer (choice).
status - Status object (status).
IERROR - Fortran only: Error status (integer).

MPI_MRECV(BUF, COUNT, DATATYPE, MESSAGE, STATUS, IERROR)
    <type>    BUF(*)
INTEGER    COUNT, DATATYPE, MESSAGE
INTEGER    STATUS(MPI_STATUS_SIZE), IERROR
```

How to read routine prototypes: 1.5.4.

4.4.2   Wildcards in the receive call

With some receive calls you know everything about the message in advance: its source, tag, and size. In other cases you want to leave some options open, and inspect the message for them after it was received. To do this, the receive call has a *status* parameter. This status is a property of the actually received messsage, so `MPI_Irecv` does not have a status parameter, but `MPI_Wait` does.

Here are some of the uses of the status:

4.4.2.0.1 Source   In some applications it makes sense that a message can come from one of a number of processes. In this case, it is possible to specify `MPI_ANY_SOURCE` as the source. To find out where the message actually came from, you would use the `MPI_SOURCE` field of the status object that is delivered by `MPI_Recv` or the `MPI_Wait...` call after an `MPI_Irecv`.

```
MPI_Recv(recv_buffer+p,1,MPI_INT, MPI_ANY_SOURCE,0,comm,
        &status);
sender = status.MPI_SOURCE;
```

There are various scenarios where receiving from 'any source' makes sense. One is that of the *master-worker model*. The master task would first send data to the worker tasks, then issues a blocking wait for the data of whichever process finishes first.

If a processor is expecting more than one messsage from a single other processor, message tags are used to distinguish between them. In that case, a value of `MPI_ANY_TAG` can be used, and the actual tag of a message can be retrieved with

```
int tag = status.MPI_TAG;
```

If the amount of data received is not known a priori, the amount received can be found as

```
MPI_Get_count(&recv_status,MPI_INT,&recv_count);
```

4.4.3   Synchronous and asynchronous communication

It is easiest to think of blocking as a form of synchronization with the other process, but that is not quite true. Synchronization is a concept in itself, and we talk about *synchronous* communication if there is actual coordination going on with the other process, and *asynchronous* communication if there is not. Blocking then only refers to the program waiting until the user data is safe to reuse; in the synchronous case a blocking call means that the data is indeed transferred, in the asynchronous case it only means that the data has been transferred to some system buffer. The four possible cases are illustrated in figure 4.9.

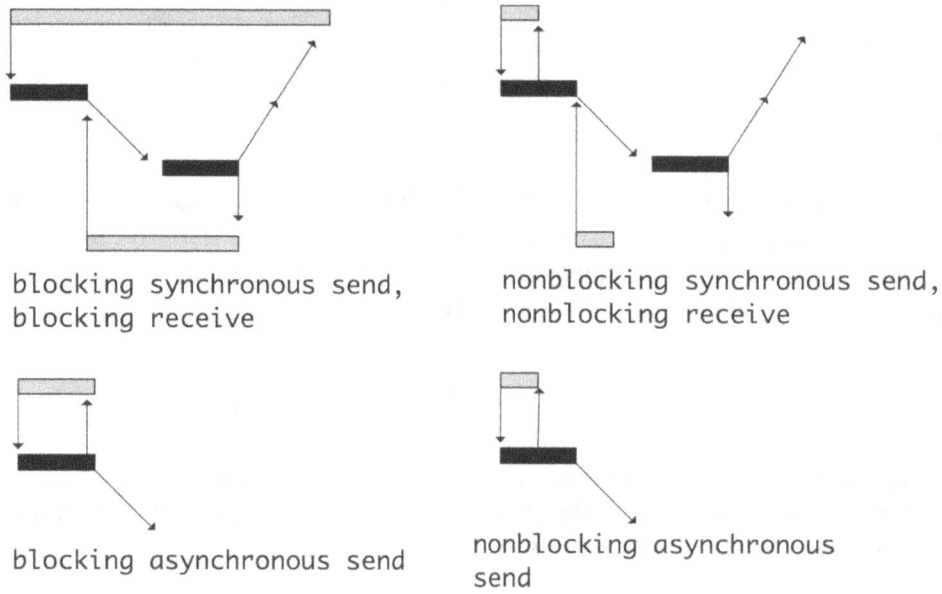

blocking synchronous send,
blocking receive

nonblocking synchronous send,
nonblocking receive

blocking asynchronous send

nonblocking asynchronous
send

Figure 4.9: Blocking and synchronicity

MPI has a number of routines for synchronous communication, such as `MPI_Ssend`.

4.4.4   Buffered communication

By now you have probably got the notion that managing buffer space in MPI is important: data has to be somewhere, either in user-allocated arrays or in system buffers. Buffered sends are yet another way of managing buffer space.

1. You allocate your own buffer space, and you attach it to your process;
2. You use the `MPI_Bsend` call for sending;
3. You detach the buffer when you're done with the buffered sends.

There can be only one buffer per process; its size should be enough for all outstanding `MPI_Bsend` calls that are simultaneously outstanding, plus `MPI_BSEND_OVERHEAD`.

`MPI_Buffer_attach`

```
int MPI_Buffer_attach(
   void *buffer,int size);
```

where the size is indicated in bytes. The possible error codes are

- `MPI_SUCCESS` the routine completed successfully.
- `MPI_ERR_BUFFER` The buffer pointer is invalid; this typically means that you have supplied a null pointer.
- `MPI_ERR_INTERN` An internal error in MPI has been detected.

The buffer is detached with `MPI_Buffer_detach`:

```
int MPI_Buffer_detach(
   void *buffer, int *size);
```

This returns the address and size of the buffer; the call blocks until all buffered messages have been delivered.

You can compute the needed size of the buffer with `MPI_Pack_size`; see section 5.4.3.

`MPI_Bsend`

```
int MPI_Bsend(
   const void *buf, int count, MPI_Datatype datatype,
   int dest, int tag, MPI_Comm comm)
```

The asynchronous version is `MPI_Ibsend`.

You can force delivery by

```
MPI_Buffer_detach( &b, &n );
MPI_Buffer_attach( b, n );
```

4.4.5 Persistent communication

An `Isend` or `Irecv` call has an `MPI_Request` parameter. This is an object that gets created in the send/recv call, and deleted in the wait call. You can imagine that this carries some overhead, and if the same communication is repeated many times you may want to avoid this overhead by reusing the request object.

To do this, MPI has *persistent communication*:

- You describe the communication with `MPI_Send_init`, which has the same calling sequence as `MPI_Isend`, or `MPI_Recv_init`, which has the same calling sequence as `MPI_Irecv`.
- The actual communication is performed by calling `MPI_Start`, for a single request, or `MPI_Startall` for an array or requests.
- Completion of the communication is confirmed with `MPI_Wait` or similar routines as you have seen in the explanation of non-blocking communication.
- The wait call does not release the request object: that is done with `MPI_Request_free`.

The calls `MPI_Send_init` and `MPI_Recv_init` for creating a persistent communication have the same syntax as those for non-blocking sends and receives. The difference is that they do not start an actual communication, they only create the request object.

```
C:
int MPI_Send_init(
    const void* buf, int count, MPI_Datatype datatype,
    int dest, int tag, MPI_Comm comm, MPI_Request *request)

Fortran:
MPI_Send_init(buf, count, datatype, dest, tag, comm, request, ierror)
TYPE(*), DIMENSION(..), INTENT(IN), ASYNCHRONOUS :: buf
INTEGER, INTENT(IN) :: count, dest, tag
TYPE(MPI_Datatype), INTENT(IN) :: datatype
TYPE(MPI_Comm), INTENT(IN) :: comm
TYPE(MPI_Request), INTENT(OUT) :: request
INTEGER, OPTIONAL, INTENT(OUT) :: ierror

Python:
MPI.Comm.Send_init(self, buf, int dest, int tag=0)

Semantics:
IN buf: initial address of send buffer (choice)
IN count: number of elements sent (non-negative integer)
IN datatype: type of each element (handle)
IN dest: rank of destination (integer)
IN tag: message tag (integer)
IN comm: communicator (handle)
OUT request: communication request (handle)
```

How to read routine prototypes: 1.5.4.

```
C:
int MPI_Recv_init(
```

```
      void* buf, int count, MPI_Datatype datatype,
      int source, int tag, MPI_Comm comm, MPI_Request *request)

Fortran:
MPI_Recv_init(buf, count, datatype, source, tag, comm, request,
ierror)
TYPE(*), DIMENSION(..), ASYNCHRONOUS :: buf
INTEGER, INTENT(IN) :: count, source, tag
TYPE(MPI_Datatype), INTENT(IN) :: datatype
TYPE(MPI_Comm), INTENT(IN) :: comm
TYPE(MPI_Request), INTENT(OUT) :: request
INTEGER, OPTIONAL, INTENT(OUT) :: ierror

Python:
MPI.Comm.Recv_init(
      self, buf, int source=ANY_SOURCE, int tag=ANY_TAG)

Semantics:
OUT buf: initial address of receive buffer (choice)
IN count: number of elements received (non-negative integer)
IN datatype: type of each element (handle)
IN source: rank of source or MPI_ANY_SOURCE (integer)
IN tag: message tag or MPI_ANY_TAG (integer)
IN com: mcommunicator (handle)
OUT request: communication request (handle)
```

How to read routine prototypes: 1.5.4.

Given these request object, a communication (both send and receive) is then started with `MPI_Start` for a single request or `MPI_Start_all` for multiple requests, given in an array.

```
      int MPI_Start(MPI_Request *request)

C:
int MPI_Startall(int count, MPI_Request array_of_requests[])

Fortran:
MPI_Startall(count, array_of_requests, ierror)
INTEGER, INTENT(IN) :: count
TYPE(MPI_Request), INTENT(INOUT) :: array_of_requests(count)
INTEGER, OPTIONAL, INTENT(OUT) :: ierror
MPI_STARTALL(COUNT, ARRAY_OF_REQUESTS, IERROR)
INTEGER COUNT, ARRAY_OF_REQUESTS(*), IERROR

Python:
MPI.Prequest.Startall(type cls, requests)

Semantics:
IN countlist length (non-negative integer)
INOUT array_of_requestsarray of requests (array of handle)
```

How to read routine prototypes: 1.5.4.

These are equivalent to starting an `Isend` or `Isend`; correspondingly, it is necessary to issue an `MPI_Wait...` call (section **??**) to determine their completion.

After a request object has been used, possibly multiple times, it can be freed; see 4.4.6.

In the following example a ping-pong is implemented with persistent communication.

```
// persist.c
if (procno==src) {
  MPI_Send_init(send,s,MPI_DOUBLE,tgt,0,comm,requests+0);
  MPI_Recv_init(recv,s,MPI_DOUBLE,tgt,0,comm,requests+1);
  printf("Size %d\n",s);
  t[cnt] = MPI_Wtime();
  for (int n=0; n<NEXPERIMENTS; n++) {
MPI_Startall(2,requests);
MPI_Waitall(2,requests,MPI_STATUSES_IGNORE);
  }
  t[cnt] = MPI_Wtime()-t[cnt];
  MPI_Request_free(requests+0); MPI_Request_free(requests+1);
} else if (procno==tgt) {
  for (int n=0; n<NEXPERIMENTS; n++) {
MPI_Recv(recv,s,MPI_DOUBLE,src,0,comm,MPI_STATUS_IGNORE);
MPI_Send(recv,s,MPI_DOUBLE,src,0,comm);
  }
}
```

As with ordinary send commands, there are the variants `MPI_Bsend_init`, `MPI_Ssend_init`, `MPI_Rsend_init`.

4.4.6   About `MPI_Request`

An `MPI_Request` object is not actually an object, unlike `MPI_Status`. Instead it is an (opaque) pointer. This meeans that when you call, for instance, `MPI_Irecv`, MPI will allocate an actual request object, and return its address in the `MPI_Request` variable.

Correspondingly, calls to `MPI_Wait...` or `MPI_Test` free this object. If your application is such that you do not use 'wait' call, you can free the request object explicitly with `MPI_Request_free`.

```
int MPI_Request_free(MPI_Request *request)
```

You can inspect the status of a request without freeing the request object with `MPI_Request_get_status`:

```
int MPI_Request_get_status(
```

```
        MPI_Request request,
        int *flag,
        MPI_Status *status
    );
```

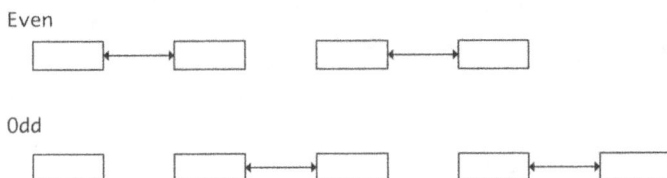

Chapter 5

MPI topic: Data types

5.1 MPI Datatypes

In the examples you have seen so far, every time data was sent, it was as a contiguous buffer with elements of a single type. In practice you may want to send heterogeneous data, or non-contiguous data.

- Communicating the real parts of an array of complex numbers means specifying every other number.
- Communicating a C structure of Fortran type with more than one type of element is not equivalent to sending an array of elements of a single type.

The datatypes you have dealt with so far are known as *elementary datatypes*; irregular objects are known as *derived datatypes*.

5.2 Elementary data types

MPI has a number of elementary data types, corresponding to the simple data types of programming languages. The names are made to resemble the types of C and Fortran, for instance `MPI_FLOAT` and `MPI_DOUBLE` versus `MPI_REAL` and `MPI_DOUBLE_PRECISION`.

MPI calls accept arrays of elements:

```
double x[20];
MPI_Send( x,20,MPI_DOUBLE, ..... )
```

so for a single element you need to take its address:

```
double x;
MPI_Send( &x,1,MPI_DOUBLE, ..... )
```

5.2.1   C/C++

`MPI_CHAR`	only for text data, do not use for small integers
`MPI_UNSIGNED_CHAR`	
`MPI_SIGNED_CHAR`	
`MPI_SHORT`	
`MPI_UNSIGNED_SHORT`	
`MPI_INT`	
`MPI_UNSIGNED`	
`MPI_LONG`	
`MPI_UNSIGNED_LONG`	
`MPI_FLOAT`	
`MPI_DOUBLE`	
`MPI_LONG_DOUBLE`	

There is some, but not complete, support for *C99* types.

5.2.2   Fortran

`MPI_CHARACTER`	Character(Len=1)
`MPI_LOGICAL`	
`MPI_INTEGER`	
`MPI_REAL`	
`MPI_DOUBLE_PRECISION`	
`MPI_COMPLEX`	
`MPI_DOUBLE_COMPLEX`	Complex(Kind=Kind(0.d0))

Addresses have type `MPI_Aint` or `INTEGER (KIND=MPI_ADDRESS_KIND)` in Fortran. The start of the address range is given in `MPI_BOTTOM`.

5.2.2.1   Fortran90 kind-defined types

If your Fortran code uses `KIND` to define scalar types with specified precision, these do not in general correspond to any predefined MPI datatypes. Hence the following routines exist to make *MPI equivalences of Fortran scalar types*:

```
C:
int MPI_Type_create_f90_integer(int r, MPI_Datatype *newtype);

Fortran:
MPI_TYPE_CREATE_F90_INTEGER(INTEGER R, INTEGER NEWTYPE, INTEGER IERROR)

Input Parameter
r : Precision, in decimal digits (integer).

Output Parameters
newtype : New data type (handle).
IERROR : Fortran only: Error status (integer).
```

How to read routine prototypes: 1.5.4.

```
C:
int MPI_Type_create_f90_real(int p, int r, MPI_Datatype *newtype)

Fortran:
MPI_TYPE_CREATE_F90_REAL (P, R, NEWTYPE, IERROR)

Input Parameters
p : Precision, in decimal digits (integer).
r : Decimal exponent range (integer).

Output Parameters
newtype : New data type (handle).
IERROR : Fortran only: Error status (integer).

Either p or r, but not both, may be omitted from calls to
SELECTED_REAL_KIND. Similarly, either argument to
MPI_Type_create_f90_real may be set to MPI_UNDEFINED.
```

How to read routine prototypes: 1.5.4.

```
C:
int MPI_Type_create_f90_real(int p, int r, MPI_Datatype *newtype)

Fortran:
MPI_TYPE_CREATE_F90_REAL (P, R, NEWTYPE, IERROR)

Input Parameters
p : Precision, in decimal digits (integer).
r : Decimal exponent range (integer).

Output Parameters
newtype : New data type (handle).
IERROR : Fortran only: Error status (integer).

Either p or r, but not both, may be omitted from calls to
SELECTED_REAL_KIND. Similarly, either argument to
MPI_Type_create_f90_complex may be set to MPI_UNDEFINED.
```

How to read routine prototypes: 1.5.4.

Examples:

```
INTEGER ( KIND = SELECTED_INTEGER_KIND(15) ) , &
 DIMENSION(100) :: array INTEGER :: root , integertype , error

CALL MPI_Type_create_f90_integer( 15 , integertype , error )
CALL MPI_Bcast ( array , 100 ,
 & integertype , root ,
```

```
        & MPI_COMM_WORLD , error )

     REAL ( KIND = SELECTED_REAL_KIND(15 ,300) ) , &
      DIMENSION(100) :: array
     CALL MPI_Type_create_f90_real( 15 , 300 , realtype , error )

     COMPLEX ( KIND = SELECTED_REAL_KIND(15 ,300) ) , &
      DIMENSION(100) :: array
     CALL MPI_Type_create_f90_complex( 15 , 300 , complextype , error )
```

5.2.3   Python

mpi4py type	NumPy type
MPI.INT	np.intc
MPI.LONG	np.int
MPI.FLOAT	np.float32
MPI.DOUBLE	np.float64

5.3   Derived datatypes

MPI allows you to create your own data types, somewhat (but not completely...) analogous to defining structures in a programming language. MPI data types are mostly of use if you want to send multiple items in one message.

There are two problems with using only elementary datatypes as you have seen so far.

- MPI communication routines can only send multiples of a single data type: it is not possible to send items of different types, even if they are contiguous in memory. It would be possible to use the MPI_BYTE data type, but this is not advisable.
- It is also ordinarily not possible to send items of one type if they are not contiguous in memory. You could of course send a contiguous memory area that contains the items you want to send, but that is wasteful of bandwidth.

With MPI data types you can solve these problems in several ways.

- You can create a new *contiguous data type* consisting of an array of elements of another data type. There is no essential difference between sending one element of such a type and multiple elements of the component type.
- You can create a *vector data type* consisting of regularly spaced blocks of elements of a component type. This is a first solution to the problem of sending non-contiguous data.
- For not regularly spaced data, there is the *indexed data type*, where you specify an array of index locations for blocks of elements of a component type. The blocks can each be of a different size.
- The *struct data type* can accomodate multiple data types.

And you can combine these mechanisms to get irregularly spaced heterogeneous data, et cetera.

5.3.1 Basic calls

The typical sequence of calls for creating a new datatype is as follows:

```
MPI_Datatype newtype;
MPI_Type_<sometype>( < oldtype specifications >, &newtype );
MPI_Type_commit( &newtype );
/* code that uses your new type */
MPI_Type_free( &newtype );
```

5.3.1.1 Datatype objects

MPI derived data types are stored in variables of type `MPI_Datatype`.

5.3.1.2 Create calls

The `MPI_Datatype` varriable gets its value by a call to one of the following routines:

- `MPI_Type_contiguous` for contiguous blocks of data; section 5.3.2;
- `MPI_Type_vector` for regularly strided data; section 5.3.3;
- `MPI_Type_create_subarray` for subsets out higher dimensional block; section 5.3.3.2;
- `MPI_Type_struct` for heterogeneous irregular data; section 5.3.5;
- `MPI_Type_indexed` and `MPI_Type_hindexed` for irregularly strided data; section 5.3.4.

These calls take an existing type, whether elementary or also derived, and produce a new type.

5.3.1.3 Commit and free

It is necessary to call `MPI_Type_commit` on a new data type, which makes MPI do the indexing calculations for the data type.

```
C:
int MPI_Type_commit(MPI_Datatype *datatype)

Fortran:
MPI_Type_commit(datatype, ierror)
TYPE(MPI_Datatype), INTENT(INOUT) :: datatype
INTEGER, OPTIONAL, INTENT(OUT) :: ierror
```

How to read routine prototypes: 1.5.4.

When you no longer need the data type, you call `MPI_Type_free`.

```
int MPI_Type_free (MPI_datatype *datatype)
```

- The definition of the datatype identifier will be changed to `MPI_DATATYPE_NULL`.
- Any communication using this data type, that was already started, will be completed succesfully.
- Datatypes that are defined in terms of this data type will still be usable.

5.3.2 Contiguous type

The simplest derived type is the 'contiguous' type, constructed with `MPI_Type_contiguous`.

```
Semantics:
MPI_TYPE_CONTIGUOUS(count, oldtype, newtype)
IN count: replication count (non-negative integer)
IN oldtype: old datatype (handle)
OUT newtype: new datatype (handle)

C:
int MPI_Type_contiguous(int count, MPI_Datatype oldtype, MPI_Datatype *newtype)

Fortran:
MPI_Type_contiguous(count, oldtype, newtype, ierror)
INTEGER, INTENT(IN) :: count
TYPE(MPI_Datatype), INTENT(IN) :: oldtype
TYPE(MPI_Datatype), INTENT(OUT) :: newtype
INTEGER, OPTIONAL, INTENT(OUT) :: ierror

Python:
Create_contiguous(self, int count)
```

How to read routine prototypes: 1.5.4.

A contigous type describes an array of items of an elementary or earlier defined type. There is no difference between sending one item of a contiguous type and multiple items of the constituent type. This is illustrated

Figure 5.1: A contiguous datatype is built up out of elements of a constituent type

in figure 5.1.

```
// contiguous.c
MPI_Datatype newvectortype;
if (procno==sender) {
  MPI_Type_contiguous(count,MPI_DOUBLE,&newvectortype);
  MPI_Type_commit(&newvectortype);
  MPI_Send(source,1,newvectortype,receiver,0,comm);
  MPI_Type_free(&newvectortype);
} else if (procno==receiver) {
  MPI_Status recv_status;
  int recv_count;
  MPI_Recv(target,count,MPI_DOUBLE,sender,0,comm,
```

```
        &recv_status);
    MPI_Get_count(&recv_status,MPI_DOUBLE,&recv_count);
    ASSERT(count==recv_count);
}
```

5.3.3   Vector type

The simplest non-contiguous datatype is the 'vector' type, constructed with `MPI_Type_vector`.

```
Semantics:
MPI_TYPE_VECTOR(count, blocklength, stride, oldtype, newtype)
IN count: number of blocks (non-negative integer)
IN blocklength: number of elements in each block (non-negative integer)
IN stride: number of elements between start of each block (integer)
IN oldtype: old datatype (handle)
OUT newtype: new datatype (handle)

C:
int MPI_Type_vector
    (int count, int blocklength, int stride,
     MPI_Datatype oldtype, MPI_Datatype *newtype)

Fortran:
MPI_Type_vector(count, blocklength, stride, oldtype, newtype, ierror)
INTEGER, INTENT(IN) :: count, blocklength, stride
TYPE(MPI_Datatype), INTENT(IN) :: oldtype
TYPE(MPI_Datatype), INTENT(OUT) :: newtype
INTEGER, OPTIONAL, INTENT(OUT) :: ierror

Python:
MPI.Datatype.Create_vector(self, int count, int blocklength, int stride)
```

How to read routine prototypes: 1.5.4.

A vector type describes a series of blocks, all of equal size, spaced with a constant stride. This is illustrated in figure 5.2.

The vector datatype gives the first non-trivial illustration that datatypes can be *different on the sender and receiver*. If the sender sends b blocks of length l each, the receiver can receive them as bl contiguous elements, either as a contiguous datatype, or as a contiguous buffer of an elementary type; see figure 5.3. In this case, the receiver has no knowledge of the stride of the datatype on the sender.

In this example a vector type is created only on the sender, in order to send a strided subset of an array; the receiver receives the data as a contiguous block.

```
// vector.c
source = (double*) malloc(stride*count*sizeof(double));
target = (double*) malloc(count*sizeof(double));
```

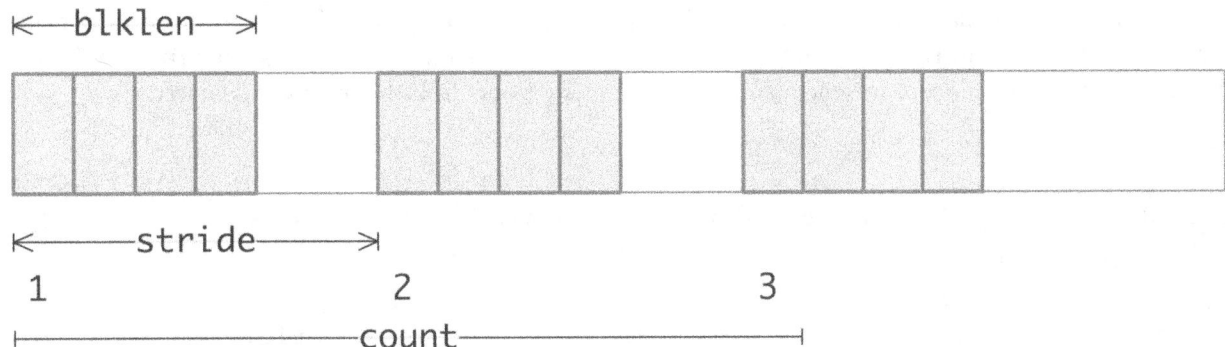

Figure 5.2: A vector datatype is built up out of strided blocks of elements of a constituent type

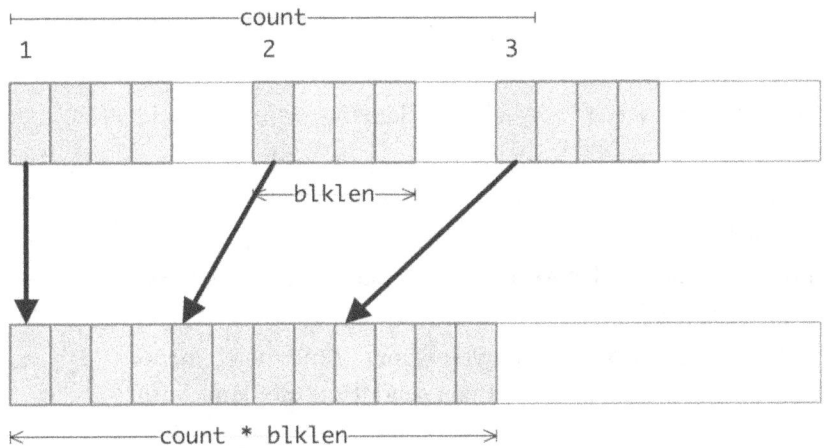

Figure 5.3: Sending a vector datatype and receiving it as elementary or contiguous

```
MPI_Datatype newvectortype;
if (procno==sender) {
  MPI_Type_vector(count,1,stride,MPI_DOUBLE,&newvectortype);
  MPI_Type_commit(&newvectortype);
  MPI_Send(source,1,newvectortype,the_other,0,comm);
  MPI_Type_free(&newvectortype);
} else if (procno==receiver) {
  MPI_Status recv_status;
  int recv_count;
  MPI_Recv(target,count,MPI_DOUBLE,the_other,0,comm,
    &recv_status);
  MPI_Get_count(&recv_status,MPI_DOUBLE,&recv_count);
  ASSERT(recv_count==count);
}
```

As an example of this datatype, consider the example of transposing a matrix, for instance to convert between C and Fortran arrays (see section HPSC-27.2). Suppose that a processor has a matrix stored in C, row-major, layout, and it needs to send a column to another processor. If the matrix is declared as

```
int M,N; double mat[M][N]
```

then a column has M blocks of one element, spaced N locations apart. In other words:

```
MPI_Datatype MPI_column;
MPI_Type_vector(
        /* count= */ M, /* blocklength= */ 1, /* stride= */ N,
    MPI_DOUBLE, &MPI_column );
```

Sending the first column is easy:

```
MPI_Send( mat, 1,MPI_column, ... );
```

The second column is just a little trickier: you now need to pick out elements with the same stride, but starting at `A[0][1]`.

```
MPI_Send( &(mat[0][1]), 1,MPI_column, ... );
```

You can make this marginally more efficient (and harder to read) by replacing the index expression by `mat+1`.

Exercise 5.1. Suppose you have a matrix of size $4N \times 4N$, and you want to send the elements `A[4*i][4*j]` with $i, j = 0, \ldots, N-1$. How would you send these elements with a single transfer?

Exercise 5.2. Allocate a matrix on processor zero, using Fortran column-major storage. Using P sendrecv calls, distribute the rows of this matrix among the processors.

Exercise 5.3. Let processor 0 have an array x of length $10P$, where P is the number of processors. Elements $0, P, 2P, \ldots, 9P$ should go to processor zero, $1, P+1, 2P+1, \ldots$ to processor 1, et cetera. Code this as a sequence of send/recv calls, using a vector datatype for the send, and a contiguous buffer for the receive. For simplicity, skip the send to/from zero. What is the most elegant solution if you want to include that case?
For testing, define the array as $x[i] = i$.

Exercise 5.4. Write code to compare the time it takes to send a strided subset from an array: copy the elements by hand to a smaller buffer, or use a vector data type. What do you find?

5.3.3.1 Subarrays as vector data

Figure 5.4 indicates one source of irregular data: with a matrix on *column-major storage*, a column is stored in contiguous memory. However, a row of such a matrix is not contiguous; its elements being separated by a *stride* equal to the column length.

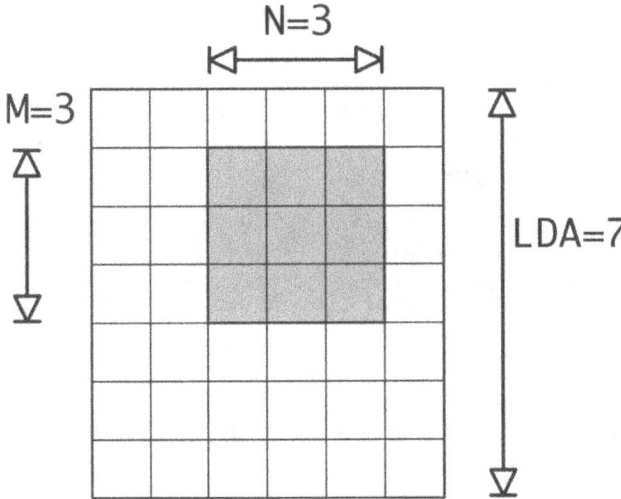

Figure 5.4: Memory layout of a row and column of a matrix in column-major storage

Exercise 5.5. How would you describe the memory layout of a submatrix, if the whole matrix has size $M \times N$ and the submatrix $m \times n$?

5.3.3.2 Subarray type

The vector datatype can be used for blocks in an array of dimension more than 2 by using it recursively. However, this gets tedious. Instead, there is an explicit subarray type

```
Semantics:
MPI_TYPE_CREATE_SUBARRAY(
    ndims, array_of_sizes, array_of_subsizes,
    array_of_starts, order, oldtype, newtype)
IN ndims: number of array dimensions (positive integer)
IN array_of_sizes: number of elements of type oldtype in each dimension
    of the full array (array of positive integers)
IN array_of_subsizes: number of elements of type oldtype in each
    dimension of the subarray (array of positive integers)
IN array_of_starts: starting coordinates of the subarray in each
    dimension (array of non-negative integers)
IN order: array storage order flag (state)
IN oldtype: array element datatype (handle)
OUT newtype: new datatype (handle)

C:
int MPI_Type_create_subarray(
    int ndims, const int array_of_sizes[],
    const int array_of_subsizes[], const int array_of_starts[],
    int order, MPI_Datatype oldtype, MPI_Datatype *newtype)

Fortran:
```

```
MPI_Type_create_subarray(ndims, array_of_sizes, array_of_subsizes,
    array_of_starts, order, oldtype, newtype, ierror)
INTEGER, INTENT(IN) :: ndims, array_of_sizes(ndims),
    array_of_subsizes(ndims), array_of_starts(ndims), order
TYPE(MPI_Datatype), INTENT(IN) :: oldtype
TYPE(MPI_Datatype), INTENT(OUT) :: newtype
INTEGER, OPTIONAL, INTENT(OUT) :: ierror

Python:
MPI.Datatype.Create_subarray(self, sizes, subsizes, starts, int order=ORDER_C)
```

How to read routine prototypes: 1.5.4.

This describes the dimensionality and extent of the array, and the starting point (the 'upper left corner') and extent of the subarray. The possibilities for the `order` parameter are `MPI_ORDER_C` and `MPI_ORDER_FORTRAN`.

Exercise 5.6.

> Assume that your number of processors is $P = Q^3$, and that each process has an array of identical size. Use `MPI_Type_create_subarray` to gather all data onto a root process. Use a sequence of send and receive calls; `MPI_Gather` does not work here.

5.3.4   Indexed type

The indexed datatype, constructed with `MPI_Type_indexed` can send arbitrarily located elements from an array of a single datatype. You need to supply an array of index locations, plus an array of blocklengths with a separate blocklength for each index. The total number of elements sent is the sum of the blocklengths.

```
Semantics:
count [in] number of blocks --
    also number of entries in indices and blocklens
blocklens [in] number of elements in each block (array of nonnegative integers
indices [in] displacement of each block in multiples of old_type
    (array of integers)
old_type [in] old datatype (handle)
newtype [out] new datatype (handle)

C:
int MPI_Type_indexed(int count, const int array_of_blocklengths[],
    const int array_of_displacements[], MPI_Datatype oldtype, MPI_Datatype
    *newtype)

Fortran:
MPI_Type_indexed(count, array_of_blocklengths, array_of_displacements,
    oldtype, newtype, ierror)
INTEGER, INTENT(IN) :: count, array_of_blocklengths(count),
array_of_displacements(count)
```

```
TYPE(MPI_Datatype), INTENT(IN) :: oldtype
TYPE(MPI_Datatype), INTENT(OUT) :: newtype
INTEGER, OPTIONAL, INTENT(OUT) :: ierror

Python:
MPI.Datatype.Create_vector(self, blocklengths,displacements )
```

How to read routine prototypes: 1.5.4.

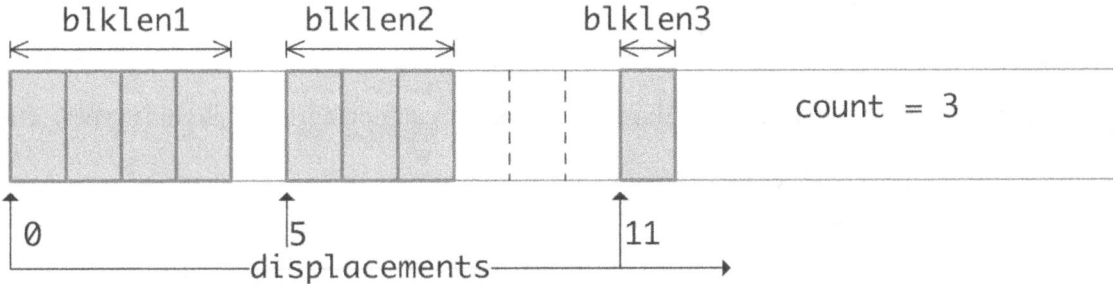

Figure 5.5: The elements of an MPI Indexed datatype

The following example picks items that are on prime number-indexed locations.

```
// indexed.c
displacements = (int*) malloc(count*sizeof(int));
blocklengths = (int*) malloc(count*sizeof(int));
source = (int*) malloc(totalcount*sizeof(int));
target = (int*) malloc(count*sizeof(int));
MPI_Datatype newvectortype;
if (procno==sender) {
  MPI_Type_indexed(count,blocklengths,displacements,MPI_INT,&newvectortype)
  MPI_Type_commit(&newvectortype);
  MPI_Send(source,1,newvectortype,the_other,0,comm);
  MPI_Type_free(&newvectortype);
} else if (procno==receiver) {
  MPI_Status recv_status;
  int recv_count;
  MPI_Recv(target,count,MPI_INT,the_other,0,comm,
    &recv_status);
  MPI_Get_count(&recv_status,MPI_INT,&recv_count);
  ASSERT(recv_count==count);
}
```

You can also `MPI_Type_create_hindexed` which describes blocks of a single old type, but with indix locations in bytes, rather than in multiples of the old type.

```
int MPI_Type_create_hindexed
```

```
(int count, int blocklens[], MPI_Aint indices[],
    MPI_Datatype old_type,MPI_Datatype *newtype)
```

You can use this to pick all occurrences of a single component out of an array of structures. However, you need to be very careful with the index calculation. Use pointer arithmetic, as in the example in section **??**. Another use of this function is in sending an `stl<vector>`, that is, a vector object from the *C++ standard library*, if the component type is a pointer. No further explanation here.

5.3.5   Struct type

The structure type, created with `MPI_Type_create_struct`, can contain multiple data types. The

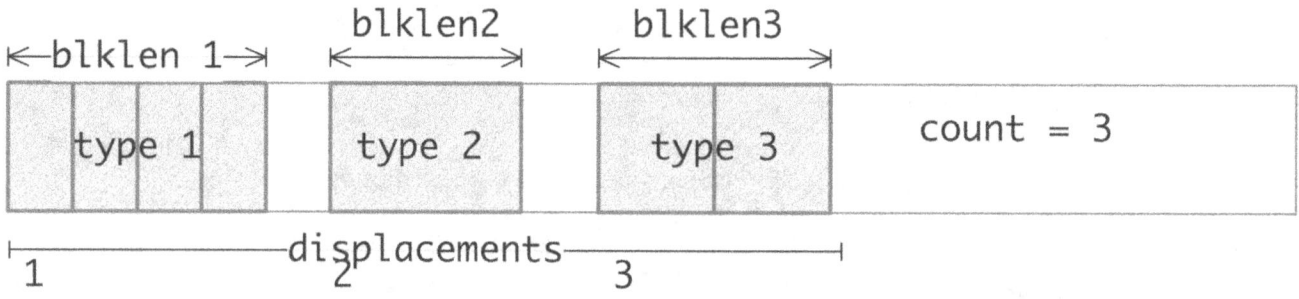

Figure 5.6: The elements of an MPI Struct datatype

specification contains a 'count' parameter that specifies how many blocks there are in a single structure. For instance,

```
struct {
  int i;
  float x,y;
} point;
```

has two blocks, one of a single integer, and one of two floats. This is illustrated in figure 5.6.

```
int MPI_Type_create_struct(
    int count, int blocklengths[], MPI_Aint displacements[],
    MPI_Datatype types[], MPI_Datatype *newtype);
```

count The number of blocks in this datatype. The `blocklengths, displacements, types` arguments have to be at least of this length.

blocklengths array containing the lengths of the blocks of each datatype.

displacements array describing the relative location of the blocks of each datatype.

types array containing the datatypes; each block in the new type is of a single datatype; there can be multiple blocks consisting of the same type.

In this example, unlike the previous ones, both sender and receiver create the structure type. With structures it is no longer possible to send as a derived type and receive as a array of a simple type. (It would be possible to send as one structure type and receive as another, as long as they have the same *datatype signature*.)

```
// struct.c
struct object {
  char c;
  double x[2];
  int i;
};
MPI_Datatype newstructuretype;
int structlen = 3;
int blocklengths[structlen]; MPI_Datatype types[structlen];
MPI_Aint displacements[structlen];
// where are the components relative to the structure?
blocklengths[0] = 1; types[0] = MPI_CHAR;
displacements[0] = (size_t)&(myobject.c) - (size_t)&myobject;
blocklengths[1] = 2; types[1] = MPI_DOUBLE;
displacements[1] = (size_t)&(myobject.x[0]) - (size_t)&myobject;
blocklengths[2] = 1; types[2] = MPI_INT;
displacements[2] = (size_t)&(myobject.i) - (size_t)&myobject;
MPI_Type_create_struct(structlen,blocklengths,displacements,types,&newstruc
MPI_Type_commit(&newstructuretype);
{
  MPI_Aint typesize;
  MPI_Type_extent(newstructuretype,&typesize);
  if (procno==0) printf("Type extent: %d bytes\n",typesize);
}
if (procno==sender) {
  MPI_Send(&myobject,1,newstructuretype,the_other,0,comm);
} else if (procno==receiver) {
  MPI_Recv(&myobject,1,newstructuretype,the_other,0,comm,MPI_STATUS_IGNORE)
}
MPI_Type_free(&newstructuretype);
```

Note the `displacement` calculations in this example, which involve some not so elegant pointer arithmetic. It would have been incorrect to write

```
displacement[0] = 0;
displacement[1] = displacement[0] + sizeof(char);
```

since you do not know the way the *compiler* lays out the structure in memory[1].

---

1.   Homework question: what does the language standard say about this?

If you want to send more than one structure, you have to worry more about padding in the structure. You can solve this by adding an extra type `MPI_UB` for the 'upper bound' on the structure:

```
displacements[3] = sizeof(myobject); types[3] = MPI_UB;
MPI_Type_create_struct(struclen+1,.....);
```

The structure type is very similar in functionality to `MPI_Type_hindexed`, which uses byte-based indexing. The structure-based type is probably cleaner in use.

5.3.6   Examples

```
Semantics:
MPI_TYPE_CONTIGUOUS(count, oldtype, newtype)
IN count: replication count (non-negative integer)
IN oldtype: old datatype (handle)
OUT newtype: new datatype (handle)

C:
int MPI_Type_contiguous(int count, MPI_Datatype oldtype, MPI_Datatype *newtype

Fortran:
MPI_Type_contiguous(count, oldtype, newtype, ierror)
INTEGER, INTENT(IN) :: count
TYPE(MPI_Datatype), INTENT(IN) :: oldtype
TYPE(MPI_Datatype), INTENT(OUT) :: newtype
INTEGER, OPTIONAL, INTENT(OUT) :: ierror

Python:
Create_contiguous(self, int count)
```

How to read routine prototypes: 1.5.4.

We send a contiguous data type of double and receive it as an array of separate doubles; we use `MPI_Get_count` to ensure that we got the right amount of data.

```
// contiguous.c
MPI_Datatype newvectortype;
if (procno==sender) {
  MPI_Type_contiguous(count,MPI_DOUBLE,&newvectortype);
  MPI_Type_commit(&newvectortype);
  MPI_Send(source,1,newvectortype,receiver,0,comm);
  MPI_Type_free(&newvectortype);
} else if (procno==receiver) {
  MPI_Status recv_status;
  int recv_count;
  MPI_Recv(target,count,MPI_DOUBLE,sender,0,comm,
    &recv_status);
  MPI_Get_count(&recv_status,MPI_DOUBLE,&recv_count);
```

```
    ASSERT(count==recv_count);
}
```

```fortran
// contiguous.F90
integer :: newvectortype
if (mytid==sender) then
   call MPI_Type_contiguous(count,MPI_DOUBLE_PRECISION,newvectortype,err)
   call MPI_Type_commit(newvectortype,err)
   call MPI_Send(source,1,newvectortype,receiver,0,comm,err)
   call MPI_Type_free(newvectortype,err)
else if (mytid==receiver) then
   call MPI_Recv(target,count,MPI_DOUBLE_PRECISION,sender,0,comm,&
       recv_status,err)
   call MPI_Get_count(recv_status,MPI_DOUBLE_PRECISION,recv_count,err)
   !ASSERT(count==recv_count);
end if
```

5.3.6.1 MPI_Type_indexed

MPI_Type_indexed

We send an indexed data type and receive as separate integers.

```c
// indexed.c
displacements = (int*) malloc(count*sizeof(int));
blocklengths = (int*) malloc(count*sizeof(int));
source = (int*) malloc(totalcount*sizeof(int));
target = (int*) malloc(count*sizeof(int));
MPI_Datatype newvectortype;
if (procno==sender) {
  MPI_Type_indexed(count,blocklengths,displacements,MPI_INT,&newvectortype)
  MPI_Type_commit(&newvectortype);
  MPI_Send(source,1,newvectortype,the_other,0,comm);
  MPI_Type_free(&newvectortype);
} else if (procno==receiver) {
  MPI_Status recv_status;
  int recv_count;
  MPI_Recv(target,count,MPI_INT,the_other,0,comm,
    &recv_status);
  MPI_Get_count(&recv_status,MPI_INT,&recv_count);
  ASSERT(recv_count==count);
}
```

```
// indexed.F90
integer :: newvectortype;
ALLOCATE(indices(count))
ALLOCATE(blocklengths(count))
ALLOCATE(source(totalcount))
ALLOCATE(targt(count))
if (mytid==sender) then
   call MPI_Type_indexed(count,blocklengths,indices,MPI_INT,&
        newvectortype,err)
   call MPI_Type_commit(newvectortype,err)
   call MPI_Send(source,1,newvectortype,receiver,0,comm,err)
   call MPI_Type_free(newvectortype,err)
else if (mytid==receiver) then
   call MPI_Recv(targt,count,MPI_INT,sender,0,comm,&
        recv_status,err)
   call MPI_Get_count(recv_status,MPI_INT,recv_count,err)
   !    ASSERT(recv_count==count);
end if
```

```
// indexed.py
displacements = np.empty(count,dtype=np.int)
blocklengths = np.empty(count,dtype=np.int)
source = np.empty(totalcount,dtype=np.float64)
target = np.empty(count,dtype=np.float64)
if procid==sender:
    newindextype = MPI.DOUBLE.Create_indexed(blocklengths,displacements)
    newindextype.Commit()
    comm.Send([source,1,newindextype],dest=the_other)
    newindextype.Free()
elif procid==receiver:
    comm.Recv([target,count,MPI.DOUBLE],source=the_other)
```

5.3.6.2 MPI_Type_struct

MPI_Type_struct

A struct data type can consist of different elementary datatypes, so in addition to the displacements and blocklengths we now have an array of MPI datatypes. Also note how the displacement computation is done in bytes.

```
// struct.c
struct object {
  char c;
  double x[2];
```

```
      int i;
};
MPI_Datatype newstructuretype;
int structlen = 3;
int blocklengths[structlen]; MPI_Datatype types[structlen];
MPI_Aint displacements[structlen];
// where are the components relative to the structure?
blocklengths[0] = 1; types[0] = MPI_CHAR;
displacements[0] = (size_t)&(myobject.c) - (size_t)&myobject;
blocklengths[1] = 2; types[1] = MPI_DOUBLE;
displacements[1] = (size_t)&(myobject.x[0]) - (size_t)&myobject;
blocklengths[2] = 1; types[2] = MPI_INT;
displacements[2] = (size_t)&(myobject.i) - (size_t)&myobject;
MPI_Type_create_struct(structlen,blocklengths,displacements,types,&newstruc
MPI_Type_commit(&newstructuretype);
{
  MPI_Aint typesize;
  MPI_Type_extent(newstructuretype,&typesize);
  if (procno==0) printf("Type extent: %d bytes\n",typesize);
}
if (procno==sender) {
  MPI_Send(&myobject,1,newstructuretype,the_other,0,comm);
} else if (procno==receiver) {
  MPI_Recv(&myobject,1,newstructuretype,the_other,0,comm,MPI_STATUS_IGNORE)
}
MPI_Type_free(&newstructuretype);
```

5.3.6.3   MPI_Type_vector

MPI_Type_vector

Send a strided data object with Type_vector and receive it as individual doubles. Use MPI_Get_ count to inspect the MPI_Status object.

```
// vector.c
source = (double*) malloc(stride*count*sizeof(double));
target = (double*) malloc(count*sizeof(double));
MPI_Datatype newvectortype;
if (procno==sender) {
  MPI_Type_vector(count,1,stride,MPI_DOUBLE,&newvectortype);
  MPI_Type_commit(&newvectortype);
  MPI_Send(source,1,newvectortype,the_other,0,comm);
  MPI_Type_free(&newvectortype);
} else if (procno==receiver) {
```

```
    MPI_Status recv_status;
    int recv_count;
    MPI_Recv(target,count,MPI_DOUBLE,the_other,0,comm,
        &recv_status);
    MPI_Get_count(&recv_status,MPI_DOUBLE,&recv_count);
    ASSERT(recv_count==count);
}
```

```
// vector.F90
integer :: newvectortype
ALLOCATE(source(stride*count))
ALLOCATE(target(stride*count))
if (mytid==sender) then
    call MPI_Type_vector(count,1,stride,MPI_DOUBLE_PRECISION,&
        newvectortype,err)
    call MPI_Type_commit(newvectortype,err)
    call MPI_Send(source,1,newvectortype,receiver,0,comm,err)
    call MPI_Type_free(newvectortype,err)
else if (mytid==receiver) then
    call MPI_Recv(target,count,MPI_DOUBLE_PRECISION,sender,0,comm,&
        recv_status,err)
    call MPI_Get_count(recv_status,MPI_DOUBLE_PRECISION,recv_count,err)
end if
```

```
// vector.py
source = np.empty(stride*count,dtype=np.float64)
target = np.empty(count,dtype=np.float64)
if procid==sender:
    newvectortype = MPI.DOUBLE.Create_vector(count,1,stride)
    newvectortype.Commit()
    comm.Send([source,1,newvectortype],dest=the_other)
    newvectortype.Free()
elif procid==receiver:
    comm.Recv([target,count,MPI.DOUBLE],source=the_other)
```

5.3.7 Type size

The space that MPI takes for a structure type can be queried in a variety of ways. First of all MPI_Type_size counts the *datatype size* as the number of bytes occupied by the data in a type. That means that in an *MPI vector datatype* it does not count the gaps.

```
// typesize.c
MPI_Type_vector(count,bs,stride,MPI_DOUBLE,&newtype);
```

```
MPI_Type_commit(&newtype);
MPI_Type_size(newtype,&size);
ASSERT( size==(count*bs)*sizeof(double) );
MPI_Type_free(&newtype);

Semantics:

int MPI_Type_size(
    MPI_Datatype datatype,
    int *size
    );

datatype: [in] datatype to get information on (handle)
size: [out] datatype size in bytes
```

How to read routine prototypes: 1.5.4.

On the other hand, the *datatype extent* is strictly the distance from the first to the last data item of the type, that is, with counting the gaps in the type.

```
MPI_Type_vector(count,bs,stride,MPI_DOUBLE,&newtype);
MPI_Type_commit(&newtype);
MPI_Type_get_extent(newtype,&lb,&asize);
ASSERT( lb==0 );
ASSERT( asize==((count-1)*stride+bs)*sizeof(double) );
MPI_Type_free(&newtype);

Semantics:

int MPI_Type_get_extent(
    MPI_Datatype datatype,
    MPI_Aint *lb, MPI_Aint *extent
    );

datatype: [in] datatype to get information on (handle)
lb: [out] lower bound of datatype (integer)
extent: [out] extent of datatype (integer)
```

How to read routine prototypes: 1.5.4.

(There is a deprecated function `MPI_Type_extent` with the same functionality.)

The *subarray datatype* need not start at the first element of the buffer, so the extent is an overstatement of how much data is involved. The routine `MPI_Type_get_true_extent` returns the lower bound, indicating where the data starts, and the extent from that point.

```
Semantics:
MPI_Type_get_true_extent(datatype,true_lb,true_extent)
```

```
Input argument:
datatype: Data type for which information is wanted (handle).
Output arguments:
true_lb: True lower bound of data type (integer).
true_extent: True size of data type (integer).

C:
int MPI_Type_get_true_extent(
    MPI_Datatype datatype,
    MPI_Aint *true_lb, MPI_Aint *true_extent)
int MPI_Type_get_true_extent_x(
    MPI_Datatype datatype,
    MPI_Count *true_lb, MPI_Count *true_extent)

Fortran
MPI_TYPE_GET_TRUE_EXTENT(DATATYPE, TRUE_LB, TRUE_EXTENT, IERROR)
    INTEGER    DATATYPE, IERROR
    INTEGER(KIND=MPI_ADDRESS_KIND) TRUE_LB, TRUE_EXTENT
MPI_TYPE_GET_TRUE_EXTENT_X(DATATYPE, TRUE_LB, TRUE_EXTENT, IERROR)
    INTEGER    DATATYPE, IERROR
    INTEGER(KIND=MPI_COUNT_KIND) TRUE_LB, TRUE_EXTENT
```

How to read routine prototypes: 1.5.4.

```
// trueextent.c
int sender = 0, receiver = 1, the_other = 1-procno,
  count = 4;
int sizes[2] = {4,6},subsizes[2] = {2,3},starts[2] = {1,2};
MPI_Datatype subarraytype;
if (procno==sender) {
  MPI_Type_create_subarray
    (2,sizes,subsizes,starts,MPI_ORDER_C,MPI_DOUBLE,&subarraytype);
  MPI_Type_commit(&subarraytype);

  MPI_Aint true_lb,true_extent,extent;
  //    MPI_Type_get_extent(subarraytype,&extent);
  MPI_Type_get_true_extent
    (subarraytype,&true_lb,&true_extent);
  MPI_Aint
    comp_lb = ( starts[0]*sizes[1]+starts[1] )*sizeof(double),
    comp_extent = ( (starts[0]+subsizes[0]-1)*sizes[1] + starts[1]+subsi
                  *sizeof(double) - comp_lb;
  //    ASSERT(extent==true_lb+extent);
  ASSERT(true_lb==comp_lb);
  ASSERT(true_extent==comp_extent);
```

```
MPI_Send(source,1,subarraytype,the_other,0,comm);
MPI_Type_free(&subarraytype);
```

5.4 More about data

5.4.1 Datatype signatures

With the primitive types it pretty much went without saying that if the sender sends an array of doubles, the receiver had to declare the datatype also as doubles. With derived types that is no longer the case: the sender and receiver can declare a different datatype for the send and receive buffer, as long as these have the same *datatype signature*.

The signature of a datatype is the internal representation of that datatype. For instance, if the sender declares a datatype consisting of two doubles, and it sends four elements of that type, the receiver can receive it as two elements of a type consisting of four doubles.

You can also look at the signature as the form 'under the hood' in which MPI sends the data.

5.4.2 Big data types

The `size` parameter in MPI send and receive calls is of type integer, meaning that it's maximally $2^{31} - 1$. These day computers are big enough that this is a limitation. Derived types offer some way out: to send a *big data type* of 10^{40} elements you would

- create a contiguous type with 10^{20} elements, and
- send 10^{20} elements of that type.

This often works, but it's not perfect. For instance, the routine   returns the total number of basic elements sent (as opposed to `MPI_Get_count` which would return the number of elements of the derived type). Since its output argument is of integer type, it can't store the right value.

The *MPI 3* standard has addressed this as follows.

- To preserve backwards compatibility, the `size` parameter keeps being of type integer.
- The trick with sending elements of a derived type still works, but
- There are new routines that can return the correct information about the total amount of data; for instance, `MPI_Get_elements_x` returns its result as a `MPI_Count`.

5.4.3 Packing

One of the reasons for derived datatypes is dealing with non-contiguous data. In older communication libraries this could only be done by *packing* data from its original containers into a buffer, and likewise unpacking it at the receiver into its destination data structures.

MPI offers this packing facility, partly for compatibility with such libraries, but also for reasons of flexibility. Unlike with derived datatypes, which transfers data atomically, packing routines add data sequentially to the buffer and unpacking takes them sequentially.

This means that one could pack an integer describing how many floating point numbers are in the rest of the packed message. Correspondingly, the unpack routine could then investigate the first integer and based on it unpack the right number of floating point numbers.

MPI offers the following:

- The `MPI_Pack` command adds data to a send buffer;
- the `MPI_Unpack` command retrieves data from a receive buffer;
- the buffer is sent with a datatype of `MPI_PACKED`.

With `MPI_PACK` data elements can be added to a buffer one at a time. The `position` parameter is updated each time by the packing routine.

```
int MPI_Pack(
    void *inbuf, int incount, MPI_Datatype datatype,
    void *outbuf, int outcount, int *position,
    MPI_Comm comm);
```

Conversely, `MPI_UNPACK` retrieves one element from the buffer at a time. You need to specify the MPI datatype.

```
int MPI_Unpack(
    void *inbuf, int insize, int *position,
    void *outbuf, int outcount, MPI_Datatype datatype,
    MPI_Comm comm);
```

A packed buffer is sent or received with a datatype of `MPI_PACKED`. The sending routine uses the `position` parameter to specify how much data is sent, but the receiving routine does not know this value a priori, so has to specify an upper bound.

```
// packtimer.c
if (mytid==sender) {
  MPI_Pack(&nsends,1,MPI_INT,buffer,buflen,&position,comm);
  for (int i=0; i<nsends; i++) {
    double value = rand()/(double)RAND_MAX;
    MPI_Pack(&value,1,MPI_DOUBLE,buffer,buflen,&position,comm);
  }
  MPI_Pack(&nsends,1,MPI_INT,buffer,buflen,&position,comm);
  MPI_Send(buffer,position,MPI_PACKED,other,0,comm);
} else if (mytid==receiver) {
  int irecv_value;
  double xrecv_value;
  MPI_Recv(buffer,buflen,MPI_PACKED,other,0,comm,MPI_STATUS_IGNORE);
  MPI_Unpack(buffer,buflen,&position,&nsends,1,MPI_INT,comm);
  for (int i=0; i<nsends; i++) {
    MPI_Unpack(buffer,buflen,&position,&xrecv_value,1,MPI_DOUBLE,comm);
  }
```

```
    MPI_Unpack(buffer,buflen,&position,&irecv_value,1,MPI_INT,comm);
    ASSERT(irecv_value==nsends);
}
```

You can precompute the size of the required buffer as follows:

```
C:
int MPI_Pack_size
    (int incount, MPI_Datatype datatype, MPI_Comm comm, int *size)

Input parameters:
incount : Count argument to packing call (integer).
datatype : Datatype argument to packing call (handle).
comm : Communicator argument to packing call (handle).

Output parameters:
size : Upper bound on size of packed message, in bytes (integer).

Fortran:
MPI_PACK_SIZE(INCOUNT, DATATYPE, COMM, SIZE, IERROR)
input parameters:
INTEGER :: INCOUNT, DATATYPE, COMM
INTEGER :: SIZE, IERROR
```

How to read routine prototypes: 1.5.4.

Add one time MPI_BSEND_OVERHEAD.

Exercise 5.7. Suppose you have a 'structure of arrays'

```
struct aos {
    int length;
    double *reals;
    double *imags;
};
```

with dynamically created arrays. Write code to send and receive this structure.

Chapter 6

MPI topic: Communicators

6.1   Subcommunications

In many scenarios you divide a large job over all the available processors. However, your job has two or more parts that can be considered as jobs by themselves. In that case it makes sense to divide your processors into subgroups accordingly.

Suppose for instance that you are running a simulation where inputs are generated, a computation is performed on them, and the results of this computation are analyzed or rendered graphically. You could then consider dividing your processors in three groups corresponding to generation, computation, rendering.

As long as you only do sends and receives, this division works fine. However, if one group of processes needs to perform a collective operation, you don't want the other groups involved in this. Thus, you really want the three groups to be really distinct from each other.

In order to make such subsets of processes, MPI has the mechanism of taking a subset of `MPI_COMM_WORLD` and turning that subset into a new communicator.

Now you understand why the MPI collective calls had an argument for the communicator: a collective involves all proceses *of that communicator*. By making a communicator that contains a subset of all available processes, you can do a collective on that subset.

6.1.1   Scenario: climate model

A climate simulation code has several components, for instance corresponding to land, air, ocean, and ice. You can imagine that each needs a different set of equations and algorithms to simulate. You can then divide your processes, where each subset simulates one component of the climate, occasionally communicating with the other components.

6.1.2   Scenario: quicksort

The popular quicksort algorithm works by splitting the data into two subsets that each can be sorted individually. If you want to sort in parallel, you could implement this by making two subcommunicators, and sorting the data on these, creating recursively more subcommunicators.

114

6.2 Communicator basics

A communicator is an object describing a group of processes. In many applications all processes work together closely coupled, and the only communicator you need is MPI_COMM_WORLD. However, there are circumstances where you want one subset of processes to operate independently of another subset. For example:

- If processors are organized in a 2×2 grid, you may want to do broadcasts inside a row or column.
- For an application that includes a producer and a consumer part, it makes sense to split the processors accordingly.

In this section we will see mechanisms for defining new communicators and sending messages between communicators.

An important reason for using communicators is the development of software libraries. If the routines in a library use their own communicator (even if it is a duplicate of the 'outside' communicator), there will never be a confusion between message tags inside and outside the library.

There are three predefined communicators:

- MPI_COMM_WORLD comprises all processes that were started together by *mpirun* (or some related program).
- MPI_COMM_SELF is the communicator that contains only the current process.
- MPI_COMM_NULL is the invalid communicator. Routines that construct communicators can give this as result if an error occurs.

In some applications you will find yourself regularly creating new communicators, using the mechanisms described below. In that case, you should de-allocate communicators with MPI_Comm_free when you're done with them.

6.3 Duplicating communicators

With MPI_Comm_dup you can make an exact duplicate of a communicator. This may seem pointless, but it is actually very useful for the design of software libraries. Image that you have a code

```
MPI_Isend(...); MPI_Irecv(...);
// library call
MPI_Waitall(...);
```

and suppose that the library has receive calls. Now it is possible that the receive in the library inadvertently catches the message that was sent in the outer environment.

In section 12.9 it was explained that MPI messages are non-overtaking. This may lead to confusing situations, witness the following. First of all, here is code where the library stores the communicator of the calling program:

```
// commdup_wrong.cxx
class library {
private:
```

```
    MPI_Comm comm;
    int procno,nprocs,other;
    MPI_Request *request;
public:
    library(MPI_Comm incomm) {
      comm = incomm;
      MPI_Comm_rank(comm,&procno);
      other = 1-procno;
      request = new MPI_Request[2];
    };
    int communication_start();
    int communication_end();
};
```

This models a main program that does a simple message exchange, and it makes two calls to library routines. Unbeknown to the user, the library also issues send and receive calls, and they turn out to interfere.

Here

- The main program does a send,
- the library call `function_start` does a send and a receive; because the receive can match either send, it is paired with the first one;
- the main program does a receive, which will be paired with the send of the library call;
- both the main program and the library do a wait call, and in both cases all requests are succesfully fulfilled, just not the way you intended.

To prevent this confusion, the library should duplicate the outer communicator, and send all messages with respect to its duplicate. Now messages from the user code can never reach the library software, since they are on different communicators.

```
Semantics:
MPI_COMM_DUP(comm, newcomm)
IN comm: communicator (handle)
OUT newcomm: copy of comm (handle)

C:
int MPI_Comm_dup(MPI_Comm comm, MPI_Comm *newcomm)

F:
MPI_Comm_dup(comm, newcomm, ierror)
TYPE(MPI_Comm), INTENT(IN) :: comm
TYPE(MPI_Comm), INTENT(OUT) :: newcomm
INTEGER, OPTIONAL, INTENT(OUT) :: ierror

Py:
newcomm = oldcomm.Dup(Info info=None)
```

How to read routine prototypes: 1.5.4.

```
// commdup_right.cxx
class library {
private:
  MPI_Comm comm;
  int procno,nprocs,other;
  MPI_Request *request;
public:
  library(MPI_Comm incomm) {
    MPI_Comm_dup(incomm,&comm);
    MPI_Comm_rank(comm,&procno);
    other = 1-procno;
    request = new MPI_Request[2];
  };
  ~library() {
    MPI_Comm_free(&comm);
  }
  int communication_start();
  int communication_end();
};
```

```
// commdup.py
class Library():
    def __init__(self,comm):
        # wrong: self.comm = comm
        self.comm = comm.Dup()
        self.other = self.comm.Get_size()-self.comm.Get_rank()-1
        self.requests = [ None ] * 2
    def communication_start(self):
        sendbuf = np.empty(1,dtype=np.int); sendbuf[0] = 37
        recvbuf = np.empty(1,dtype=np.int)
        self.requests[0] = self.comm.Isend( sendbuf, dest=other,tag=2 )
        self.requests[1] = self.comm.Irecv( recvbuf, source=other )
    def communication_end(self):
        MPI.Request.Waitall(self.requests)

mylibrary = Library(comm)
my_requests[0] = comm.Isend( sendbuffer,dest=other,tag=1 )
mylibrary.communication_start()
my_requests[1] = comm.Irecv( recvbuffer,source=other )
MPI.Request.Waitall(my_requests,my_status)
mylibrary.communication_end()
```

Newly created communicators should be released again with MPI_Comm_free.

6.4   Splitting a communicator

Splitting a communicator into multiple disjoint communicators can be done with `MPI_Comm_split`. This uses a 'colour':

```
Semantics:
MPI_COMM_SPLIT(comm, color, key, newcomm)
IN comm: communicator (handle)
IN color: control of subset assignment (integer)
IN key: control of rank assigment (integer)
OUT newcomm: new communicator (handle)

C:
int MPI_Comm_split(
    MPI_Comm comm, int color, int key,
    MPI_Comm *newcomm)

F:
MPI_Comm_split(comm, color, key, newcomm, ierror)
TYPE(MPI_Comm), INTENT(IN) :: comm
INTEGER, INTENT(IN) :: color, key
TYPE(MPI_Comm), INTENT(OUT) :: newcomm
INTEGER, OPTIONAL, INTENT(OUT) :: ierror
MPI_COMM_SPLIT(COMM, COLOR, KEY, NEWCOMM, IERROR)
INTEGER COMM, COLOR, KEY, NEWCOMM, IERROR

Py:
newcomm = comm.Split(int color=0, int key=0)
```

How to read routine prototypes: 1.5.4.

and all processes in the old communicator with the same colour wind up in a new communicator together. The old communicator still exists, so processes now have two different contexts in which to communicate.

The ranking of processes in the new communicator is determined by a 'key' value. Most of the time, there is no reason to use a relative ranking that is different from the global ranking, so the `MPI_Comm_rank` value of the global communicator is a good choice.

Here is one example of communicator splitting. Suppose your processors are in a two-dimensional grid:

```
MPI_Comm_rank( MPI_COMM_WORLD, &mytid );
proc_i = mytid % proc_column_length;
proc_j = mytid / proc_column_length;
```

You can now create a communicator per column:

```
MPI_Comm column_comm;
MPI_Comm_split( MPI_COMM_WORLD, proc_j, mytid, &column_comm );
```

and do a broadcast in that column:

```
MPI_Bcast( data, /* tag: */ 0, column_comm );
```

Because of the SPMD nature of the program, you are now doing in parallel a broadcast in every processor column. Such operations often appear in *dense linear algebra*.

The `MPI_Comm_split` routine has a 'key' parameter, which controls how the processes in the new communicator are ordered. By supplying the rank from the original communicator you let them be arranged in the same order.

Exercise 6.1. Organize your processes in a grid, and make subcommunicators for the rows and columns. For this compute the row and column number of each process.
In the row and column communicator, compute the rank. For instance, on a 2×3 processor grid you should find:

```
Global ranks:   Ranks in row:   Ranks in colum:
  0   1   2       0   1   2         0   0
  3   4   5       0   1   2         1   1
```

Check that the rank in the row communicator is the column number, and the other way around.
Run your code on different number of processes, for instance a number of rows and columns that is a power of 2, or that is a prime number.

As an example of communicator splitting, consider the recursive algorithm for *matrix transposition*. Processors are organized in a square grid. The matrix is divided on 2×2 block form.

Exercise 6.2. Implement a recursive algorithm for matrix transposition:

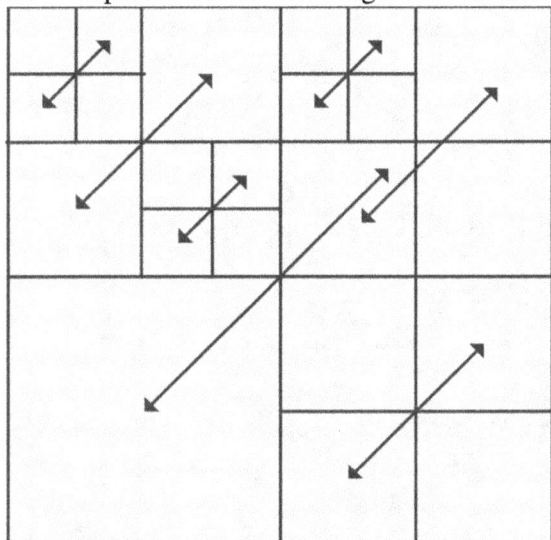

- Swap blocks $(1, 2)$ and $(2, 1)$; then
- Divide the processors into four subcommunicators, and apply this algorithm recursively on each;
- If the communicator has only one process, transpose the matrix in place.

There is an important application of communicator splitting in the context of one-sided communication, grouping processes by whether they access the same shared memory area; see section 11.1.

6.4.1   Process groups

The most general mechanism is based on groups: you can extract the group from a communicator, combine different groups, and form a new communicator from the resulting group.

The group mechanism is more involved. You get the group from a communicator, or conversely make a communicator from a group with `MPI_Comm_group` and `MPI_Comm_create`:

```
MPI_Comm_group( comm, &group);
MPI_Comm_create( old_comm, group, &new_comm );
```

and groups are manipulated with `MPI_Group_incl`, `MPI_Group_excl`, `MPI_Group_difference` and a few more.

You can name your communicators with `MPI_Comm_set_name`, which could improve the quality of error messages when they arise.

6.4.2   Intra-communicators

We start by exploring the mechanisms for creating a communicator that encompasses a subset of `MPI_COMM_WORLD`.

The most general mechanism for creating communicators is through process groups: you can query the group of processes of a communicator, manipulate groups, and make a new communicator out of a group you have formed.

```
MPI_COMM_GROUP (comm, group, ierr)
MPI_COMM_CREATE (MPI_Comm comm, MPI_Group group, MPI_Comm newcomm, ierr)

MPI_GROUP_UNION(group1, group2, newgroup, ierr)
MPI_GROUP_INTERSECTION(group1, group2, newgroup, ierr)
MPI_GROUP_DIFFERENCE(group1, group2, newgroup, ierr)

MPI_GROUP_INCL(group, n, ranks, newgroup, ierr)
MPI_GROUP_EXCL(group, n, ranks, newgroup, ierr)

MPI_GROUP_SIZE(group, size, ierr)
MPI_GROUP_RANK(group, rank, ierr)
```

6.5   Inter-communicators

If two disjoint communicators exist, it may be necessary to communicate between them. This can of course be done by creating a new communicator that overlaps them, but this would be complicated: since the 'inter' communication happens in the overlap communicator, you have to translate its ordering into those of the two worker communicators. It would be easier to express messages directly in terms of those communicators, and this can be done with 'inter-communicators'.

```
MPI_Intercomm_create (local_comm, local_leader, bridge_comm, remote_leader,
```

After this, the intercommunicator can be used in collectives such as

```
MPI_Bcast (buff, count, dtype, root, comm, ierr)
```

- In group A, the root process passes `MPI_ROOT` as 'root' value; all others use `MPI_NULL_PROC`.
- In group B, all processes use a 'root' value that is the rank of the root process in the root group.

Gather and scatter behave similarly; the allgather is different: all send buffers of group A are concatenated in rank order, and places on all processes of group B.

Inter-communicators can be used if two groups of process work asynchronously with respect to each other; another application is fault tolerance (section 12.5).

Chapter 7

MPI topic: Process management

7.1   Process management

The first version of MPI did not contain any process management routines, even though the earlier *PVM* project did have that functionality. Process management was later added with MPI-2.

Unlike what you might think, newly added processes do not become part of MPI_COMM_WORLD; rather, they get their own communicator, and an *intercommunicator* is established between this new group and the existing one. The first routine is MPI_Comm_spawn, which tries to fire up multiple copies of a single named executable. You could imagine using this mechanism to start the whole of your MPI code, but that is likely to be inefficient.

```
Semantics:
MPI_COMM_SPAWN(command, argv, maxprocs, info, root, comm,
    intercomm,array_of_errcodes)

IN command: name of program to be spawned
    (string, significant only at root)
IN argv: arguments to command
    (array of strings, significant only at root)
IN maxprocs: maximum number of processes to start
    (integer, significant only at root)
IN info: a set of key-value pairs telling the runtime system where and
    how to start the processes (handle, significant only at root)
IN root: rank of process in which previous arguments are examined
    (integer)
IN comm: intracommunicator containing group of spawning processes
    (handle)
OUT intercomm: intercommunicator between original group and the
    newly spawned group (handle)
OUT array_of_errcodes: one code per process (array of integer)

C:
int MPI_Comm_spawn(const char *command, char *argv[], int maxprocs,
    MPI_Info info, int root, MPI_Comm comm,
    MPI_Comm *intercomm, int array_of_errcodes[])
```

```
Fortran:
MPI_Comm_spawn(command, argv, maxprocs, info, root, comm, intercomm,
array_of_errcodes, ierror)
CHARACTER(LEN=*), INTENT(IN) :: command, argv(*)
INTEGER, INTENT(IN) :: maxprocs, root
TYPE(MPI_Info), INTENT(IN) :: info
TYPE(MPI_Comm), INTENT(IN) :: comm
TYPE(MPI_Comm), INTENT(OUT) :: intercomm
INTEGER :: array_of_errcodes(*)
INTEGER, OPTIONAL, INTENT(OUT) :: ierror

Python:

MPI.Intracomm.Spawn(self,
    command, args=None, int maxprocs=1, Info info=INFO_NULL,
    int root=0, errcodes=None)
returns an intracommunicator
```

How to read routine prototypes: *1.5.4.*

(If you're feeling sure of yourself, specify `MPI_ERRCODES_IGNORE`.)

Here is an example of a work manager.

```
// spawn_manager.c
MPI_Comm_size(MPI_COMM_WORLD, &world_size);
MPI_Comm_rank(MPI_COMM_WORLD, &manager_rank);

MPI_Attr_get(MPI_COMM_WORLD, MPI_UNIVERSE_SIZE,
        (void*)&universe_sizep, &flag);
if (!flag) {
  if (manager_rank==0) {
    printf("This MPI does not support UNIVERSE_SIZE.\nHow many processes to
    scanf("%d", &universe_size);
  }
  MPI_Bcast(&universe_size,1,MPI_INTEGER,0,MPI_COMM_WORLD);
} else {
  universe_size = *universe_sizep;
  if (manager_rank==0)
    printf("Universe size deduced as %d\n",universe_size);
}
ASSERTm(universe_size>world_size,"No room to start workers");
int nworkers = universe_size-world_size;

/*
 * Now spawn the workers. Note that there is a run-time determination
```

```
* of what type of worker to spawn, and presumably this calculation mus
* be done at run time and cannot be calculated before starting
* the program. If everything is known when the application is
* first started, it is generally better to start them all at once
* in a single MPI_COMM_WORLD.
*/

const char *worker_program = "spawn_worker";
int errorcodes[nworkers];
MPI_Comm_spawn(worker_program, MPI_ARGV_NULL, nworkers,
 MPI_INFO_NULL, 0, MPI_COMM_WORLD, &everyone,
 errorcodes);

// spawn_manager.py
nworkers = universe_size - nprocs

itercomm = comm.Spawn("spawn_worker.py", maxprocs=nworkers)
```

You could start up a single copy of this program with

```
mpirun -np 1 spawn_manager
```

but with a hostfile that has more than one host. In that case the `MPI_UNIVERSE_SIZE` will tell you to the total number of hosts available. If this option is not supported, you can determine yourself how many processes you want to spawn. If you exceed the hardware resources, your multi-tasking operating system (which is some variant of Unix for almost everyone) will use *time-slicing*, but you will not gain any performance.

The spawned program looks very much like a regular MPI program, with its own initialization and finalize calls.

```
// spawn_worker.c
MPI_Comm_size(MPI_COMM_WORLD,&nworkers);
MPI_Comm_rank(MPI_COMM_WORLD,&workerno);
MPI_Comm_get_parent(&parent);
ASSERTm(parent!=MPI_COMM_NULL,"No parent!");

MPI_Comm_remote_size(parent, &remotesize);
if (workerno==0) {
  printf("Deducing %d workers and %d parents\n",nworkers,remotesize);
}
// ASSERTm(nworkers==size-1,"nworkers mismatch. probably misunderstand

// spawn_worker.py
parentcomm = comm.Get_parent()
```

```
nparents = parentcomm.Get_remote_size()
```

Spawned processes wind up with a value of `MPI_COMM_WORLD` of their own, but managers and workers can find each other regardless. The spawn routine returns the intercommunicator to the parent; the children can find it through `MPI_Comm_get_parent`. The number of spawning processes can be found through `MPI_Comm_remote_size` on the parent communicator.

```
Semantics:
MPI_COMM_REMOTE_SIZE(comm, size)
IN comm: inter-communicator (handle)
OUT size: number of processes in the remote group of comm (integer)

C:
int MPI_Comm_remote_size(MPI_Comm comm, int *size)

Fortran:
MPI_Comm_remote_size(comm, size, ierror)
TYPE(MPI_Comm), INTENT(IN) :: comm
INTEGER, INTENT(OUT) :: size
INTEGER, OPTIONAL, INTENT(OUT) :: ierror

Python:
Intercomm.Get_remote_size(self)
```

How to read routine prototypes: 1.5.4.

7.1.1 MPMD

Instead of spawning a single executable, you can spawn multiple with `MPI_Comm_spawn_multiple`.

7.1.2 Socket-style communications

`MPI_Comm_connect MPI_Comm_accept`

`MPI_Open_port MPI_Close_port MPI_Publish_name MPI_Unpublish_name MPI_Comm_join MPI_Comm_disconnect`

Chapter 8

MPI topic: One-sided communication

Above, you saw point-to-point operations of the two-sided type: they require the co-operation of a sender and receiver. This co-operation could be loose: you can post a receive with MPI_ANY_SOURCE as sender, but there had to be both a send and receive call. In this section, you will see one-sided communication routines where a process can do a 'put' or 'get' operation, writing data to or reading it from another processor, without that other processor's involvement.

In one-sided MPI operations, also known as Remote Direct Memory Access (RDMA) or Remote Memory Access (RMA) operations, there are still two processes involved: the *origin*, which is the process that originates the transfer, whether this is a 'put' or a 'get', and the *target* whose memory is being accessed. Unlike with two-sided operations, the target does not perform an action that is the counterpart of the action on the origin.

That does not mean that the origin can access arbitrary data on the target at arbitrary times. First of all, one-sided communication in MPI is limited to accessing only a specifically declared memory area on the target: the target declares an area of user-space memory that is accessible to other processes. This is known as a *window*. Windows limit how origin processes can access the target's memory: you can only 'get' data from a window or 'put' it into a window; all the other memory is not reachable from other processes.

The alternative to having windows is to use *distributed shared memory* or *virtual shared memory*: memory is distributed but acts as if it shared. The so-called Partitioned Global Address Space (PGAS) languages such as Unified Parallel C (UPC) use this model. The MPI RMA model makes it possible to lock a window which makes programming slightly more cumbersome, but the implementation more efficient.

Within one-sided communication, MPI has two modes: active RMA and passive RMA. In *active RMA*, or *active target synchronization*, the target sets boundaries on the time period (the 'epoch') during which its window can be accessed. The main advantage of this mode is that the origin program can perform many small transfers, which are aggregated behind the scenes. Active RMA acts much like asynchronous transfer with a concluding `Waitall`.

In *passive RMA*, or *passive target synchronization*, the target process puts no limitation on when its window can be accessed. (PGAS languages such as UPC are based on this model: data is simply read or written at will.) While intuitively it is attractive to be able to write to and read from a target at arbitrary time, there are problems. For instance, it requires a remote agent on the target, which may interfere with execution of

126

the main thread, or conversely it may not be activated at the optimal time. Passive RMA is also very hard to debug and can lead to strange deadlocks.

8.1   Windows

In one-sided communication, each processor can make an area of memory, called a *window*, available to one-sided transfers. This has the following characteristics:

- The window is defined on a communicator, so the create call is collective.
- The window size can be set individually on each process. A zero size is allowed, but since window creation is collective, it is not possible to skip the create call.

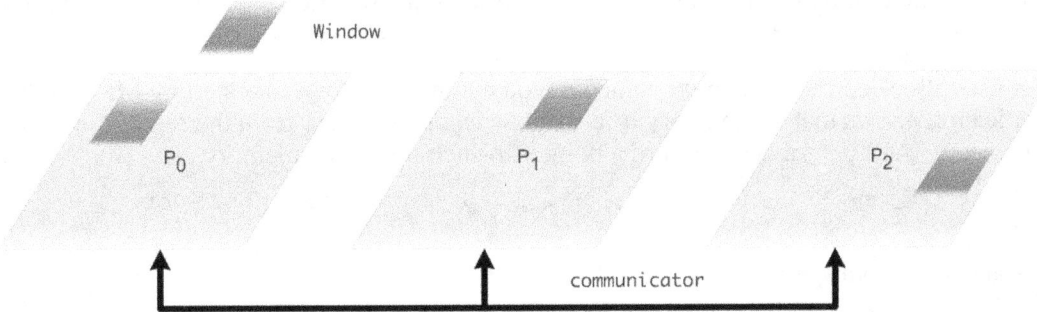

Figure 8.1: Collective definition of a window for one-sided data access

defined with respect to a communicator: each process specifies a memory area. Routine for creating and releasing windows are collective, so each process *has* to call them; see figure 8.1.

```
MPI_Info info;
MPI_Win window;
MPI_Win_create( /* memory area */, info, comm, &window );
MPI_Win_free( &window );
```

(For the `info` parameter you can often use `MPI_INFO_NULL`.) While the creation of a window is collective, each processor can specify its own window size, including zero, and even the type of the elements in it.

```
C:
int MPI_Win_create
    (void *base, MPI_Aint size, int disp_unit,
     MPI_Info info, MPI_Comm comm, MPI_Win *win)

Fortran:
MPI_Win_create(base, size, disp_unit, info, comm, win, ierror)
TYPE(*), DIMENSION(..), ASYNCHRONOUS :: base
INTEGER(KIND=MPI_ADDRESS_KIND), INTENT(IN) :: size
INTEGER, INTENT(IN) :: disp_unit
TYPE(MPI_Info), INTENT(IN) :: info
```

```
TYPE(MPI_Comm), INTENT(IN) :: comm
TYPE(MPI_Win), INTENT(OUT) :: win
INTEGER, OPTIONAL, INTENT(OUT) :: ierror

Python:
MPI.Win.Create
    (memory, int disp_unit=1,
     Info info=INFO_NULL, Intracomm comm=COMM_SELF)
```

How to read routine prototypes: 1.5.4.

The data array must not be PARAMETER or static const.

The size parameter is measured in bytes. In C this is easily done with the sizeof operator; for doing this calculation in Fortran, see section 13.4.3.3.

Instead of exposing user-allocated memory in the window, you can use memory allocated by MPI. In that case, the MPI specification allows that the memory of a window can be separate from the regular program memory. The routine MPI_Alloc_mem can return a pointer to such priviliged memory.

```
int MPI_Alloc_mem(MPI_Aint size, MPI_Info info, void *baseptr)
```

How to read routine prototypes: 1.5.4.

This memory is freed with

```
MPI_Free_mem()
```

These calls reduce to malloc and free if there is no special memory area; SGI is an example where such memory does exist.

There will be more discussion of window memory in section 8.6.1.

8.2 Active target synchronization: epochs

There are two mechanisms for *active target synchronization*, that is, one-sided communications where both sides are involved to the extent that they declare the communication epoch. In this section we look at the first mechanism, which is to use a *fence* operation:

```
MPI_Win_fence (int assert, MPI_Win win)
```

This operation is collective on the communicator of the window. It is comparable to MPI_Wait calls for non-blocking communication.

The use of fences is somewhat complicated. The interval between two fences is known as an *epoch*. You can give various hints to the system about this epoch versus the ones before and after through the assert parameter.

```
MPI_Win_fence((MPI_MODE_NOPUT | MPI_MODE_NOPRECEDE), win);
MPI_Get( /* operands */, win);
MPI_Win_fence(MPI_MODE_NOSUCCEED, win);
```

In between the two fences the window is exposed, and while it is you should not access it locally. If you absolutely need to access it locally, you can use an RMA operation for that. Also, there can be only one remote process that does a `put`; multiple `accumulate` accesses are allowed.

Fences are, together with other window calls, collective operations. That means they imply some amount of synchronization between processes. Consider:

```
MPI_Win_fence( ... win ... ); // start an epoch
if (mytid==0) // do lots of work
else // do almost nothing
MPI_Win_fence( ... win ... ); // end the epoch
```

and assume that all processes execute the first fence more or less at the same time. The zero process does work before it can do the second fence call, but all other processes can call it immediately. However, they can not finish that second fence call until all one-sided communication is finished, which means they wait for the zero process.

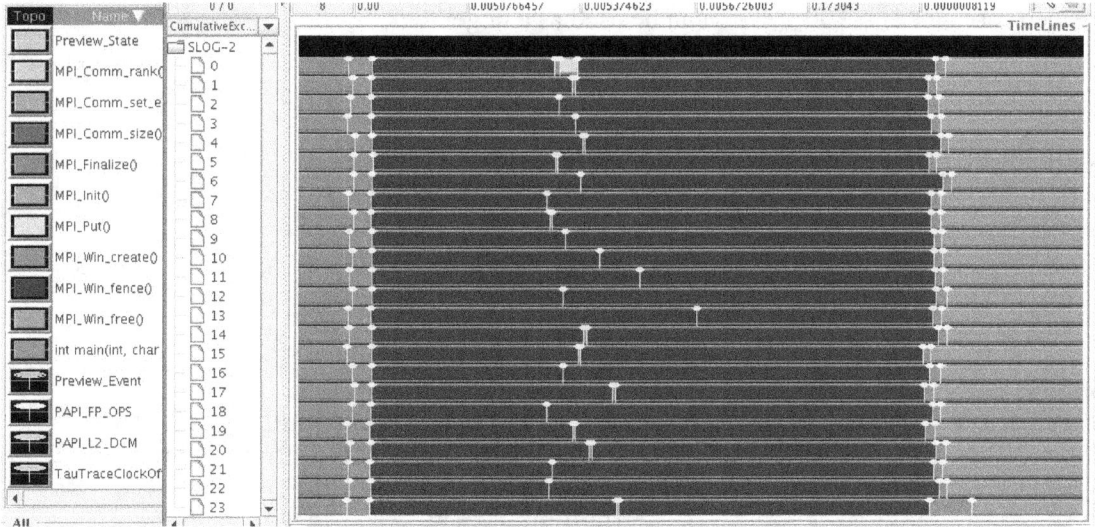

Figure 8.2: A trace of a one-sided communication epoch where process zero only originates a one-sided transfer

```
// putblock.c
MPI_Win_create(&other_number,1,sizeof(int),
              MPI_INFO_NULL,comm,&the_window);
MPI_Win_fence(0,the_window);
if (mytid==0) {
```

```
        MPI_Put( /* data on origin: */   &my_number, 1,MPI_INT,
            /* data on target: */   1,0,           1,MPI_INT,
            the_window);
      sleep(.5);
    }
    MPI_Win_fence(0,the_window);
    if (mytid==1)
      printf("I got the following: %d\n",other_number);
```

As a further restriction, you can not mix `Get` with `Put` or `Accumulate` calls in a single epoch. Hence, we can characterize an epoch as an *access epoch* on the origin, and as an *exposure epoch* on the target.

Assertions are an integer parameter: you can add or logical-or values. The value zero is always correct. For further information, see section 8.3.7.

8.3   Put, get, accumulate

Window areas are accessible to other processes in the communicator by specifying the process rank and an offset from the base of the window.

As in the two-sided case, `MPI_PROC_NULL` can be used as a target rank.

8.3.1   Put

The `MPI_Put` routine is used to put data in the window of a target process

```
C:
int MPI_Put(
  const void *origin_addr, int origin_count, MPI_Datatype origin_datatype,
  int target_rank, MPI_Aint target_disp, int target_count, MPI_Datatype target_
  MPI_Win win)

Semantics:
IN origin_addr: initial address of origin buffer (choice)
IN origin_count: number of entries in origin buffer (non-negative integer)
IN origin_datatype: datatype of each entry in origin buffer (handle)
IN target_rank: rank of target (non-negative integer)
IN target_disp: displacement from start of window to target buffer (non-negativ
IN target_count: number of entries in target buffer (non-negative integer)
IN target_datatype: datatype of each entry in target buffer (handle)
IN win: window object used for communication (handle)

Fortran:
MPI_Put(origin_addr, origin_count, origin_datatype,
  target_rank, target_disp, target_count, target_datatype, win, ierror)
TYPE(*), DIMENSION(..), INTENT(IN), ASYNCHRONOUS :: origin_addr
INTEGER, INTENT(IN) :: origin_count, target_rank, target_count
```

```
TYPE(MPI_Datatype), INTENT(IN) :: origin_datatype, target_datatype
INTEGER(KIND=MPI_ADDRESS_KIND), INTENT(IN) :: target_disp
TYPE(MPI_Win), INTENT(IN) :: win
INTEGER, OPTIONAL, INTENT(OUT) :: ierror

Python:

win.Put(self, origin, int target_rank, target=None)
```

How to read routine prototypes: 1.5.4.

The data is written in the buffer of the target window, using the window parameters that were specified on the target. Specifically, data is written starting at

window_base + target_disp × disp_unit.

Fortran note The disp_unit variable is declared as

```
integer(kind=MPI_ADDRESS_KIND) :: displacement
```

Specifying a literal constant, such as 0, can lead to bizarre runtime errors.

Here is a single put operation. Note that the window create and window fence calls are collective, so they have to be performed on all processors of the communicator that was used in the create call.

```
// putblock.c
MPI_Win_create(&other_number,1,sizeof(int),
               MPI_INFO_NULL,comm,&the_window);
MPI_Win_fence(0,the_window);
if (mytid==0) {
  MPI_Put( /* data on origin: */   &my_number, 1,MPI_INT,
       /* data on target: */   1,0,          1,MPI_INT,
       the_window);
  sleep(.5);
}
MPI_Win_fence(0,the_window);
if (mytid==1)
  printf("I got the following: %d\n",other_number);
```

Exercise 8.1. Write code where process 0 randomly writes in the window on 1 or 2.

8.3.2 Get

The MPI_Get call is very similar.

```
int MPI_Get(void *origin_addr, int origin_count, MPI_Datatype
            origin_datatype, int target_rank, MPI_Aint target_disp,
            int target_count, MPI_Datatype target_datatype, MPI_Win
            win)
```

8.3.3 Accumulate

A third one-sided routine is `MPI_Accumulate` which does a reduction operation on the results that are being put:

```
MPI_Accumulate (
  void *origin_addr, int origin_count, MPI_Datatype origin_datatype,
  int target_rank,
  MPI_Aint target_disp, int target_count, MPI_Datatype target_datatype,
  MPI_Op op,MPI_Win window)
```

Exercise 8.2. Implement an 'all-gather' operation using one-sided communication: each processor stores a single number, and you want each processor to build up an array that contains the values from all processors. Note that you do not need a special case for a processor collecting its own value: doing 'communication' between a processor and itself is perfectly legal.

Accumulate is a reduction with remote result. As with `MPI_Reduce`, the order in which the operands are accumulated is undefined. The same predefined operators are available, but no user-defined ones. There is one extra operator: `MPI_REPLACE`, this has the effect that only the last result to arrive is retained.

8.3.4 Put vs Get

```
while(!converged(A)){
  update(A);
  MPI_Win_fence(MPI_MODE_NOPRECEDE, win);
  for(i=0; i < toneighbors; i++)
    MPI_Put(&frombuf[i], 1, fromtype[i], toneighbor[i],
                        todisp[i], 1, totype[i], win);
  MPI_Win_fence((MPI_MODE_NOSTORE | MPI_MODE_NOSUCCEED), win);
  }
```

```
while(!converged(A)){
  update_boundary(A);
  MPI_Win_fence((MPI_MODE_NOPUT | MPI_MODE_NOPRECEDE), win);
  for(i=0; i < fromneighbors; i++)
    MPI_Get(&tobuf[i], 1, totype[i], fromneighbor[i],
                    fromdisp[i], 1, fromtype[i], win);
  update_core(A);
  MPI_Win_fence(MPI_MODE_NOSUCCEED, win);
  }
```

8.3.5 Accumulate

```
C:
```

```
int MPI_Accumulate
    (const void *origin_addr, int origin_count,MPI_Datatype origin_datatype,
     int target_rank,MPI_Aint target_disp, int target_count,MPI_Datatype target_dat
     MPI_Op op, MPI_Win win)
int MPI_Raccumulate
    (const void *origin_addr, int origin_count,MPI_Datatype origin_datatype,
     int target_rank,MPI_Aint target_disp, int target_count,MPI_Datatype target_dat
     MPI_Op op, MPI_Win win,MPI_Request *request)
```

Input Parameters

origin_addr : Initial address of buffer (choice).
origin_count : Number of entries in buffer (nonnegative integer).
origin_datatype : Data type of each buffer entry (handle).
target_rank : Rank of target (nonnegative integer).
target_disp : Displacement from start of window to beginning of target buffer (non
target_count : Number of entries in target buffer (nonnegative integer).
target_datatype : Data type of each entry in target buffer (handle).
op : Reduce operation (handle).
win : Window object (handle).

Output Parameter

MPI_Raccumulate: RMA request
IERROR (Fortran only): Error status (integer).

Fortran:

```
MPI_ACCUMULATE
    (ORIGIN_ADDR, ORIGIN_COUNT, ORIGIN_DATATYPE,
     TARGET_RANK,TARGET_DISP, TARGET_COUNT, TARGET_DATATYPE,
     OP, WIN, IERROR)
<type> ORIGIN_ADDR(*)
INTEGER(KIND=MPI_ADDRESS_KIND) :: TARGET_DISP
INTEGER :: ORIGIN_COUNT, ORIGIN_DATATYPE,
           TARGET_RANK, TARGET_COUNT,TARGET_DATATYPE,
           OP, WIN, IERROR
MPI_RACCUMULATE
    (ORIGIN_ADDR, ORIGIN_COUNT, ORIGIN_DATATYPE,
     TARGET_RANK,TARGET_DISP, TARGET_COUNT, TARGET_DATATYPE,
     OP, WIN, REQUEST, IERROR)
<type> ORIGIN_ADDR(*)
INTEGER(KIND=MPI_ADDRESS_KIND) :: TARGET_DISP
INTEGER :: ORIGIN_COUNT, ORIGIN_DATATYPE, TARGET_RANK, TARGET_COUNT, TARGET_DATATY
           OP, WIN, REQUEST, IERROR
```

Python:
MPI.Win.Accumulate(self, origin, int target_rank, target=None, Op op=SUM)

How to read routine prototypes: 1.5.4.

Exercise 8.3.

Implement a shared counter:

- One process maintains a counter;
- Iterate: all others at random moments update this counter.
- When the counter is zero, everyone stops iterating.

The problem here is data synchronization: does everyone see the counter the same way?

8.3.6 Request-based operations

Analogous to `MPI_Isend` there are request based one-sided operations:

```
C:
int MPI_Rput(
    const void *origin_addr, int origin_count, MPI_Datatype origin_datatype,
    int target_rank, MPI_Aint target_disp, int target_count, MPI_Datatype target_
    MPI_Win win, MPI_Request *request)

Semantics:
IN origin_addr: initial address of origin buffer (choice)
IN origin_count: number of entries in origin buffer (non-negative integer)
IN origin_datatype: datatype of each entry in origin buffer (handle)
IN target_rank: rank of target (non-negative integer)
IN target_disp: displacement from start of window to target buffer (non-negativ
IN target_count: number of entries in target buffer (non-negative integer)
IN target_datatype: datatype of each entry in target buffer (handle)
IN win: window object used for communication (handle)
OUT request: RMA request (handle)
```

How to read routine prototypes: 1.5.4.

and similarly `MPI_Rget` and `MPI_Raccumulate`.

These only apply to passive target synchronization. Any `MPI_Win_flush...` call also terminates these transfers.

8.3.7 Assertions

The `MPI_Win_fence` call, as well `MPI_Win_start` and such, take an argument through which assertions can be passed about the activity before, after, and during the epoch. The value zero is always allowed, by you can make your program more efficient by specifying one or more of the following, combined by bitwise OR in C/C++ or `IOR` in Fortran.

MPI_WIN_START Supports the option:

MPI_MODE_NOCHECK the matching calls to `MPI_WIN_POST` have already completed on all target processes when the call to `MPI_WIN_START` is made. The nocheck option can be specified in a start call if and only if it is specified in each matching post call. This is similar to the optimization of "ready-send" that may save a handshake when the handshake is implicit in the code. (However, ready-send is matched by a regular receive, whereas both start and post must specify the nocheck option.)

MPI_WIN_POST supports the following options:

MPI_MODE_NOCHECK the matching calls to `MPI_WIN_START` have not yet occurred on any origin processes when the call to `MPI_WIN_POST` is made. The nocheck option can be specified by a post call if and only if it is specified by each matching start call.

MPI_MODE_NOSTORE the local window was not updated by local stores (or local get or receive calls) since last synchronization. This may avoid the need for cache synchronization at the post call.

MPI_MODE_NOPUT the local window will not be updated by put or accumulate calls after the post call, until the ensuing (wait) synchronization. This may avoid the need for cache synchronization at the wait call.

MPI_WIN_FENCE supports the following options:

MPI_MODE_NOSTORE the local window was not updated by local stores (or local get or receive calls) since last synchronization.

MPI_MODE_NOPUT the local window will not be updated by put or accumulate calls after the fence call, until the ensuing (fence) synchronization.

MPI_MODE_NOPRECEDE the fence does not complete any sequence of locally issued RMA calls. If this assertion is given by any process in the window group, then it must be given by all processes in the group.

MPI_MODE_NOSUCCEED the fence does not start any sequence of locally issued RMA calls. If the assertion is given by any process in the window group, then it must be given by all processes in the group.

MPI_WIN_LOCK supports the following option:

MPI_MODE_NOCHECK no other process holds, or will attempt to acquire a conflicting lock, while the caller holds the window lock. This is useful when mutual exclusion is achieved by other means, but the coherence operations that may be attached to the lock and unlock calls are still required.

As an example, let's look at *halo update*. The array A is updated using the local values and the halo that comes from bordering processors, either through Put or Get operations.

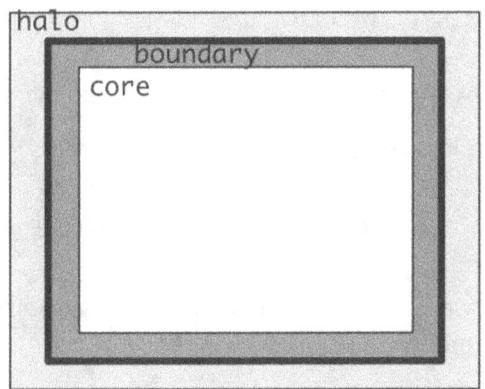

In a first version we separate computation and communication. Each iteration has two fences. Between the two fences in the loop body we do the `MPI_Put` operation; between the second and and first one of the next iteration there is only computation, so we add the `NOPRECEDE` and `NOSUCCEED` assertions. The `NOSTORE` assertion states that the local window was not updated: the Put operation only works on remote windows.

```
for ( .... ) {
  update(A);
  MPI_Win_fence(MPI_MODE_NOPRECEDE, win);
  for(i=0; i < toneighbors; i++)
    MPI_Put( ... );
  MPI_Win_fence((MPI_MODE_NOSTORE | MPI_MODE_NOSUCCEED), win);
  }
```

Next, we split the update in the core part, which can be done purely from local values, and the boundary, which needs local and halo values. Update of the core can overlap the communication of the halo.

```
for ( .... ) {
  update_boundary(A);
  MPI_Win_fence((MPI_MODE_NOPUT | MPI_MODE_NOPRECEDE), win);
  for(i=0; i < fromneighbors; i++)
    MPI_Get( ... );
  update_core(A);
  MPI_Win_fence(MPI_MODE_NOSUCCEED, win);
  }
```

The NOPRECEDE and NOSUCCEED assertions still hold, but the Get operation implies that instead of NOSTORE in the second fence, we use NOPUT in the first.

8.3.8 More active target synchronization

The 'fence' mechanism (section **??**) uses a global synchronization on the communicator of the window, which may lead to performance inefficiencies if processors are not in step which each other. There is a mechanism that is more fine-grained, by using synchronization only on a processor *group*. This takes four different calls, two for starting and two for ending the epoch, separately for target and origin.

You start and complete an *exposure epoch* with :

```
int MPI_Win_post(MPI_Group group, int assert, MPI_Win win)
int MPI_Win_wait(MPI_Win win)
```

In other words, this turns your window into the *target* for a remote access.

You start and complete an *access epoch* with :

```
int MPI_Win_start(MPI_Group group, int assert, MPI_Win win)
int MPI_Win_complete(MPI_Win win)
```

In other words, these calls border the access to a remote window, with the current processor being the *origin* of the remote access.

In the following snippet a single processor puts data on one other. Note that they both have their own definition of the group, and that the receiving process only does the post and wait calls.

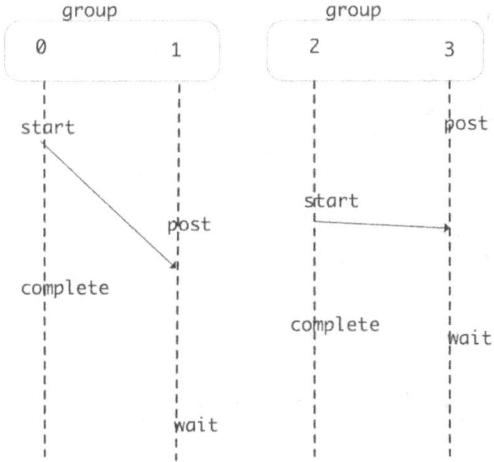

Figure 8.3: Window locking calls in fine-grained active target synchronization

```
// postwaitwin.c
if (procno==origin) {
  MPI_Group_incl(all_group,1,&target,&two_group);
  // access
  MPI_Win_start(two_group,0,the_window);
  MPI_Put( /* data on origin: */   &my_number, 1,MPI_INT,
           /* data on target: */   target,0,   1,MPI_INT,
      the_window);
  MPI_Win_complete(the_window);
}

if (procno==target) {
  MPI_Group_incl(all_group,1,&origin,&two_group);
  // exposure
  MPI_Win_post(two_group,0,the_window);
  MPI_Win_wait(the_window);
}
```

8.3.9   Atomic operations

The   call atomically retrieves an item from the window indicated, and replaces the item on the target by doing an accumulate on it with the data on the origin.

```
Semantics:

MPI_FETCH_AND_OP(origin_addr, result_addr, datatype, target_rank,
    target_disp, op, win)
IN origin_addr: initial address of buffer (choice)
```

```
OUT result_addr: initial address of result buffer (choice)
IN datatype: datatype of the entry in origin, result, and target buffers
(handle)
IN target_rank: rank of target (non-negative integer)
IN target_disp: displacement from start of window to beginning of target
buffer (non-negative integer)
IN op: reduce operation (handle)
IN win: window object (handle)

C:
int MPI_Fetch_and_op
    (const void *origin_addr, void *result_addr,
     MPI_Datatype datatype, int target_rank, MPI_Aint target_disp,
     MPI_Op op, MPI_Win win)

Fortran:
MPI_Fetch_and_op(origin_addr, result_addr, datatype, target_rank,
     target_disp, op, win, ierror)
TYPE(*), DIMENSION(..), INTENT(IN), ASYNCHRONOUS :: origin_addr
TYPE(*), DIMENSION(..), ASYNCHRONOUS :: result_addr
TYPE(MPI_Datatype), INTENT(IN) :: datatype
INTEGER, INTENT(IN) :: target_rank
INTEGER(KIND=MPI_ADDRESS_KIND), INTENT(IN) :: target_disp
TYPE(MPI_Op), INTENT(IN) :: op
TYPE(MPI_Win), INTENT(IN) :: win
INTEGER, OPTIONAL, INTENT(OUT) :: ierror
```

How to read routine prototypes: 1.5.4.

Exercise 8.4.   Redo exercise 8.3 using `MPI_Fetch_and_op`. The problem is again to make sure all processes have the same view of the shared counter.
Does it work to make the fetch-and-op conditional? Is there a way to do it unconditionally? What should the 'break' test be, seeing that multiple processes can update the counter at the same time?

8.4   More active target synchronization

There is a more fine-grained ways of doing *active target synchronization*. While fences corresponded to a global synchronization of one-sided calls, the `MPI_Win_start`, `MPI_Win_complete`, `MPI_Win_post`, `Win_wait` routines are suitable, and possibly more efficient, if only a small number of processor pairs is involved. Which routines you use depends on whether the processor is an *origin* or *target*.

If the current process is going to have the data in its window accessed, you define an *exposure epoch* by:

```
MPI_Win_post( /* group of origin processes */ )
MPI_Win_wait()
```

This turns the current processor into a target for access operations issued by a different process.

If the current process is going to be issuing one-sided operations, you define an *access epoch* by:

```
MPI_Win_start( /* group of target processes */ )
// access operations
MPI_Win_complete()
```

This turns the current process into the origin of a number of one-sided access operations.

Both pairs of operations declare a *group of processors*; see section 6.4.2 for how to get such a group from a communicator. On an origin processor you would specify a group that includes the targets you will interact with, on a target processor you specify a group that includes the possible origins.

8.5 Passive target synchronization

In *passive target synchronization* only the origin is actively involved: the target makes no calls whatsoever. This means that the origin process remotely locks the window on the target.

During an access epoch, a process can initiate and finish a one-sided transfer.

```
If (rank == 0) {
  MPI_Win_lock (MPI_LOCK_EXCLUSIVE, 1, 0, win);
  MPI_Put (outbuf, n, MPI_INT, 1, 0, n, MPI_INT, win);
  MPI_Win_unlock (1, win);
}
```

The two lock types are:

- MPI_LOCK_SHARED which should be used for Get calls: since multiple processors are allowed to read from a window in the same epoch, the lock can be shared.
- MPI_LOCK_EXCLUSIVE which should be used for Put and Accumulate calls: since only one processor is allowed to write to a window during one epoch, the lock should be exclusive.

These routines make MPI behave like a shared memory system; the instructions between locking and un-locking the window effectively become *atomic operations*.

```
C:
int MPI_Win_lock(int lock_type, int rank, int assert, MPI_Win win)

Input Parameters:
lock_type - Indicates whether other processes may access the target window at the
    same time (if MPI_LOCK_SHARED) or not (MPI_LOCK_EXCLUSIVE)
rank - rank of locked window (nonnegative integer)
assert - Used to optimize this call; zero may be used as a default. (integer)
win - window object (handle)

Python:
MPI.Win.Lock(self,
```

```
                    int rank, int lock_type=LOCK_EXCLUSIVE, int assertion=0)
```

How to read routine prototypes: 1.5.4.

To lock the windows of all processes in the group of the windows, use `MPI_Win_lock_all`:

```
C:
int MPI_Win_lock( int assert, MPI_Win win)

Input Parameters:
assert - Used to optimize this call; zero may be used as a default. (integer)
win - window object (handle)
```

How to read routine prototypes: 1.5.4.

To unlock a window, use `MPI_Win_unlock` and `MPI_Win_unlock_all`.

```
C:


Py:
MPI.Win.Unlock(self, int rank)
MPI.Win.Unlock_all(self)
```

How to read routine prototypes: 1.5.4.

The RMA epoch is now defined between the lock and unlock calls, and operations are only guaranteed to be concluded after the unlock call.

8.5.1   Atomic shared memory operations

The above example is of limited use. Suppose processor zero has a data structure `work_table` with items that need to be processed. A counter `first_work` keeps track of the lowest numbered item that still needs processing. You can imagine the following *master-worker* scenario:

- Each process connects to the master,
- inspects the `first_work` variable,
- retrieves the corresponding work item, and
- increments the `first_work` variable.

It is important here to avoid a *race condition* (see section HPSC-2.6.1.5) that would result from a second process reading the `first_work` variable before the first process could have updated it. Therefore, the reading and updating needs to be an *atomic operation*.

Unfortunately, you can not have a put and get call in the same access epoch. For this reason, MPI version 3 has added certain atomic operations, such as `MPI_Fetch_and_op`.

Exercise 8.5.

- Let each process have an empty array of sufficient length and a stack pointer that maintains the first free location.
- Now let each process randomly put data in a free location of another process' array.
- Use window locking. (Why is active target synchronization not possible?)

8.6   Details

8.6.1   Window memory

An MPI Window is built around a buffer. There are four possible treatments of that buffer:

- You can pass a user buffer to MPI_Win_create. This buffer can be an ordinary array, or it can be created with MPI_Alloc_mem.
- With MPI_Win_create_dynamic you can attach the buffer later, when its size has been dynamically determined.
- You can leave the buffer allocation to mpi with MPI_Win_allocate; and
- If a communicator is on a shared memory (see section 11.1) you can create a winow in that shared memory with MPI_Win_allocate_shared.

We looked at the first case, passing a buffer to the window create call, in section 8.1. This buffer could be allocated with new or MPI_Alloc_mem. An easier way to let MPI do the allocation is

```
Semantics:
MPI_WIN_ALLOCATE(size, disp_unit, info, comm, baseptr, win)

Input parameters:
size: size of local window in bytes (non-negative integer)
disp_unit local unit size for displacements, in bytes (positive
integer)
info: info argument (handle)
comm: intra-communicator (handle)

Output parameters:
baseptr: address of local allocated window segment (choice)
win: window object returned by the call (handle)

C:
int MPI_Win_allocate
    (MPI_Aint size, int disp_unit, MPI_Info info,
     MPI_Comm comm, void *baseptr, MPI_Win *win)

Fortran:
MPI_Win_allocate
    (size, disp_unit, info, comm, baseptr, win, ierror)
USE, INTRINSIC :: ISO_C_BINDING, ONLY : C_PTR
INTEGER(KIND=MPI_ADDRESS_KIND), INTENT(IN) :: size
INTEGER, INTENT(IN) :: disp_unit
TYPE(MPI_Info), INTENT(IN) :: info
TYPE(MPI_Comm), INTENT(IN) :: comm
TYPE(C_PTR), INTENT(OUT) :: baseptr
TYPE(MPI_Win), INTENT(OUT) :: win
INTEGER, OPTIONAL, INTENT(OUT) :: ierror
```

How to read routine prototypes: 1.5.4.

which returns a pointer to the data area created. The data allocated is freed by MPI_Win_free.

It is also possible to have windows where the size is dynamically set.

```
int MPI_Win_create_dynamic(MPI_Info info, MPI_Comm comm, MPI_Win *win)

Input Parameters
info : info argument (handle)
comm : communicator (handle)

Output Parameters
win : window object returned by the call (handle)
```

How to read routine prototypes: 1.5.4.

Memory is attached to the window:

```
Semantics:
MPI_Win_attach(win, base, size)

Input Parameters:
win : window object (handle)
base : initial address of memory to be attached
size : size of memory to be attached in bytes

C:
int MPI_Win_attach(MPI_Win win, void *base, MPI_Aint size)

Fortran:
MPI_Win_attach(win, base, size, ierror)
TYPE(MPI_Win), INTENT(IN) :: win
TYPE(*), DIMENSION(..), ASYNCHRONOUS :: base
INTEGER(KIND=MPI_ADDRESS_KIND), INTENT(IN) :: size
INTEGER, OPTIONAL, INTENT(OUT) :: ierror
```

How to read routine prototypes: 1.5.4.

and its inverse:

```
Semantics:
MPI_Win_detach(win, base)

Input parameters:
win : window object (handle)
base : initial address of memory to be detached

C:
int MPI_Win_detach(MPI_Win win, const void *base)

Fortran:
MPI_Win_detach(win, base, ierror)
TYPE(MPI_Win), INTENT(IN) :: win
TYPE(*), DIMENSION(..), ASYNCHRONOUS :: base
INTEGER, OPTIONAL, INTENT(OUT) :: ierror
```

How to read routine prototypes: 1.5.4.

8.6.2   Window information

The `MPI_Info` parameter can be used to pass implementation-dependent information; see section 12.3.

```
MPI_Win_get_attr(win, MPI_WIN_BASE, &base, &flag),
MPI_Win_get_attr(win, MPI_WIN_SIZE, &size, &flag),
MPI_Win_get_attr(win, MPI_WIN_DISP_UNIT, &disp_unit, &flag),
MPI_Win_get_attr(win, MPI_WIN_CREATE_FLAVOR, &create_kind, &flag), and
MPI_Win_get_attr(win, MPI_WIN_MODEL, &memory_model, &flag) will return in b


int MPI_Win_get_group(MPI_Win win, MPI_Group *group)
MPI_Win_get_group(win, group, ierror)
TYPE(MPI_Win), INTENT(IN) :: win
TYPE(MPI_Group), INTENT(OUT) :: group
INTEGER, OPTIONAL, INTENT(OUT) :: ierror


int MPI_Win_set_info(MPI_Win win, MPI_Info info)
MPI_Win_set_info(win, info, ierror)
TYPE(MPI_Win), INTENT(IN) :: win
TYPE(MPI_Info), INTENT(IN) :: info
INTEGER, OPTIONAL, INTENT(OUT) :: ierror


int MPI_Win_get_info(MPI_Win win, MPI_Info *info_used)
MPI_Win_get_info(win, info_used, ierror)
TYPE(MPI_Win), INTENT(IN) :: win
TYPE(MPI_Info), INTENT(OUT) :: info_used
INTEGER, OPTIONAL, INTENT(OUT) :: ierror
```

8.7   Implementation

You may wonder how one-sided communication is realized[1]. Can a processor somehow get at another processor's data? Unfortunately, no.

Active target synchronization is implemented in terms of two-sided communication. Imagine that the first fence operation does nothing, unless it concludes prior one-sided operations. The Put and Get calls do nothing involving communication, except for marking with what processors they exchange data. The concluding fence is where everything happens: first a global operation determines which targets need to issue send or receive calls, then the actual sends and receive are executed.

_____

1.   For more on this subject, see [ ].

Exercise 8.6. Assume that only Get operations are performed during an epoch. Sketch how these are translated to send/receive pairs. The problem here is how the senders find out that they need to send. Show that you can solve this with an `MPI_Scatter_reduce` call.

The previous paragraph noted that a collective operation was necessary to determine the two-sided traffic. Since collective operations induce some amount of synchronization, you may want to limit this.

Exercise 8.7. Argue that the mechanism with window post/wait/start/complete operations still needs a collective, but that this is less burdensome.

Passive target synchronization needs another mechanism entirely. Here the target process needs to have a background task (process, thread, daemon,...) running that listens for requests to lock the window. This can potentially be expensive.

Chapter 9

MPI topic: File I/O

9.1 MPI file I/O

File input and output in parallel is a little more complicated than sequentially.

- There is nothing against every process opening an existing file for reading, and using an individual file pointer to get its unique data.
- ... but having every process open the same file for output is probably not a good idea.
- Based on the process rank it is easy enough to have every process create a unique file, but that can put a lot of strain on the file system, and it means you may have to post-process to get all the data in one file.

Wouldn't it be nice if there was a way to open one file in parallel, and have every process read from and write to its own location? That's where *MPI/O* comes in.

MPI has its own file handle: `MPI_File`

> *Fortran note* Use an `integer` to store the file handle.

File open:

```
Semantics:
MPI_FILE_OPEN(comm, filename, amode, info, fh)
IN comm: communicator (handle)
IN filename: name of file to open (string)
IN amode: file access mode (integer)
IN info: info object (handle)
OUT fh: new file handle (handle)

C:
int MPI_File_open
    (MPI_Comm comm, char *filename, int amode,
     MPI_Info info, MPI_File *fh)

Fortran:
MPI_FILE_OPEN(COMM, FILENAME, AMODE, INFO, FH, IERROR)
CHARACTER*(*) FILENAME
INTEGER COMM, AMODE, INFO, FH, IERROR
```

```
Python:
Open(type cls, Intracomm comm, filename,
     int amode=MODE_RDONLY, Info info=INFO_NULL)
```

How to read routine prototypes: 1.5.4.

This routine is collective, even if only certain processes will access the file with a read or write call. Similarly, `MPI_File_close` is collective.

> *Python note* Note the slightly unusual syntax for opening a file: even though the file is opened on a communicator, it is a class method for the `MPI.File` class, rather than for the communicator object. The latter is passed in as an argument.

File access modes:

- `MPI_MODE_RDONLY`: read only,
- `MPI_MODE_RDWR`: reading and writing,
- `MPI_MODE_WRONLY`: write only,
- `MPI_MODE_CREATE`: create the file if it does not exist,
- `MPI_MODE_EXCL`: error if creating file that already exists,
- `MPI_MODE_DELETE_ON_CLOSE`: delete file on close,
- `MPI_MODE_UNIQUE_OPEN`: file will not be concurrently opened elsewhere,
- `MPI_MODE_SEQUENTIAL`: file will only be accessed sequentially,
- `MPI_MODE_APPEND`: set initial position of all file pointers to end of file.

These modes can be added or bitwise-or'ed.

Writing to and reading from a parallel file is rather similar to sending a receiving:

- The process uses an elementary data type or a derived datatype to describe what elements in an array go to file, or are read from file.
- In the simplest case, your read or write that data to the file using an offset, or first having done a seek operation.
- But you can also set a 'file view' to describe explicitly what elements in the file will be involved.

File accesses:

- `MPI_File_seek`
- `MPI_File_read`
- `MPI_File_read_all`
- `MPI_File_read_ordered`
- `MPI_File_read_shared`
- `MPI_File_read_at`: combine read and seek.
- `MPI_File_write`
- `MPI_File_write_all`
- `MPI_File_write_ordered`
- `MPI_File_write_shared`
- `MPI_File_write_at`: combine write and seek

These modes are enough for writing simple contiguous blocks. However, you can also access non-contiguous areas in the file. For this you use

```
Semantics:
MPI_FILE_SET_VIEW(fh, disp, etype, filetype, datarep, info)
INOUT fh: file handle (handle)
IN disp: displacement (integer)
IN etype: elementary datatype (handle)
IN filetype: filetype (handle)
IN datarep: data representation (string)
IN info: info object (handle)

C:
int MPI_File_set_view
    (MPI_File fh,
     MPI_Offset disp, MPI_Datatype etype, MPI_Datatype filetype,
     char *datarep, MPI_Info info)

Fortran:
MPI_FILE_SET_VIEW(FH, DISP, ETYPE, FILETYPE, DATAREP, INFO, IERROR)
INTEGER FH, ETYPE, FILETYPE, INFO, IERROR
CHARACTER*(*) DATAREP
INTEGER(KIND=MPI_OFFSET_KIND) DISP

Python:
mpifile = MPI.File.Open( .... )
mpifile.Set_view
    (self,
     Offset disp=0, Datatype etype=None, Datatype filetype=None,
     datarep=None, Info info=INFO_NULL)
```

How to read routine prototypes: 1.5.4.

This call is collective, even if not all processes access the file.

- The `etype` describes the data type of the file, it needs to be the same on all processes.
- The `filetype` describes how this process sees the file, so it can differ between processes.
- The `disp` displacement parameters is measured in bytes. It can differ between processes. On sequential files such as tapes or network streams it does not make sense to set a displacement; for those the `MPI_DISPLACEMENT_CURRENT` value can be used.

  Fortran note In Fortran you have to assure that the displacement parameter is of 'kind' . In particular, you can not specify a literal zero '0' as the displacement; use `0_MPI_OFFSET_KIND` instead.

More: `MPI_File_delete MPI_File_set_size MPI_File_get_size MPI_File_preallocate MPI_File_get_view`

```
MPI_File_write_at(fh,offset,buf,count,datatype)

Semantics:
Input Parameters
fh : File handle (handle).
offset : File offset (integer).
```

```
buf : Initial address of buffer (choice).
count : Number of elements in buffer (integer).
datatype : Data type of each buffer element (handle).

Output Parameters:
status : Status object (status).

C:
int MPI_File_write_at
    (MPI_File fh, MPI_Offset offset, const void *buf,
     int count, MPI_Datatype datatype, MPI_Status *status)

Fortran:
MPI_FILE_WRITE_AT
    (FH,  OFFSET,  BUF, COUNT, DATATYPE, STATUS,  IERROR)
<type>    BUF(*)
INTEGER :: FH, COUNT, DATATYPE, STATUS(MPI_STATUS_SIZE), IERROR
INTEGER(KIND=MPI_OFFSET_KIND) :: OFFSET

Python:
MPI.File.Write_at(self, Offset offset, buf, Status status=None)
```

How to read routine prototypes: *1.5.4.*

9.1.1 Constants

MPI_SEEK_SET used to be called SEEK_SET which gave conflicts with the C++ library. This had to be circumvented with

```
make CPPFLAGS="-DMPICH_IGNORE_CXX_SEEK -DMPICH_SKIP_MPICXX"
```

and such.

Chapter 10

MPI topic: Topologies

In the communicators you have seen so far, processes are linearly ordered. In some circumstances the problem you are coding has some structure, and expressing the program in terms of that structure would be convenient. For this purpose, MPI can define a virtual *topology*. There are two types:

- regular, Cartesian, grids; and
- general graphs.

```
int MPI_Topo_test(MPI_Comm comm, int *status)

status:
MPI_UNDEFINED
MPI_CART
MPI_GRAPH
MPI_DIST_GRAPH
```

How to read routine prototypes: 1.5.4.

10.1   Cartesian grid topology

A *Cartesian grid* is a structure, typically in 2 or 3 dimensions, of points that have two neighbours in each of the dimensions. Thus, if a Cartesian grid has sizes $K \times M \times N$, its points have coordinates (k, m, n) with $0 \le k < K$ et cetera. Most points have six neighbours $(k \pm 1, m, n)$, $(k, m \pm 1, n)$, $(k, m, n \pm 1)$; the exception are the edge points. A grid where edge processors are connected through *wraparound connections* is called a *periodic grid*.

The most common use of Cartesian coordinates is to find the rank of process by referring to it in grid terms. For instance, one could ask 'what are my neighbours offset by $(1, 0, 0)$, $(-1, 0, 0)$, $(0, 1, 0)$ et cetera'.

While the Cartesian topology interface is fairly easy to use, as opposed to the more complicated general graph topology below, it is not actually sufficient for all Cartesian graph uses. Notably, in a so-called *star stencil*, such as the *nine-point stencil*, there are diagonal connections, which can not be described in a single step. Instead, it is necessary to take a separate step along each coordinate dimension. In higher dimensions this is of course fairly awkward.

Thus, even for Cartesian structures, it may be advisable to use the general graph topology interface.

10.1.1 Cartesian routines

The cartesian topology is specified by giving `MPI_Cart_create` the sizes of the processor grid along each axis, and whether the grid is periodic along that axis.

```
int MPI_Cart_create(
   MPI_Comm comm_old, int ndims, int *dims, int *periods,
   int reorder, MPI_Comm *comm_cart)
```

Each point in this new communicator has a coordinate and a rank. They can be queried with `MPI_Cart_coord` and `MPI_Cart_rank` respectively.

```
int MPI_Cart_coords(
   MPI_Comm comm, int rank, int maxdims,
   int *coords);
int MPI_Cart_rank(
   MPI_Comm comm, init *coords,
   int *rank);
```

Note that these routines can give the coordinates for any rank, not just for the current process.

```
// cart.c
MPI_Comm comm2d;
ndim = 2; periodic[0] = periodic[1] = 0;
dimensions[0] = idim; dimensions[1] = jdim;
MPI_Cart_create(comm,ndim,dimensions,periodic,1,&comm2d);
MPI_Cart_coords(comm2d,procno,ndim,coord_2d);
MPI_Cart_rank(comm2d,coord_2d,&rank_2d);
printf("I am %d: (%d,%d); originally %d\n",rank_2d,coord_2d[0],coord_2d
```

The `reorder` parameter to `MPI_Cart_create` indicates whether processes can have a rank in the new communicator that is different from in the old one.

Strangely enough you can only shift in one direction, you can not specify a shift vector.

```
int MPI_Cart_shift(MPI_Comm comm, int direction, int displ, int *source,
                   int *dest)
```

If you specify a processor outside the grid the result is `MPI_PROC_NULL`.

10.2 Distributed graph topology

MPI communicators have a topology type associated. This is tested with `MPI_Topo_test` and possible values are:

- `MPI_UNDEFINED` for communicators where nothing topology has explicitly been specified.

- MPI_CART for Cartesian toppologies; section 10.1.
- MPI_GRAPH for the MPI-1 graph topology; section 10.3.
- MPI_DIST_GRAPH for the distributed graph topology; section 10.2.

10.2.1   Creation

There are two creation routines for process graphs.

- MPI_Dist_graph_create_adjacent assumes that a process knows both who it is sending it, and who will send to it. This means that every edge in the communication graph is represented twice, so the memory footprint is double of what is strictly necessary. However, no communication is needed to build the graph.
- MPI_Dist_graph_create specifies on each process only its 'sources'. Consequently, some amount of processing – including communication – is needed to build the full graph.

```
int MPI_Dist_graph_create
    (MPI_Comm comm_old, int n, const int sources[],
     const int degrees[], const int destinations[], const int weights[],
     MPI_Info info, int reorder,
     MPI_Comm *comm_dist_graph)


Input Parameters:
comm_old : input communicator (handle)
n : number of source nodes for which this process specifies edges (non-negative in
sources : array containing the n source nodes for which this process specifies edg
degrees : array specifying the number of destinations for each source node in the
destinations : destination nodes for the source nodes in the source
node array (array of
non-negative
integers)
weights : weights for source to destination edges (array of
non-negative integers or MPI_UNWEIGHTED)
info : hints on optimization and interpretation of weights (handle)
reorder : the process may be reordered (true) or not (false) (logical)


Output Parameters:
comm_dist_graph : communicator with distributed graph topology added (handle)
```

How to read routine prototypes: 1.5.4.

10.2.2   Query

Statistics query: MPI_Dist_graph_neighbors_count

10.3   Graph topology (deprecated)

The original *MPI 1* had a graph topology interface which required each process to specify the full process graph. Since this is not scalable, it should be considered deprecated. Use the distributed graph topology (section 10.2) instead.

```
int MPI_Graph_create
    (MPI_Comm comm_old, int nnodes, const int indx[],
     const int edges[], int reorder,
     MPI_Comm *comm_graph)

Input Parameters:
comm_old : input communicator without topology (handle)
nnodes : number of nodes in graph (integer)
indx : array of integers describing node degrees
edges : array of integers describing graph edges
reorder : ranking may be reordered (true) or not (false) (logical)

Output Parameters:
comm_graph : communicator with graph topology added (handle)
```

How to read routine prototypes: 1.5.4.

Chapter 11

MPI topic: Shared memory

The one-sided MPI calls (chapter 8) can be used to emulate shared memory. In this chapter we will look at the ways MPI can interact with the presence of actual shared memory. Many MPI implementations have optimizations that detect shared memory and can exploit it, but that is not exposed to the programmer. The *MPI 3* standard added routines that do give the programmer that knowledge.

11.1 Recognizing shared memory

MPI's one-sided routines take a very symmetric view of processes: each process can access the window of every other process (within a communicator). Of course, in practice there will be a difference in performance depending on whether the origin and target are actually on the same shared memory, or whether they can only communicate through the network. For this reason MPI makes it easy to group processes by shared memory domains using `MPI_Comm_split_type`.

```
C:
int MPI_Comm_split_type(
   MPI_Comm comm, int split_type, int key,
   MPI_Info info, MPI_Comm *newcomm)

Fortran:
MPI_Comm_split_type(comm, split_type, key, info, newcomm, ierror)
TYPE(MPI_Comm), INTENT(IN) :: comm
INTEGER, INTENT(IN) :: split_type, key
TYPE(MPI_Info), INTENT(IN) :: info
TYPE(MPI_Comm), INTENT(OUT) :: newcomm
INTEGER, OPTIONAL, INTENT(OUT) :: ierror

Python:
MPI.Comm.Split_type(
   self, int split_type, int key=0, Info info=INFO_NULL)
```

How to read routine prototypes: 1.5.4.

Here the `split_type` parameter has to be from the following (short) list:

- `MPI_COMM_TYPE_SHARED`: split the communicator into subcommunicators of processes sharing a memory area.

In the following example, `CORES_PER_NODE` is a platform-dependent constant:

```
// commsplittype.c
MPI_Info info;
MPI_Comm_split_type(MPI_COMM_WORLD,MPI_COMM_TYPE_SHARED,procno,info,&sha
MPI_Comm_size(sharedcomm,&new_nprocs);
MPI_Comm_rank(sharedcomm,&new_procno);

ASSERT(new_procno<CORES_PER_NODE);
```

11.2 Shared memory for windows

Processes that exist on the same physical shared memory should be able to move data by copying, rather than through MPI send/receive calls – which of course will do a copy operation under the hood. In order to do such user-level copying:

1. We need to create a shared memory area with `MPI_Win_allocate_shared`, and
2. We need to get pointers to where a process' area is in this shared space; this is done with `MPI_Win_shared_query`.

11.2.1 Creating a shared window

First we create a window with memory that is allocated by the MPI library. Presumably this places the memory close the *socket* on which the process runs.

```
Semantics:
MPI_WIN_ALLOCATE_SHARED(size, disp_unit, info, comm, baseptr, win)

Input parameters:
size: size of local window in bytes (non-negative integer)
disp_unit local unit size for displacements, in bytes (positive
integer)
info: info argument (handle)
comm: intra-communicator (handle)

Output parameters:
baseptr: address of local allocated window segment (choice)
win: window object returned by the call (handle)

C:
int MPI_Win_allocate_shared
    (MPI_Aint size, int disp_unit, MPI_Info info,
     MPI_Comm comm, void *baseptr, MPI_Win *win)
```

```
Fortran:
MPI_Win_allocate_shared
    (size, disp_unit, info, comm, baseptr, win, ierror)
USE, INTRINSIC :: ISO_C_BINDING, ONLY : C_PTR
INTEGER(KIND=MPI_ADDRESS_KIND), INTENT(IN) :: size
INTEGER, INTENT(IN) :: disp_unit
TYPE(MPI_Info), INTENT(IN) :: info
TYPE(MPI_Comm), INTENT(IN) :: comm
TYPE(C_PTR), INTENT(OUT) :: baseptr
TYPE(MPI_Win), INTENT(OUT) :: win
INTEGER, OPTIONAL, INTENT(OUT) :: ierror
```

How to read routine prototypes: 1.5.4.

As an example, which consider the 1D heat equation. On each process we create a local area of three point:

```
// sharedshared.c
MPI_Win_allocate_shared(3,sizeof(int),info,sharedcomm,&shared_baseptr,&shar
```

11.2.2   Querying the shared structure

Even though the window created above is shared, that doesn't mean it's contiguous. Hence it is necessary to retrieve the pointer to the area of each process that you want to communicate with.

```
Semantics:
MPI_WIN_SHARED_QUERY(win, rank, size, disp_unit, baseptr)

Input arguments:
win:   shared memory window object (handle)
rank:  rank in the group of window win (non-negative integer)
       or MPI_PROC_NULL

Output arguments:
size: size of the window segment (non-negative integer)
disp_unit: local unit size for displacements,
           in bytes (positive integer)
baseptr: address for load/store access to window segment (choice)

C:
int MPI_Win_shared_query
    (MPI_Win win, int rank, MPI_Aint *size, int *disp_unit,
     void *baseptr)

Fortran:
MPI_Win_shared_query(win, rank, size, disp_unit, baseptr, ierror)
USE, INTRINSIC :: ISO_C_BINDING, ONLY : C_PTR
TYPE(MPI_Win), INTENT(IN) :: win
INTEGER, INTENT(IN) :: rank
INTEGER(KIND=MPI_ADDRESS_KIND), INTENT(OUT) :: size
```

```
INTEGER, INTENT(OUT) :: disp_unit
TYPE(C_PTR), INTENT(OUT) :: baseptr
INTEGER, OPTIONAL, INTENT(OUT) :: ierror
```

How to read routine prototypes: 1.5.4.

Chapter 12

MPI leftover topics

12.1   Synchronization

MPI programs conform to the SPMD model, and this means that events in one process can be unrelated in time to events in another process. Any *synchronization* that happens is induced by communication and other MPI mechanisms. By synchronization here we mean any sort of temporal ordering of events in different processes.

You have already seen some mechanisms.

1. In blocking communication, the receive call does not return until the send call has completed.
2. In non-blocking communication, the wait on a receive request will not return until the send has been completed.
3. In one-sided communication, the fence mechanism impose a certain ordering on events.

Another synchronization mechanism is induced by the *barrier* mechanism. However, while an `MPI_Barrier` call guarantees that all processes have reached a certain location in their source, this does not necessarily imply anything about message traffic. Consider this example

Proc 0	Proc 1	Proc 2
Isend to 1	Irecv from any source	
Barrier	Barrier	Barrier
Wait for send request	wait for recv request	Isend to 1
	(another wildcard recv)	wait for send request

The unexpected behaviour here is that the (first) receive on process 1 can be matched with the send on process 2: the barrier on process 1 only guarantees that the receive instruction was performed, not the actual transfer. For that you need the `MPI_Wait` call, which is after the barrier.

12.2   Error handling

Errors in normal programs can be tricky to deal with; errors in parallel programs can be even harder. This is because in addition to everything that can go wrong with a single executable (floating point errors, memory violation) you now get errors that come from faulty interaction between multiple executables.

A few examples of what can go wrong:

- MPI errors: an MPI routine can abort for various reasons, such as receiving much more data than its buffer can accomodate. Such errors, as well as the more common type mentioned above, typically cause your whole execution to abort. That is, if one incarnation of your executable aborts, the MPI runtime will kill all others.
- Deadlocks and other hanging executions: there are various scenarios where your processes individually do not abort, but are all waiting for each other. This can happen if two processes are both waiting for a message from each other, and this can be helped by using non-blocking calls. In another scenario, through an error in program logic, one process will be waiting for more messages (including non-blocking ones) than are sent to it.

The MPI library has a general mechanism for dealing with errors that it detects. The default behaviour, where the full run is aborted, is equivalent to your code having the following call [1]:

```
MPI_Comm_set_errhandler(MPI_COMM_WORLD,MPI_ERRORS_ARE_FATAL);
```

Another simple possibility is to specify

```
MPI_Comm_set_errhandler(MPI_COMM_WORLD,MPI_ERRORS_RETURN);
```

which gives you the opportunity to write code that handles the error return value. The values `MPI_ERRORS_ARE_FATAL` and `MPI_ERRORS_RETURN` are of type `MPI_Errhandler`.

In most cases where an MPI error occurs a complete abort is the sensible thing, since there are few ways to recover. The second possibility can for instance be used to print out debugging information:

```
int ierr;
ierr = MPI_Something();
if (ierr!=0) {
    // print out information about what your programming is doing
    MPI_Abort();
}
```

For instance,

```
Fatal error in MPI_Waitall:
See the MPI_ERROR field in MPI_Status for the error code
```

You could then retrieve the `MPI_ERROR` field of the status, and print out an error string with `MPI_Error_string`:

```
MPI_Comm_set_errhandler(MPI_COMM_WORLD,MPI_ERRORS_RETURN);
ierr = MPI_Waitall(2*ntids-2,requests,status);
if (ierr!=0) {
    char errtxt[200];
    for (int i=0; i<2*ntids-2; i++) {
        int err = status[i].MPI_ERROR; int len=200;
```

---

1.   The routine `MPI_Errhandler_set` is deprecated.

```
            MPI_Error_string(err,errtxt,&len);
            printf("Waitall error: %d %s\n",err,errtxt);
        }
    MPI_Abort(MPI_COMM_WORLD,0);
}
```

One cases where errors can be handled is that of *MPI file I/O MPI!I/O*: if an output file has the wrong permissions, code can possibly progress without writing data, or writing to a temporary file.

MPI operators (MPI_Op) do not return an error code. In case of an error they call MPI_Abort; if MPI_ERRORS_RETURN is the error handler, errors may be silently ignore.

You can create your own error handler with MPI_Comm_create_errhandler, which is then installed with MPI_Comm_set_errhandler. You can retrieve the error handler with MPI_Comm_get_errhandler.

12.3   Machine-specific information

```
MPI_Info info ;

int MPI_Info_create ( MPI_Info *info )

int MPI_Info_set ( MPI_Info info , const char *key, const char *value )

int MPI_Info_free ( MPI_Info *info )
```

How to read routine prototypes: 1.5.4.

12.4   Fortran issues

MPI is typically written in C, what if you program *Fortran*?

See section 5.2.2.1 for MPI types corresponding to *Fortran90 types*.

12.4.1   Assumed-shape arrays

Use of other than contiguous data, for instance A(1:N:2), was a problem in MPI calls, especially non-blocking ones. In that case it was best to copy the data to a contiguous array. This has been fixed in MPI3.

- Fortran routines have the same prototype as C routines except for the addition of an integer error parameter.
- The call for MPI_Init in Fortran does not have the commandline arguments; they need to be handled separately.
- The routine MPI_Sizeof is only available in Fortran, it provides the functionality of the C/C++ operator sizeof.

12.5   Fault tolerance

Processors are not completely reliable, so it may happen that one 'breaks': for software or hardware reasons it becomes unresponsive. For an MPI program this means that it becomes impossible to send data to it, and any collective operation involving it will hang. Can we deal with this case? Yes, but it involves some programming.

First of all, one of the possible MPI error return codes (section **??**) is `MPI_ERR_COMM`, which can be returned if a processor in the communicator is unavailable. You may want to catch this error, and add a 'replacement processor' to the program. For this, the `MPI_Comm_spawn` can be used (see 7.1 for details). But this requires a change of program design: the communicator containing the new process(es) is not part of the old `MPI_COMM_WORLD`, so it is better to set up your code as a collection of inter-communicators to begin with.

12.6   Context information

The *MPI version* is available through two parameters `MPI_VERSION` and `MPI_SUBVERSION` or the function `MPI_Get_version`.

12.7   Timing

Timing of parallel programs is tricky. On each node you can use a timer, typically based on some Operating System (OS) call. MPI supplies its own routine `MPI_Wtime` which gives *wall clock time*. Normally you don't worry about the starting point for this timer: you call it before and after an event and subtract the values.

```
t = MPI_Wtime();
// something happens here
t = MPI_Wtime()-t;
```

If you execute this on a single processor you get fairly reliable timings, except that you would need to subtract the overhead for the timer. This is the usual way to measure timer overhead:

```
t = MPI_Wtime();
// absolutely nothing here
t = MPI_Wtime()-t;
```

12.7.1   Global timing

However, if you try to time a parallel application you will most likely get different times for each process, so you would have to take the average or maximum. Another solution is to synchronize the processors by using a *barrier* :

```
MPI_Barrier(comm)
t = MPI_Wtime();
// something happens here
MPI_Barrier(comm)
t = MPI_Wtime()-t;
```

Exercise 12.1.   This scheme also has some overhead associated with it. How would you
measure that?

12.7.2   Local timing

Now suppose you want to measure the time for a single send. It is not possible to start a clock on the sender
and do the second measurement on the receiver, because the two clocks need not be synchronized. Usually
a *ping-pong* is done:

```
if ( proc_source ) {
  MPI_Send( /* to target */ );
  MPI_Recv( /* from target */ );
else if ( proc_target ) {
  MPI_Recv( /* from source */ );
  MPI_Send( /* to source */ );
}
```

Exercise 12.2.   Why is it generally not a good idea to use processes 0 and 1 for the source and
target processor? Can you come up with a better guess?

No matter what sort of timing you are doing, it is good to know the accuracy of your timer. The routine
`MPI_Wtick` gives the smallest possible timer increment. If you find that your timing result is too close to
this 'tick', you need to find a better timer (for CPU measurements there are cycle-accurate timers), or you
need to increase your running time, for instance by increasing the amount of data.

12.8   Profiling

MPI allows you to write your own profiling interface. To make this possible, every routine `MPI_Something`
calls a routine `PMPI_Something` that does the actual work. You can now write your `MPI_...` routine
which calls `PMPI_...`, and inserting your own profiling calls. As you can see in figure 12.1, normally
only the `PMPI` routines show up in the stack trace.

Does the standard mandate this?

12.9   Determinism

MPI processes are only synchronized to a certain extent, so you may wonder what guarantees there are that
running a code twice will give the same result. You need to consider two cases: first of all, if the two runs
are on different numbers of processors there are already numerical problems; see HPSC-3.3.7.

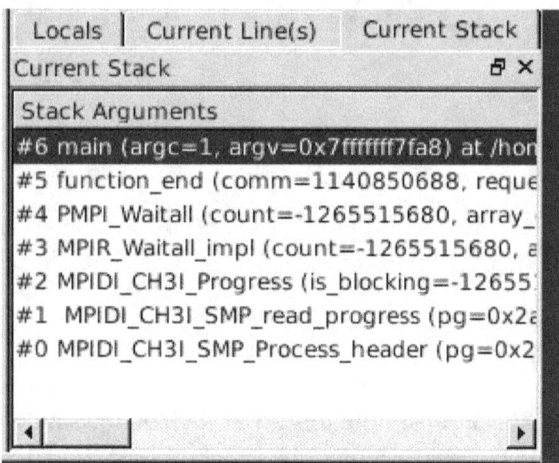

Figure 12.1: A stack trace, showing the PMPI calls.

Let us then limit ourselves to two runs on the same set of processors. In that case, MPI is deterministic as long as you do not use wildcards such as MPI_ANY_SOURCE. Formally, MPI messages are 'non-overtaking': two messages between the same sender-receiver pair will arrive in sequence. Actually, they may not arrive in sequence: they are *matched* in sequence in the user program. If the second message is much smaller than the first, it may actually arrive earlier in the lower transport layer.

12.10 Progress

Non-blocking communication implies that messages make *progress* while computation is going on. However, communication of this sort can typically not be off-loaded to the network card, so it has to be done by a process. This requires a separate thread of execution, with obvious performance problems. Therefore, in practice overlap may not actually happen, and for the message to make progress it is necessary for the MPI library to become active occasionally. For instance, people have inserted dummy MPI_Probe calls.

A similar problem arises with passive target synchronization: it is possible that the origin process may hang until the target process makes an MPI call.

12.11 Subtleties with processor synchronization

Blocking communication involves a complicated dialog between the two processors involved. Processor one says 'I have this much data to send; do you have space for that?', to which processor two replies 'yes, I do; go ahead and send', upon which processor one does the actual send. This back-and-forth (technically known as a *handshake*) takes a certain amount of communication overhead. For this reason, network hardware will sometimes forgo the handshake for small messages, and just send them regardless, knowing that the other process has a small buffer for such occasions.

One strange side-effect of this strategy is that a code that should *deadlock* according to the MPI specification does not do so. In effect, you may be shielded from you own programming mistake! Of course, if you then run a larger problem, and the small message becomes larger than the threshold, the deadlock will suddenly occur. So you find yourself in the situation that a bug only manifests itself on large problems, which are usually harder to debug. In this case, replacing every MPI_Send with a MPI_Ssend will force the handshake, even for small messages.

Conversely, you may sometimes wish to avoid the handshake on large messages. MPI as a solution for this: the MPI_Rsend ('ready send') routine sends its data immediately, but it needs the receiver to be ready for this. How can you guarantee that the receiving process is ready? You could for instance do the following (this uses non-blocking routines, which are explained below in section 4.3.2):

```
if ( receiving ) {
  MPI_Irecv()    // post non-blocking receive
  MPI_Barrier() // synchronize
else if ( sending ) {
  MPI_Barrier() // synchronize
  MPI_Rsend()    // send data fast
```

When the barrier is reached, the receive has been posted, so it is safe to do a ready send. However, global barriers are not a good idea. Instead you would just synchronize the two processes involved.

Exercise 12.3.   Give pseudo-code for a scheme where you synchronize the two processes through the exchange of a blocking zero-size message.

12.12   Leftover topics

12.12.1   MPI constants

MPI has a number of built-in *constants*. These do not all behave the same.

- Some are *compile-time* constants. Examples are MPI_VERSION and MPI_MAX_PROCESSOR_NAME. Thus, they can be used in array size declarations, even before MPI_Init.
- Some *link-time* constants get their value by MPI initialization, such as MPI_COMM_WORLD. Such symbols, which include all predefined handles, can be used in initialization expressions.
- Some link-time symbols can not be used in initialization expressions, such as MPI_BOTTOM and MPI_STATUS_IGNORE.

For symbols, the binary realization is not defined. For instance, MPI_COMM_WORLD is of type MPI_Comm, but the implementation of that type is not specified.

See Annex A of the 3.1 standard for full lists.

The following are the compile-time constants:

```
MPI_MAX_PROCESSOR_NAME
MPI_MAX_LIBRARY_VERSION_STRING
MPI_MAX_ERROR_STRING
```

```
MPI_MAX_DATAREP_STRING
MPI_MAX_INFO_KEY
MPI_MAX_INFO_VAL
MPI_MAX_OBJECT_NAME
MPI_MAX_PORT_NAME
MPI_VERSION
MPI_SUBVERSION
MPI_STATUS_SIZE (Fortran only)
MPI_ADDRESS_KIND (Fortran only)
MPI_COUNT_KIND (Fortran only)
MPI_INTEGER_KIND (Fortran only)
MPI_OFFSET_KIND (Fortran only)
MPI_SUBARRAYS_SUPPORTED (Fortran only)
MPI_ASYNC_PROTECTS_NONBLOCKING (Fortran only)
```

The following are the link-time constants:

```
MPI_BOTTOM
MPI_STATUS_IGNORE
MPI_STATUSES_IGNORE
MPI_ERRCODES_IGNORE
MPI_IN_PLACE
MPI_ARGV_NULL
MPI_ARGVS_NULL
MPI_UNWEIGHTED
MPI_WEIGHTS_EMPTY
```

Assorted constants:

```
C type: const int (or unnamed enum)
Fortran type: INTEGER

MPI_PROC_NULL
MPI_ANY_SOURCE
MPI_ANY_TAG
MPI_UNDEFINED
MPI_BSEND_OVERHEAD
MPI_KEYVAL_INVALID
MPI_LOCK_EXCLUSIVE
MPI_LOCK_SHARED
MPI_ROOT
```

(This section was inspired by http://blogs.cisco.com/performance/mpi-outside-of-c-and-for

12.12.2   32-bit size issues

The `size` parameter in MPI routines is defined as an `int`, meaning that it is limited to 32-bit quantities. There are ways around this, such as sending a number of `MPI_Type_contiguous` blocks that add up to more than 2^{31}.

12.12.3   Fortran issues

12.12.3.1 Data types

The equivalent of `MPI_Aint in Fortran` is

```
integer(kind=MPI_ADDRESS_KIND) :: winsize
```

12.12.3.2 Type issues

Fortran90 is a strongly typed language, so it is not possible to pass argument by reference to their address, as C/C++ do with the `void*` type for send and receive buffers. In Fortran this is solved by having separate routines for each datatype, and providing an `Interface` block in the MPI module. If you manage to request a version that does not exist, the compiler will display a message like

```
There is no matching specific
subroutine for this generic subroutine call [MPI_Send]
```

12.12.3.3 Byte calculations

Fortran lacks a `sizeof` operator to query the sizes of datatypes. Since sometimes exact byte counts are necessary, for instance in one-sided communication, Fortran can use the `MPI_Sizeof` routine, for instance for `MPI_Win_create`:

```
call MPI_Sizeof(windowdata,window_element_size,ierr)
window_size = window_element_size*500
call MPI_Win_create( windowdata,window_size,window_element_size,... );
```

12.12.4   Python issues

12.12.4.1 Byte calculations

The `MPI_Win_create` routine needs a displacement in bytes. Here is a good way for finding the size of *numpy* datatypes:

```
numpy.dtype('i').itemsize
```

12.12.4.2 *Arrays of objects*

Objects of type `MPI.Status` or `MPI.Request` often need to be created in an array, for instance when looping through a number of `Isend` calls. In that case the following idiom may come in handy:

```
requests = [ None ] * nprocs
for p in range(nprocs):
  requests[p] = comm.Irecv( ... )
```

12.12.5 Cancelling messages

In section **??** we showed a master-worker example where the master accepts in arbitrary order the messages from the workers. Here we will show a slightly more complicated example, where only the result of the first task to complete is needed. Thus, we issue an `MPI_Recv` with `MPI_ANY_SOURCE` as source. When a result comes, we broadcast its source to all processes. All the other workers then use this information to cancel their message with an `MPI_Cancel` operation.

```
// cancel.c
if (procno==nprocs-1) {
  MPI_Status status;
  ierr = MPI_Recv(dummy,0,MPI_INT, MPI_ANY_SOURCE,0,comm,
                  &status); CHK(ierr);
  first_tid = status.MPI_SOURCE;
  ierr = MPI_Bcast(&first_tid,1,MPI_INT, nprocs-1,comm); CHK(ierr);
  printf("first msg came from %d\n",first_tid);
} else {
  float randomfraction = (rand() / (double)RAND_MAX);
  int randomwait = (int) ( nprocs * randomfraction );
  MPI_Request request;
  printf("process %d waits for %e/%d=%d\n",
   procno,randomfraction,nprocs,randomwait);
  sleep(randomwait);
  ierr = MPI_Isend(dummy,0,MPI_INT, nprocs-1,0,comm,
                  &request); CHK(ierr);
  ierr = MPI_Bcast(&first_tid,1,MPI_INT, nprocs-1,comm
                  ); CHK(ierr);
  if (procno!=first_tid) {
    ierr = MPI_Cancel(&request); CHK(ierr);
  }
}
```

12.12.6 Constants

MPI constants such as `MPI_COMM_WORLD` or `MPI_INT` are not necessarily statitally defined, such as by a `#define` statement: the best you can say is that they have a value after `MPI_Init` or `MPI_`

`Init_thread`. That means you can not transfer a compiled MPI file between platforms, or even between compilers on one platform. However, a working MPI source on one MPI implementation will also work on another.

12.13   Context information

12.13.1   Processor name

You can query the *hostname* of a processor. This name need not be unique between different processor ranks.

```
C:
int MPI_Get_processor_name(char *name, int *resultlen)
name : buffer char[MPI_MAX_PROCESSOR_NAME]

Fortran:
MPI_Get_processor_name(name, resultlen, ierror)
CHARACTER(LEN=MPI_MAX_PROCESSOR_NAME), INTENT(OUT) :: name
INTEGER, INTENT(OUT) :: resultlen
INTEGER, OPTIONAL, INTENT(OUT) :: ierror

Python:
MPI.Get_processor_name()
```

How to read routine prototypes: 1.5.4.

You have to pass in the character storage: the character array must be at least `MPI_MAX_PROCESSOR_NAME` characters long. The actual length of the name is returned in the `resultlen` parameter.

12.13.2   Version information

```
C and C++:

#define MPI_VERSION 2
#define MPI_SUBVERSION 2

Fortran:

INTEGER MPI_VERSION, MPI_SUBVERSION
PARAMETER (MPI_VERSION = 2)
PARAMETER (MPI_SUBVERSION = 2)
```

How to read routine prototypes: 1.5.4.

For runtime determination,

```
Semantics:
  MPI_GET_VERSION( version, subversion )
  OUT version version number (integer)
  OUT subversion subversion number (integer)

C:
  int MPI_Get_version(int *version, int *subversion)

Fortran:
  MPI_GET_VERSION(VERSION, SUBVERSION, IERROR)
  INTEGER VERSION, SUBVERSION, IERROR
```

How to read routine prototypes: 1.5.4.

12.13.3   Attributes

```
int MPI_Attr_get(
    MPI_Comm comm, int keyval, void *attribute_val, int *flag)
```

How to read routine prototypes: 1.5.4.

Attributes are:

- `MPI_UNIVERSE_SIZE`: the total number of processes that can be created. This can be more than the size of `MPI_COMM_WORLD` if the host list is larger than the number of initially started processes. See section 7.1.
- `MPI_APPNUM`: if MPI is used in **MPMD! (MPMD!)** mode, or if `MPI_Comm_spawn_multiple` is used, this attribute reports the how-manieth program we are in.

12.14   Timing

MPI has a *wall clock* timer: `MPI_Wtime`

```
 C:
double MPI_Wtime(void);

Fortran:
DOUBLE PRECISION MPI_WTIME()

Python:
MPI.Wtime()
```

How to read routine prototypes: 1.5.4.

which gives the number of seconds from a certain point in the past. (Note the absence of the error parameter in the fortran call.)

```
// pingpong.c
int src = 0,tgt = nprocs/2;
double t, send=1.1,recv;
if (procno==src) {
  t = MPI_Wtime();
  for (int n=0; n<NEXPERIMENTS; n++) {
    MPI_Send(&send,1,MPI_DOUBLE,tgt,0,comm);
    MPI_Recv(&recv,1,MPI_DOUBLE,tgt,0,comm,MPI_STATUS_IGNORE);
  }
  t = MPI_Wtime()-t; t /= NEXPERIMENTS;
  printf("Time for pingpong: %e\n",t);
} else if (procno==tgt) {
  for (int n=0; n<NEXPERIMENTS; n++) {
    MPI_Recv(&recv,1,MPI_DOUBLE,src,0,comm,MPI_STATUS_IGNORE);
    MPI_Send(&recv,1,MPI_DOUBLE,src,0,comm);
  }
}
```

The timer has a resolution of `MPI_Wtick`:

```
C:
double MPI_Wtick(void);

Fortran:
DOUBLE PRECISION MPI_WTICK()

Python
MPI.Wtick()
```

How to read routine prototypes: 1.5.4.

Timing in parallel is a tricky issue. For instance, most clusters do not have a central clock, so you can not relate start and stop times on one process to those on another. You can test for a global clock as follows :

```
int *v,flag;
MPI_Attr_get( comm, MPI_WTIME_IS_GLOBAL, &v, &flag );
if (mytid==0) printf(``Time synchronized? %d->%d\n'',flag,*v);
```

12.15   Multi-threading

Hybrid MPI/threaded codes need to replace `MPI_Init` by `MPI_Init_thread`:

```
C:
int MPI_Init_thread(int *argc, char ***argv, int required, int *provided)
```

```
Fortran:
MPI_Init_thread(required, provided, ierror)
INTEGER, INTENT(IN) :: required
INTEGER, INTENT(OUT) :: provided
INTEGER, OPTIONAL, INTENT(OUT) :: ierror
```

How to read routine prototypes: 1.5.4.

With the `required` parameter the user requests a certain level of support, and MPI reports the actual capabilities in the `provided` parameter.

The following constants are defined:

- `MPI_THREAD_SINGLE`: each MPI process can only have a single thread.
- `MPI_THREAD_FUNNELED`: an MPI process can be multithreaded, but all MPI calls need to be done from a single thread.
- `MPI_THREAD_SERIALIZED`: a processes can sustain multiple threads that make MPI calls, but these threads can not be simultaneous: they need to be for instance in an OpenMP *critical section*.
- `MPI_THREAD_MULTIPLE`: processes can be fully generally multi-threaded.

These values are monotonically increasing.

After the initialization call, you can query the support level with `MPI_Query_thread`:

```
C:
int MPI_Query_thread(int *provided)

Fortran:
MPI_Query_thread(provided, ierror)
INTEGER, INTENT(OUT) :: provided
INTEGER, OPTIONAL, INTENT(OUT) :: ierror
```

How to read routine prototypes: 1.5.4.

In case more than one thread performs communication, the following routine can determine whether a thread is the main thread:

```
C:
int MPI_Is_thread_main(int *flag)

Fortran:
MPI_Is_thread_main(flag, ierror)
LOGICAL, INTENT(OUT) :: flag
INTEGER, OPTIONAL, INTENT(OUT) :: ierror
```

How to read routine prototypes: 1.5.4.

12.16   The origin of one-sided communication in ShMem

The *Cray T3E* had a library called *shmem* which offered a type of shared memory. Rather than having a true global address space it worked by supporting variables that were guaranteed to be identical between processors, and indeed, were guaranteed to occupy the same location in memory. Variables could be declared to be shared a 'symmetric' pragma or directive; their values could be retrieved or set by `shmem_get` and `shmem_put` calls.

12.17   Literature

Online resources:

- MPI 1 Complete reference:
  `http://www.netlib.org/utk/papers/mpi-book/mpi-book.html`
- Official MPI documents:
  `http://www.mpi-forum.org/docs/`
- List of all MPI routines:
  `http://www.mcs.anl.gov/research/projects/mpi/www/www3/`

Tutorial books on MPI:

- Using MPI [ ] by some of the original authors.

Chapter 13

MPI Reference

This section gives reference information and illustrative examples of the use of MPI. While the code snippets given here should be enough, full programs can be found in the repository for this book `https://bitbucket.org/VictorEijkhout/parallel-computing-book`.

13.1   Elementary datatypes

List of predefined `MPI_Datatype` values:

C	Fortran	meaning
MPI_CHAR	MPI_CHARACTER	
MPI_SHORT	MPI_BYTE	
MPI_INT	MPI_INTEGER	
MPI_LONG		
MPI_UNSIGNED_CHAR		
MPI_UNSIGNED_SHORT		
MPI_UNSIGNED		
MPI_UNSIGNED_LONG		
MPI_FLOAT	MPI_REAL	
MPI_DOUBLE	MPI_DOUBLE_PRECISION	
MPI_LONG_DOUBLE		
MPI_BYTE		
MPI_PACKED	MPI_PACKED	
	MPI_COMPLEX	
	MPI_DOUBLE_COMPLEX	
	MPI_LOGICAL	
		optional
MPI_LONG_LONG_INT		
	MPI_INTEGER1	
	MPI_INTEGER2	
	MPI_INTEGER4	
	MPI_REAL2	
	MPI_REAL4	
	MPI_REAL8	

13.2 Mpi operations

The following is the list of predefined MPI_OP values.

MPI operator	description
MPI_MAX	maximum
MPI_MIN	minimum
MPI_SUM	sum
MPI_PROD	product
MPI_LAND	logical and
MPI_BAND	bitwise and
MPI_LOR	logical or
MPI_BOR	bitwise or
MPI_LXOR	logical xor
MPI_BXOR	bitwise xor
MPI_MAXLOC	max value and location
MPI_MINLOC	min value and location

All except the last two operate on MPI datatypes; the last two operate on a value/index pair.

13.3 Communicators

13.3.1 Process topologies

13.3.1.1 *Cartesian grid topology*

13.4 Leftover topics

13.4.1 MPI constants

MPI has a number of built-in *constants*. These do not all behave the same.

- Some are *compile-time* constants. Examples are `MPI_VERSION` and `MPI_MAX_PROCESSOR_NAME`. Thus, they can be used in array size declarations, even before `MPI_Init`.
- Some *link-time* constants get their value by MPI initialization, such as `MPI_COMM_WORLD`. Such symbols, which include all predefined handles, can be used in initialization expressions.
- Some link-time symbols can not be used in initialization expressions, such as `MPI_BOTTOM` and `MPI_STATUS_IGNORE`.

For symbols, the binary realization is not defined. For instance, `MPI_COMM_WORLD` is of type `MPI_Comm`, but the implementation of that type is not specified.

See Annex A of the 3.1 standard for full lists.

The following are the compile-time constants:

```
MPI_MAX_PROCESSOR_NAME
MPI_MAX_LIBRARY_VERSION_STRING
MPI_MAX_ERROR_STRING
MPI_MAX_DATAREP_STRING
MPI_MAX_INFO_KEY
MPI_MAX_INFO_VAL
MPI_MAX_OBJECT_NAME
MPI_MAX_PORT_NAME
MPI_VERSION
MPI_SUBVERSION
MPI_STATUS_SIZE (Fortran only)
MPI_ADDRESS_KIND (Fortran only)
MPI_COUNT_KIND (Fortran only)
MPI_INTEGER_KIND (Fortran only)
MPI_OFFSET_KIND (Fortran only)
MPI_SUBARRAYS_SUPPORTED (Fortran only)
MPI_ASYNC_PROTECTS_NONBLOCKING (Fortran only)
```

The following are the link-time constants:

```
MPI_BOTTOM
MPI_STATUS_IGNORE
MPI_STATUSES_IGNORE
MPI_ERRCODES_IGNORE
```

```
MPI_IN_PLACE
MPI_ARGV_NULL
MPI_ARGVS_NULL
MPI_UNWEIGHTED
MPI_WEIGHTS_EMPTY
```

Assorted constants:

```
C type: const int (or unnamed enum)
Fortran type: INTEGER

MPI_PROC_NULL
MPI_ANY_SOURCE
MPI_ANY_TAG
MPI_UNDEFINED
MPI_BSEND_OVERHEAD
MPI_KEYVAL_INVALID
MPI_LOCK_EXCLUSIVE
MPI_LOCK_SHARED
MPI_ROOT
```

(This section was inspired by `http://blogs.cisco.com/performance/mpi-outside-of-c-and-fortra`

13.4.2   32-bit size issues

The `size` parameter in MPI routines is defined as an `int`, meaning that it is limited to 32-bit quantities. There are ways around this, such as sending a number of `MPI_Type_contiguous` blocks that add up to more than 2^{31}.

13.4.3   Fortran issues

13.4.3.1   Data types

The equivalent of `MPI_Aint in Fortran` is

```
integer(kind=MPI_ADDRESS_KIND) :: winsize
```

13.4.3.2   Type issues

Fortran90 is a strongly typed language, so it is not possible to pass argument by reference to their address, as C/C++ do with the `void*` type for send and receive buffers. In Fortran this is solved by having separate routines for each datatype, and providing an `Interface` block in the MPI module. If you manage to request a version that does not exist, the compiler will display a message like

```
There is no matching specific
subroutine for this generic subroutine call [MPI_Send]
```

13.4.3.3 Byte calculations

Fortran lacks a `sizeof` operator to query the sizes of datatypes. Since sometimes exact byte counts are necessary, for instance in one-sided communication, Fortran can use the `MPI_Sizeof` routine, for instance for `MPI_Win_create`:

```
call MPI_Sizeof(windowdata,window_element_size,ierr)
window_size = window_element_size*500
call MPI_Win_create( windowdata,window_size,window_element_size,... );
```

13.4.4 Python issues

13.4.4.1 Byte calculations

The `MPI_Win_create` routine needs a displacement in bytes. Here is a good way for finding the size of *numpy* datatypes:

```
numpy.dtype('i').itemsize
```

13.4.4.2 Arrays of objects

Objects of type `MPI.Status` or `MPI.Request` often need to be created in an array, for instance when looping through a number of `Isend` calls. In that case the following idiom may come in handy:

```
requests = [ None ] * nprocs
for p in range(nprocs):
  requests[p] = comm.Irecv( ... )
```

13.4.5 Cancelling messages

In section **??** we showed a master-worker example where the master accepts in arbitrary order the messages from the workers. Here we will show a slightly more complicated example, where only the result of the first task to complete is needed. Thus, we issue an `MPI_Recv` with `MPI_ANY_SOURCE` as source. When a result comes, we broadcast its source to all processes. All the other workers then use this information to cancel their message with an `MPI_Cancel` operation.

```
// cancel.c
if (procno==nprocs-1) {
  MPI_Status status;
  ierr = MPI_Recv(dummy,0,MPI_INT, MPI_ANY_SOURCE,0,comm,
                  &status); CHK(ierr);
```

```
      first_tid = status.MPI_SOURCE;
      ierr = MPI_Bcast(&first_tid,1,MPI_INT, nprocs-1,comm); CHK(ierr);
      printf("first msg came from %d\n",first_tid);
    } else {
      float randomfraction = (rand() / (double)RAND_MAX);
      int randomwait = (int) ( nprocs * randomfraction );
      MPI_Request request;
      printf("process %d waits for %e/%d=%d\n",
       procno,randomfraction,nprocs,randomwait);
      sleep(randomwait);
      ierr = MPI_Isend(dummy,0,MPI_INT, nprocs-1,0,comm,
                       &request); CHK(ierr);
      ierr = MPI_Bcast(&first_tid,1,MPI_INT, nprocs-1,comm
                       ); CHK(ierr);
      if (procno!=first_tid) {
        ierr = MPI_Cancel(&request); CHK(ierr);
      }
    }
```

13.4.6   Constants

MPI constants such as MPI_COMM_WORLD or MPI_INT are not necessarily statitally defined, such as by a #define statement: the best you can say is that they have a value after MPI_Init or MPI_Init_thread. That means you can not transfer a compiled MPI file between platforms, or even between compilers on one platform. However, a working MPI source on one MPI implementation will also work on another.

13.5   Context information

13.5.1   Processor name

You can query the *hostname* of a processor. This name need not be unique between different processor ranks.

```
C:
int MPI_Get_processor_name(char *name, int *resultlen)
name : buffer char[MPI_MAX_PROCESSOR_NAME]

Fortran:
MPI_Get_processor_name(name, resultlen, ierror)
CHARACTER(LEN=MPI_MAX_PROCESSOR_NAME), INTENT(OUT) :: name
INTEGER, INTENT(OUT) :: resultlen
INTEGER, OPTIONAL, INTENT(OUT) :: ierror
```

```
Python:
MPI.Get_processor_name()
```

How to read routine prototypes: 1.5.4.

You have to pass in the character storage: the character array must be at least `MPI_MAX_PROCESSOR_NAME` characters long. The actual length of the name is returned in the `resultlen` parameter.

13.5.2 Version information

```
C and C++:

#define MPI_VERSION 2
#define MPI_SUBVERSION 2

Fortran:

INTEGER MPI_VERSION, MPI_SUBVERSION
PARAMETER (MPI_VERSION = 2)
PARAMETER (MPI_SUBVERSION = 2)
```

How to read routine prototypes: 1.5.4.

For runtime determination,

```
Semantics:
  MPI_GET_VERSION( version, subversion )
  OUT version version number (integer)
  OUT subversion subversion number (integer)

C:
  int MPI_Get_version(int *version, int *subversion)

Fortran:
  MPI_GET_VERSION(VERSION, SUBVERSION, IERROR)
  INTEGER VERSION, SUBVERSION, IERROR
```

How to read routine prototypes: 1.5.4.

13.5.3 Attributes

```
int MPI_Attr_get(
    MPI_Comm comm, int keyval, void *attribute_val, int *flag)
```

How to read routine prototypes: 1.5.4.

Attributes are:

- MPI_UNIVERSE_SIZE: the total number of processes that can be created. This can be more than the size of MPI_COMM_WORLD if the host list is larger than the number of initially started processes. See section 7.1.
- MPI_APPNUM: if MPI is used in **MPMD!** mode, or if MPI_Comm_spawn_multiple is used, this attribute reports the how-manieth program we are in.

13.6 Timing

MPI has a *wall clock* timer: MPI_Wtime

```
 C:
double MPI_Wtime(void);


Fortran:
DOUBLE PRECISION MPI_WTIME()


Python:
MPI.Wtime()
```

How to read routine prototypes: 1.5.4.

which gives the number of seconds from a certain point in the past. (Note the absence of the error parameter in the fortran call.)

```
// pingpong.c
int src = 0,tgt = nprocs/2;
double t, send=1.1,recv;
if (procno==src) {
  t = MPI_Wtime();
  for (int n=0; n<NEXPERIMENTS; n++) {
    MPI_Send(&send,1,MPI_DOUBLE,tgt,0,comm);
    MPI_Recv(&recv,1,MPI_DOUBLE,tgt,0,comm,MPI_STATUS_IGNORE);
  }
  t = MPI_Wtime()-t; t /= NEXPERIMENTS;
  printf("Time for pingpong: %e\n",t);
} else if (procno==tgt) {
  for (int n=0; n<NEXPERIMENTS; n++) {
    MPI_Recv(&recv,1,MPI_DOUBLE,src,0,comm,MPI_STATUS_IGNORE);
    MPI_Send(&recv,1,MPI_DOUBLE,src,0,comm);
  }
}
```

The timer has a resolution of MPI_Wtick:

```
 C:
double MPI_Wtick(void);
```

```
Fortran:
DOUBLE PRECISION MPI_WTICK()

Python
MPI.Wtick()
```

How to read routine prototypes: 1.5.4.

Timing in parallel is a tricky issue. For instance, most clusters do not have a central clock, so you can not relate start and stop times on one process to those on another. You can test for a global clock as follows :

```
int *v,flag;
MPI_Attr_get( comm, MPI_WTIME_IS_GLOBAL, &v, &flag );
if (mytid==0) printf(``Time synchronized? %d->%d\n'',flag,*v);
```

13.7   Multi-threading

Hybrid MPI/threaded codes need to replace `MPI_Init` by `MPI_Init_thread`:

```
C:
int MPI_Init_thread(int *argc, char ***argv, int required, int *provided)

Fortran:
MPI_Init_thread(required, provided, ierror)
INTEGER, INTENT(IN) :: required
INTEGER, INTENT(OUT) :: provided
INTEGER, OPTIONAL, INTENT(OUT) :: ierror
```

How to read routine prototypes: 1.5.4.

With the `required` parameter the user requests a certain level of support, and MPI reports the actual capabilities in the `provided` parameter.

The following constants are defined:

- `MPI_THREAD_SINGLE`: each MPI process can only have a single thread.
- `MPI_THREAD_FUNNELED`: an MPI process can be multithreaded, but all MPI calls need to be done from a single thread.
- `MPI_THREAD_SERIALIZED`: a processes can sustain multiple threads that make MPI calls, but these threads can not be simultaneous: they need to be for instance in an OpenMP *critical section*.
- `MPI_THREAD_MULTIPLE`: processes can be fully generally multi-threaded.

These values are monotonically increasing.

After the initialization call, you can query the support level with `MPI_Query_thread`:

```
C:
int MPI_Query_thread(int *provided)
```

```
Fortran:
MPI_Query_thread(provided, ierror)
INTEGER, INTENT(OUT) :: provided
INTEGER, OPTIONAL, INTENT(OUT) :: ierror
```

How to read routine prototypes: 1.5.4.

In case more than one thread performs communication, the following routine can determine whether a thread is the main thread:

```
C:
int MPI_Is_thread_main(int *flag)
```

```
Fortran:
MPI_Is_thread_main(flag, ierror)
LOGICAL, INTENT(OUT) :: flag
INTEGER, OPTIONAL, INTENT(OUT) :: ierror
```

How to read routine prototypes: 1.5.4.

Chapter 14

MPI Examples

14.1   C

14.1.0.1 `MPI_Cancel`

`MPI_Cancel`

Cancelling a send operation:

```
// cancel.c
if (procno==nprocs-1) {
  MPI_Status status;
  ierr = MPI_Recv(dummy,0,MPI_INT, MPI_ANY_SOURCE,0,comm,
                  &status); CHK(ierr);
  first_tid = status.MPI_SOURCE;
  ierr = MPI_Bcast(&first_tid,1,MPI_INT, nprocs-1,comm); CHK(ierr);
  printf("first msg came from %d\n",first_tid);
} else {
  float randomfraction = (rand() / (double)RAND_MAX);
  int randomwait = (int) ( nprocs * randomfraction );
  MPI_Request request;
  printf("process %d waits for %e/%d=%d\n",
   procno,randomfraction,nprocs,randomwait);
  sleep(randomwait);
  ierr = MPI_Isend(dummy,0,MPI_INT, nprocs-1,0,comm,
                   &request); CHK(ierr);
  ierr = MPI_Bcast(&first_tid,1,MPI_INT, nprocs-1,comm
                   ); CHK(ierr);
  if (procno!=first_tid) {
    ierr = MPI_Cancel(&request); CHK(ierr);
  }
}
```

14.1.0.2 `MPI_Cart...`

`MPI_Cart...`

```
// cart.c
MPI_Comm comm2d;
ndim = 2; periodic[0] = periodic[1] = 0;
dimensions[0] = idim; dimensions[1] = jdim;
MPI_Cart_create(comm,ndim,dimensions,periodic,1,&comm2d);
MPI_Cart_coords(comm2d,procno,ndim,coord_2d);
MPI_Cart_rank(comm2d,coord_2d,&rank_2d);
printf("I am %d: (%d,%d); originally %d\n",rank_2d,coord_2d[0],coord_2d[1],

char mychar = 65+procno;
MPI_Cart_shift(comm2d,0,+1,&rank_2d,&rank_right);
MPI_Cart_shift(comm2d,0,-1,&rank_2d,&rank_left);
MPI_Cart_shift(comm2d,1,+1,&rank_2d,&rank_up);
MPI_Cart_shift(comm2d,1,-1,&rank_2d,&rank_down);
int irequest = 0; MPI_Request *requests = malloc(8*sizeof(MPI_Request));
MPI_Isend(&mychar,1,MPI_CHAR,rank_right, 0,comm, requests+irequest++);
MPI_Isend(&mychar,1,MPI_CHAR,rank_left,  0,comm, requests+irequest++);
MPI_Isend(&mychar,1,MPI_CHAR,rank_up,    0,comm, requests+irequest++);
MPI_Isend(&mychar,1,MPI_CHAR,rank_down,  0,comm, requests+irequest++);
MPI_Irecv( indata+idata++, 1,MPI_CHAR, rank_right, 0,comm, requests+ireques
MPI_Irecv( indata+idata++, 1,MPI_CHAR, rank_left,  0,comm, requests+ireques
MPI_Irecv( indata+idata++, 1,MPI_CHAR, rank_up,    0,comm, requests+ireques
MPI_Irecv( indata+idata++, 1,MPI_CHAR, rank_down,  0,comm, requests+ireques
```

14.1.0.3 `MPI_Comm_dup`

`MPI_Comm_dup`

Giving a library its own communicator.

```
// commdup_right.cxx
class library {
private:
  MPI_Comm comm;
  int procno,nprocs,other;
  MPI_Request *request;
public:
  library(MPI_Comm incomm) {
    MPI_Comm_dup(incomm,&comm);
    MPI_Comm_rank(comm,&procno);
    other = 1-procno;
```

```
      request = new MPI_Request[2];
    };
    ~library() {
      MPI_Comm_free(&comm);
    }
    int communication_start();
    int communication_end();
  };


  library my_library(comm);
  MPI_Isend(&sdata,1,MPI_INT,other,1,comm,&(request[0]));
  my_library.communication_start();
  MPI_Irecv(&rdata,1,MPI_INT,other,MPI_ANY_TAG,
      comm,&(request[1]));
  MPI_Waitall(2,request,status);
  my_library.communication_end();
```

14.1.0.4 MPI_Comm_split

MPI_Comm_split

First we take all processes module two, then again recursively.

```
// commsplit.c
int mydata = procno;
// create sub communicator modulo 2
color = procno%2;
MPI_Comm_split(MPI_COMM_WORLD,color,procno,&mod2comm);
MPI_Comm_rank(mod2comm,&new_procno);

// create sub communicator modulo 4 recursively
color = new_procno%2;
MPI_Comm_split(mod2comm,color,new_procno,&mod4comm);
MPI_Comm_rank(mod4comm,&new_procno);

if (mydata/4!=new_procno)
  printf("Error %d %d %d\n",procno,new_procno,mydata/4);

// commsplit.py
mydata = procid

# communicator modulo 2
color = procid%2
```

```
mod2comm = comm.Split(color)
new_procid = mod2comm.Get_rank()

# communicator modulo 4 recursively
color = new_procid%2
mod4comm = mod2comm.Split(color)
new_procid = mod4comm.Get_rank()

if mydata/4!=new_procid:
    print "Error",procid,new_procid,mydata/4
```

14.2   F

14.2.0.1 MPI_Fetch_and_op

`MPI_Fetch_and_op`

A root process has a table of data; the other processes do atomic gets and update of that data using *passive target synchronization* through `MPI_Win_lock`.

```
// passive.cxx
if (procno==repository) {
  // Repository processor creates a table of inputs
  // and associates that with the window
}
if (procno!=repository) {
  float contribution=(float)procno,table_element;
  int loc=0;
  MPI_Win_lock(MPI_LOCK_EXCLUSIVE,repository,0,the_window);
  // read the table element by getting the result from adding zero
  err = MPI_Fetch_and_op
    (&contribution,&table_element,MPI_FLOAT,
     repository,loc,MPI_SUM,the_window); CHK(err);
  MPI_Win_unlock(repository,the_window);
}

// passive.py
if procid==repository:
    # repository process creates a table of inputs
    # and associates it with the window
    win_mem = np.empty( ninputs,dtype=np.float32 )
    win = MPI.Win.Create( win_mem,comm=comm )
else:
```

```
        # everyone else has an empty window
        win = MPI.Win.Create( None,comm=comm )
    if procid!=repository:
        contribution = np.empty( 1,dtype=np.float32 )
        contribution[0] = 1.*procid
        table_element = np.empty( 1,dtype=np.float32 )
        win.Lock( repository,lock_type=MPI.LOCK_EXCLUSIVE )
        win.Fetch_and_op( contribution,table_element,repository,0,MPI.SUM)
        win.Unlock( repository )
```

14.3   G

14.3.0.1 `MPI_Gather`

`MPI_Gather`

Gather data onto a root. Only the root allocates the gather buffer.

```
// gather.c
// we assume that each process has a value "localsize"
// the root process collectes these values

if (procno==root)
  localsizes = (int*) malloc( (nprocs+1)*sizeof(int) );

// everyone contributes their info
MPI_Gather(&localsize,1,MPI_INT,
           localsizes,1,MPI_INT,root,comm);
```

14.3.0.2 `MPI_Get`

`MPI_Get`

One process does a one-sided get from another. This also illustrates setting size parameters in `MPI_Win_create`. Synchronization is done with `MPI_Win_fence`.

```
// getfence.c
MPI_Win_create(&other_number,2*sizeof(int),sizeof(int),
               MPI_INFO_NULL,comm,&the_window);
MPI_Win_fence(0,the_window);
if (procno==0) {
  MPI_Get( /* data on origin: */   &my_number, 1,MPI_INT,
       /* data on target: */   other,1,    1,MPI_INT,
       the_window);
```

```
}
MPI_Win_fence(0,the_window);
```

We make a null window on processes that do not participate.

```
// getfence.py
if procid==0 or procid==nprocs-1:
    win_mem = np.empty( 1,dtype=np.float64 )
    win = MPI.Win.Create( win_mem,comm=comm )
else:
    win = MPI.Win.Create( None,comm=comm )

# put data on another process
win.Fence()
if procid==0 or procid==nprocs-1:
    putdata = np.empty( 1,dtype=np.float64 )
    putdata[0] = mydata
    print "[%d] putting %e" % (procid,mydata)
    win.Put( putdata,other )
win.Fence()
```

14.4   I

14.4.0.1 MPI_Init_thread

MPI_Init_thread

The Init_thread call takes the requested level of thread support and reports back what the provided level is.

```
// thread.c
MPI_Init_thread(&argc,&argv,MPI_THREAD_MULTIPLE,&threading);
comm = MPI_COMM_WORLD;
MPI_Comm_rank(comm,&procno);
MPI_Comm_size(comm,&nprocs);

if (procno==0) {
  switch (threading) {
  case MPI_THREAD_MULTIPLE : printf("Glorious multithreaded MPI\n"); break;
  case MPI_THREAD_SERIALIZED : printf("No simultaneous MPI from threads\n")
  case MPI_THREAD_FUNNELED : printf("MPI from main thread\n"); break;
  case MPI_THREAD_SINGLE : printf("no threading supported\n"); break;
  }
}
```

```
MPI_Finalize();
```

14.5   P

14.5.0.1 `MPI_Put`

`MPI_Put`

A one-sided `MPI_Put` with active target synchronization through the use of fences. This is more or less the same as the `MPI_Get` example above.

```
// putblock.c
MPI_Win_create(&other_number,1,sizeof(int),
                 MPI_INFO_NULL,comm,&the_window);
MPI_Win_fence(0,the_window);
if (mytid==0) {
  MPI_Put( /* data on origin: */   &my_number, 1,MPI_INT,
       /* data on target: */   1,0,          1,MPI_INT,
       the_window);
  sleep(.5);
}
MPI_Win_fence(0,the_window);
if (mytid==1)
  printf("I got the following: %d\n",other_number);


// putfence.py
window_data = np.zeros(2,dtype=np.int)
my_number = np.empty(1,dtype=np.int)
src = 0; tgt = nprocs-1
if procid==src:
    my_number[0] = 37
else:
    my_number[0] = 1

intsize = np.dtype('int').itemsize
win = MPI.Win.Create(window_data,intsize,comm=comm)

win.Fence()
if procid==src:
    # put data in the second element of the window
    win.Put(my_number,tgt,target=1)
win.Fence()
```

14.6   R

14.7   S

14.7.0.1 `MPI_Send_init`

`MPI_Send_init`

Persistent communication is setup up on the sending process with `MPI_Send_init` and `MPI_Recv_init`, then performed with `MPI_Startall`. The receiver is using regular sends and receives.

```
// persist.c
if (procno==src) {
  MPI_Send_init(send,s,MPI_DOUBLE,tgt,0,comm,requests+0);
  MPI_Recv_init(recv,s,MPI_DOUBLE,tgt,0,comm,requests+1);
  printf("Size %d\n",s);
  t[cnt] = MPI_Wtime();
  for (int n=0; n<NEXPERIMENTS; n++) {
MPI_Startall(2,requests);
MPI_Waitall(2,requests,MPI_STATUSES_IGNORE);
  }
  t[cnt] = MPI_Wtime()-t[cnt];
  MPI_Request_free(requests+0); MPI_Request_free(requests+1);
} else if (procno==tgt) {
  for (int n=0; n<NEXPERIMENTS; n++) {
MPI_Recv(recv,s,MPI_DOUBLE,src,0,comm,MPI_STATUS_IGNORE);
MPI_Send(recv,s,MPI_DOUBLE,src,0,comm);
  }
}
```

```
// persist.py
sendbuf = np.ones(size,dtype=np.int)
recvbuf = np.ones(size,dtype=np.int)
if procid==src:
    print "Size:",size
    times[isize] = MPI.Wtime()
    for n in range(nexperiments):
        requests[0] = comm.Isend(sendbuf[0:size],dest=tgt)
        requests[1] = comm.Irecv(recvbuf[0:size],source=tgt)
        MPI.Request.Waitall(requests)
        sendbuf[0] = sendbuf[0]+1
    times[isize] = MPI.Wtime()-times[isize]
elif procid==tgt:
    for n in range(nexperiments):
        comm.Recv(recvbuf[0:size],source=src)
        comm.Send(recvbuf[0:size],dest=src)
```

14.7.0.2 `MPI_Ssend`

`MPI_Ssend`

Using `MPI_Ssend` messages that would fall under the *eager limit* do block.

```
// ssendblock.c
other = 1-procno;
sendbuf = (int*) malloc(sizeof(int));
recvbuf = (int*) malloc(sizeof(int));
size = 1;
MPI_Ssend(sendbuf,size,MPI_INT,other,0,comm);
MPI_Recv(recvbuf,size,MPI_INT,other,0,comm,&status);
printf("This statement is not reached\n");
```

14.8   T

14.9   W

14.9.0.1 `MPI_Win_lock`

`MPI_Win_lock`

See the `Fetch_and_op` example.

14.9.0.2 `MPI_Win_start`

`MPI_Win_start`

A one-sided `MPI_Put` using active target synchronization: use `MPI_Win_start` and `MPI_Win_complete` on the origin, and `MPI_Win_post` and `MPI_Win_wait` on the target.

```
// postwaitwin.c
if (procno==origin) {
  MPI_Group_incl(all_group,1,&target,&two_group);
  // access
  MPI_Win_start(two_group,0,the_window);
  MPI_Put( /* data on origin: */   &my_number, 1,MPI_INT,
         /* data on target: */   target,0,   1,MPI_INT,
     the_window);
  MPI_Win_complete(the_window);
}

if (procno==target) {
```

```
MPI_Group_incl(all_group,1,&origin,&two_group);
// exposure
MPI_Win_post(two_group,0,the_window);
MPI_Win_wait(the_window);
}
```

14.9.0.3 MPI_Win_create

`MPI_Win_create`

See the `MPI_Get` example.

14.9.0.4 MPI_Win_fence

`MPI_Win_fence`

One process does `MPI_Put` operations, randomly on one of two other processes. We use a fence for active target synchronization.

```
// randomput.c
MPI_Win_create(&window_data,sizeof(int),sizeof(int),
               MPI_INFO_NULL,comm,&the_window);

for (int c=0; c<10; c++) {
  if (mytid==0) { // decide where to put data
float randomfraction = (rand() / (double)RAND_MAX);
if (randomfraction>.5)
    other = 2;
else
    other = 1;
my_number = 1;
  } else {
window_data = 0;
my_number = 0;
  }
  my_sum += window_data;
}

if (mytid>0 && mytid<3)
  printf("Sum on %d: %d\n",mytid,my_sum);
if (mytid==0) printf("(sum should be 10)\n");
```

Chapter 15

MPI Review

For all true/false questions, if you answer that a statement is false, give a one-line explanation.

15.1 Conceptual

Exercise 15.1. True or false: `mpicc` is a compiler.

Exercise 15.2. What is the function of a hostfile?

15.2 Communicators

1. True or false: in each communicator, processes are numbered consecutively from zero.
2. If a process is in two communicators, it has the same rank in both.

15.3 Point-to-point

1. Describe a deadlock scenario involving three processors.
2. True or false: a message sent with `MPI_Isend` from one processor can be received with an `MPI_Recv` call on another processor.
3. True or false: a message sent with `MPI_Send` from one processor can be received with an `MPI_Irecv` on another processor.
4. Why does the `MPI_Irecv` call not have an `MPI_Status` argument?
5. What is the relation between the concepts of 'origin', 'target', 'fence', and 'window' in one-sided communication.
6. What are the three routines for one-sided data transfer?
7. In the following fragments assume that all buffers have been allocated with sufficient size. For each fragment note whether it deadlocks or not. Discuss performance issues.

```
// block1.c
for (int p=0; p<nprocs; p++)
  if (p!=procid)
    MPI_Send(sbuffer,buflen,MPI_INT,p,0,comm);
for (int p=0; p<nprocs; p++)
  if (p!=procid)
    MPI_Recv(rbuffer,buflen,MPI_INT,p,0,comm,MPI_STATUS_IGNORE);
```

```
// block2.c
for (int p=0; p<nprocs; p++)
  if (p!=procid)
    MPI_Recv(rbuffer,buflen,MPI_INT,p,0,comm,MPI_STATUS_IGNORE);
for (int p=0; p<nprocs; p++)
  if (p!=procid)
    MPI_Send(sbuffer,buflen,MPI_INT,p,0,comm);
```

```
// block3.c
int ireq = 0;
for (int p=0; p<nprocs; p++)
  if (p!=procid)
    MPI_Isend(sbuffers[p],buflen,MPI_INT,p,0,comm,&(requests[ireq++]));
for (int p=0; p<nprocs; p++)
  if (p!=procid)
    MPI_Recv(rbuffer,buflen,MPI_INT,p,0,comm,MPI_STATUS_IGNORE);
MPI_Waitall(nprocs-1,requests,MPI_STATUSES_IGNORE);
```

```
// block4.c
int ireq = 0;
for (int p=0; p<nprocs; p++)
  if (p!=procid)
    MPI_Irecv(rbuffers[p],buflen,MPI_INT,p,0,comm,&(requests[ireq++]));
for (int p=0; p<nprocs; p++)
  if (p!=procid)
    MPI_Send(sbuffer,buflen,MPI_INT,p,0,comm);
MPI_Waitall(nprocs-1,requests,MPI_STATUSES_IGNORE);
```

```
// block5.c
int ireq = 0;
for (int p=0; p<nprocs; p++)
  if (p!=procid)
    MPI_Irecv(rbuffers[p],buflen,MPI_INT,p,0,comm,&(requests[ireq++]));
MPI_Waitall(nprocs-1,requests,MPI_STATUSES_IGNORE);
for (int p=0; p<nprocs; p++)
  if (p!=procid)
    MPI_Send(sbuffer,buflen,MPI_INT,p,0,comm);
```

Fortran codes:

```fortran
// block1.F90
do p=0,nprocs-1
   if (p/=procid) then
      call MPI_Send(sbuffer,buflen,MPI_INT,p,0,comm,ierr)
   end if
end do
do p=0,nprocs-1
   if (p/=procid) then
      call MPI_Recv(rbuffer,buflen,MPI_INT,p,0,comm,MPI_STATUS_IGNORE,ierr)
   end if
end do
```

```fortran
// block2.F90
do p=0,nprocs-1
   if (p/=procid) then
      call MPI_Recv(rbuffer,buflen,MPI_INT,p,0,comm,MPI_STATUS_IGNORE,ierr)
   end if
end do
do p=0,nprocs-1
   if (p/=procid) then
      call MPI_Send(sbuffer,buflen,MPI_INT,p,0,comm,ierr)
   end if
end do
```

```fortran
// block3.F90
ireq = 0
do p=0,nprocs-1
   if (p/=procid) then
      call MPI_Isend(sbuffers(1,p+1),buflen,MPI_INT,p,0,comm,&
            requests(ireq+1),ierr)
      ireq = ireq+1
   end if
end do
do p=0,nprocs-1
   if (p/=procid) then
      call MPI_Recv(rbuffer,buflen,MPI_INT,p,0,comm,MPI_STATUS_IGNORE,ierr)
   end if
end do
call MPI_Waitall(nprocs-1,requests,MPI_STATUSES_IGNORE,ierr)
```

```fortran
// block4.F90
ireq = 0
do p=0,nprocs-1
   if (p/=procid) then
      call MPI_Irecv(rbuffers(1,p+1),buflen,MPI_INT,p,0,comm,&
            requests(ireq+1),ierr)
      ireq = ireq+1
   end if
end do
do p=0,nprocs-1
   if (p/=procid) then
      call MPI_Send(sbuffer,buflen,MPI_INT,p,0,comm,ierr)
```

```
        end if
    end do
    call MPI_Waitall(nprocs-1,requests,MPI_STATUSES_IGNORE,ierr)

    // block5.F90
    ireq = 0
    do p=0,nprocs-1
        if (p/=procid) then
            call MPI_Irecv(rbuffers(1,p+1),buflen,MPI_INT,p,0,comm,&
                requests(ireq+1),ierr)
            ireq = ireq+1
        end if
    end do
    call MPI_Waitall(nprocs-1,requests,MPI_STATUSES_IGNORE,ierr)
    do p=0,nprocs-1
        if (p/=procid) then
            call MPI_Send(sbuffer,buflen,MPI_INT,p,0,comm,ierr)
        end if
    end do
```

15.4 Collectives

1. MPI collectives can be divided into (a) rooted vs rootless (b) using uniform buffer lengths vs variable length buffers (c) blocking vs non-blocking. Give examples of each type.
2. True or false: an `MPI_Scatter` call puts the same data on each process.
3. Given a distributed array, with every processor storing
   ```
   double x[N]; // N can vary per processor
   ```
   give the approximate MPI-based code that computes the maximum value in the array, and leaves the result on every processor.
4. With data as in the previous question, given the code for normalizing the array.

15.5 Datatypes

1. Give two examples of MPI derived datatypes. What parameters are used to describe them?
2. Give a practical example where the sender uses a different type to send than the receiver uses in the corresponding receive call. Name the types involved.

15.6 Theory

1. Give a simple model for the time a send operation takes.
2. Give a simple model for the time a broadcast of a single scalar takes.

PART II

OPENMP

Chapter 16

Getting started with OpenMP

This chapter explains the basic concepts of OpenMP, and helps you get started on running your first OpenMP program.

16.1 The OpenMP model

We start by establishing a mental picture of the hardware and software that OpenMP targets.

16.1.1 Target hardware

Modern computers have a multi-layered design. Maybe you have access to a cluster, and maybe you have learned how to use MPI to communicate between cluster nodes. OpenMP, the topic of this chapter, is concerned with a single *cluster node* or *motherboard*, and getting the most out of the available parallelism available there.

Figure 16.1: A node with two sockets and a co-processor

Figure 16.1 pictures a typical design of a node: within one enclosure you find two *sockets*: single processor chips. Your personal laptop of computer will probably have one socket, most supercomputers have nodes with two or four sockets (the picture is of a *Stampede node* with two sockets)[1], although the recent *Intel Knight's Landing* is again a single-socket design.

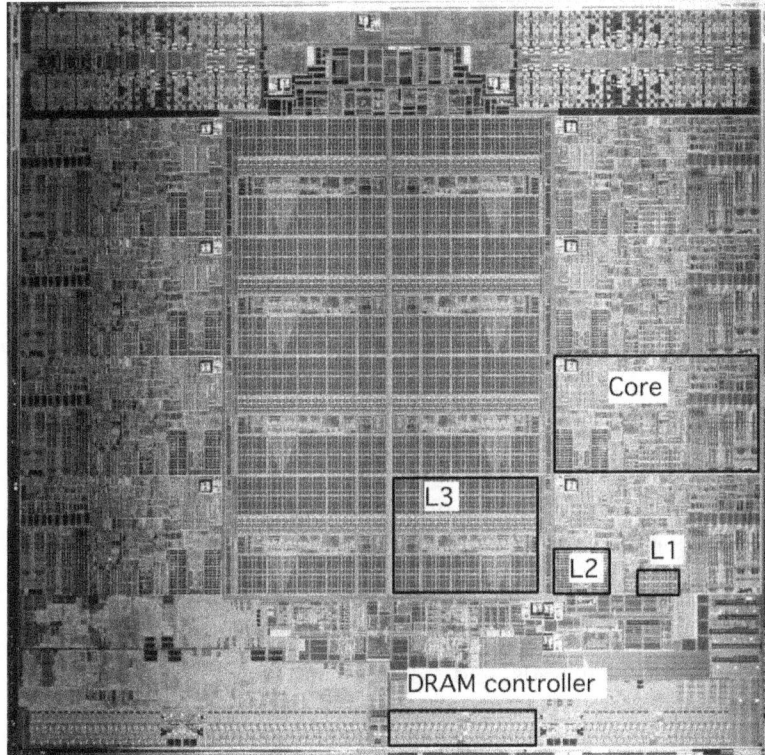

Figure 16.2: Structure of an Intel Sandybridge eight-core socket

To see where OpenMP operates we need to dig into the sockets. Figure 16.2 shows a picture of an *Intel Sandybridge* socket. You recognize a structure with eight *cores core*: independent processing units, that all have access to the same memory. (In figure 16.1 you saw four memory banks attached to each of the two sockets; all of the sixteen cores have access to all that memory.)

To summarize the structure of the architecture that OpenMP targets:

- A node has up to four sockets;
- each socket has up to 60 cores;
- each core is an independent processing unit, with access to all the memory on the node.

16.1.2 Target software

OpenMP is based on on two concepts: the use of *threads* and the *fork/join model* of parallelism. For now you can think of a thread as a sort of process: the computer executes a sequence of instructions. The fork/join model says that a thread can split itself ('fork') into a number of threads that are identical copies. At some point these copies go away and the original thread is left ('join'), but while the *team of threads*

---

1.   In that picture you also see a co-processor: OpenMP is increasingly targeting those too.

created by the fork exists, you have parallelism available to you. The part of the execution between fork and join is known as a *parallel region*.

Figure 16.3 gives a simple picture of this: a thread forks into a team of threads, and these threads themselves can fork again.

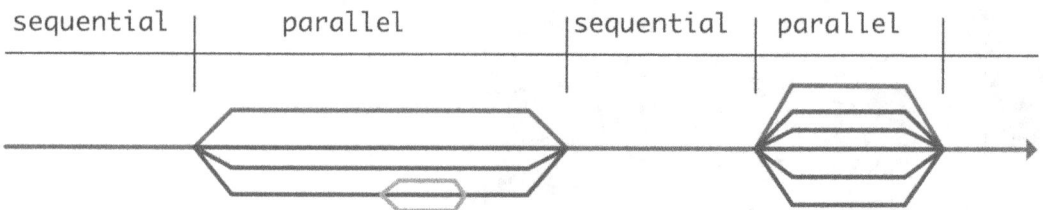

Figure 16.3: Thread creation and deletion during parallel execution

The threads that are forked are all copies of the *master thread*: they have access to all that was computed so far; this is their *shared data*. Of course, if the threads were completely identical the parallelism would be pointless, so they also have private data, and they can identify themselves: they know their thread number. This allows you to do meaningful parallel computations with threads.

This brings us to the third important concept: that of *work sharing* constructs. In a team of threads, initially there will be replicated execution; a work sharing construct divides available parallelism over the threads.

> So there you have it: OpenMP uses teams of threads, and inside a parallel region the work is distributed over the threads with a work sharing construct. Threads can access shared data, and they have some private data.

An important difference between OpenMP and MPI is that parallelism in OpenMP is dynamically activated by a thread spawning a team of threads. Furthermore, the number of threads used can differ between parallel regions, and threads can create threads recursively. This is known as as *dynamic mode*. By contrast, in an MPI program the number of running processes is (mostly) constant throughout the run, and determined by factors external to the program.

16.1.3   About threads and cores

OpenMP programming is typically done to take advantage of *multicore* processors. Thus, to get a good speedup you would typically let your number of threads be equal to the number of cores. However, there is nothing to prevent you from creating more threads: the operating system will use *time slicing* to let them all be executed. You just don't get a speedup beyond the number of actually available cores.

On some modern processors there are *hardware threads*, meaning that a core can actually let more than thread be executed, with some speedup over the single thread. To use such a processor efficiently you would let the number of OpenMP threads be $2\times$ or $4\times$ the number of cores, depending on the hardware.

16.1.4   About thread data

In most programming languages, visibility of data is governed by rules on the *scope of variables*: a variable is declared in a block, and it is then visible to any statement in that block and blocks with a *lexical scope* contained in it, but not in surrounding blocks:

```
main () {
  // no variable 'x' define here
  {
    int x = 5;
    if (somecondition) { x = 6; }
    printf("x=%e\n",x); // prints 5 or 6
  }
  printf("x=%e\n",x); // syntax error: 'x' undefined
}
```

In C, you can redeclare a variable inside a nested scope:

```
{
  int x;
  if (something) {
    double x; // same name, different entity
  }
  x = ... // this refers to the integer again
}
```

Doing so makes the outer variable inaccessible.

Fortran has simpler rules, since it does not have blocks inside blocks.

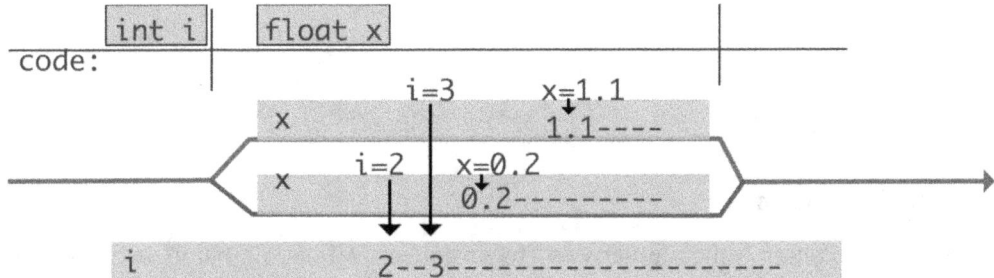

Figure 16.4: Locality of variables in threads

In OpenMP the situation is a bit more tricky because of the threads. When a team of threads is created they can all see the data of the master thread. However, they can also create data of their own. This is illustrated in figure 16.4. We will go into the details later.

16.2 Compiling and running an OpenMP program

16.2.1 Compiling

Your file or Fortran module needs to contain

```
#include "omp.h"
```

in C, and

```
use omp_lib
```

or

```
#include "omp_lib.h"
```

for Fortran.

OpenMP is handled by extensions to your regular compiler, typically by adding an option to your command-line:

```
# gcc
gcc -o foo foo.c -fopenmp
# Intel compiler
icc -o foo foo.c -openmp
```

If you have separate compile and link stages, you need that option in both.

When you use the openmp compiler option, a *cpp* variable _OPENMP will be defined. Thus, you can have conditional compilation by writing

```
#ifdef _OPENMP
   ...
#else
   ...
#endif
```

16.2.2   Running an OpenMP program

You run an OpenMP program by invoking it the regular way (for instance ./a.out), but its behaviour is influenced by some *OpenMP environment variables*. The most important one is OMP_NUM_THREADS:

```
export OMP_NUM_THREADS=8
```

which sets the number of threads that a program will use. See section 27.1 for a list of all environment variables.

16.3   Your first OpenMP program

In this section you will see just enough of OpenMP to write a first program and to explore its behaviour. For this we need to introduce a couple of OpenMP language constructs. They will all be discussed in much greater detail in later chapters.

16.3.1 Directives

OpenMP is not magic, so you have to tell it when something can be done in parallel. This is mostly done through *directives*; additional specifications can be done through library calls.

In C/C++ the *pragma* mechanism is used: annotations for the benefit of the compiler that are otherwise not part of the language. This looks like:

```
#pragma omp somedirective clause(value,othervalue)
  parallel statement;

#pragma omp somedirective clause(value,othervalue)
  {
  parallel statement 1;
  parallel statement 2;
  }
```

with

- the `#pragma omp` *sentinel* to indicate that an OpenMP directive is coming;
- a directive, such as `parallel`;
- and possibly clauses with values.
- After the directive comes either a single statement or a block in *curly braces*.

Directives in C/C++ are case-sensitive. Directives can be broken over multiple lines by escaping the line end.

The sentinel in Fortran looks like a comment:

```
!$omp directive clause(value)
  statements
!$omp end directive
```

The difference with the C directive is that Fortran can not have a block, so there is an explicit *end-of directive* line.

If you break a directive over more than one line, all but the last line need to have a continuation character, and each line needs to have the sentinel:

```
!$OMP parallel do &
!%OMP    copyin(x),copyout(y)
```

The directives are case-insensitive. In *Fortran fixed-form source* files, `c$omp` and `*$omp` are allowed too.

16.3.2 Parallel regions

The simplest way to create parallelism in OpenMP is to use the `parallel` pragma. A block preceded by the `omp parallel` pragma is called a *parallel region*; it is executed by a newly created team of threads. This is an instance of the *Single Program Multiple Data (SPMD)* model: all threads execute the same segment of code.

```
#pragma omp parallel
{
  // this is executed by a team of threads
}
```

We will go into much more detail in section 17.

16.3.3   An actual OpenMP program!

Exercise 16.1.   Write a program that contains the following lines:
```
        printf("There are %d processors\n",omp_get_num_procs());
    #pragma omp parallel
        printf("There are %d threads\n",
                /* !!!! something missing here !!!! */ );
```

The first print statement tells you the number of available cores in the hardware. Your assignment is to supply the missing function that reports the number of threads used. Compile and run the program. Experiment with the OMP_NUM_THREADS environment variable. What do you notice about the number of lines printed?

Exercise 16.2.   Extend the program from exercise 16.1. Make a complete program based on these lines:
```
    int tsum=0;
    #pragma omp parallel
      tsum += /* the thread number */
    printf("Sum is %d\n",tsum);
```

Compile and run again. (In fact, run your program a number of times.) Do you see something unexpected? Can you think of an explanation?

16.3.4   Code and execution structure

Here are a couple of important concepts:

Definition 1

structured block An OpenMP directive is followed by an structured block; *in C this is a single statement, a compound statement, or a block in braces; In Fortran it is delimited by the directive and its matching 'end' directive.*

A structured block can not be jumped into, so it can not start with a labeled statement, or contain a jump statement leaving the block.

construct An OpenMP construct is the section of code starting with a directive and spanning the following structured block, plus in Fortran the end-directive. This is a lexical concept: it contains the statements directly enclosed, and not any subroutines called from them.

region of code A region of code *is defined as all statements that are dynamically encountered while execut-ing the code of an OpenMP construct. This is a dynamic concept: unlike a 'construct', it does include any subroutines that are called from the code in the structured block.*

Chapter 17

OpenMP topic: Parallel regions

The simplest way to create parallelism in OpenMP is to use the `parallel` pragma. A block preceded by the `omp parallel` pragma is called a *parallel region*; it is executed by a newly created team of threads. This is an instance of the *SPMD* model: all threads execute the same segment of code.

```
#pragma omp parallel
{
    // this is executed by a team of threads
}
```

It would be pointless to have the block be executed identically by all threads. One way to get a meaningful parallel code is to use the function `omp_get_thread_num`, to find out which thread you are, and execute work that is individual to that thread. There is also a function `omp_get_num_threads` to find out the total number of threads. Both these functions give a number relative to the current team; recall from figure 16.3 that new teams can be created recursively.

For instance, if you program computes

```
result = f(x)+g(x)+h(x)
```

you could parallelize this as

```
double result,fresult,gresult,hresult;
#pragma omp parallel
{ int num = omp_get_thread_num();
  if (num==0)      fresult = f(x);
  else if (num==1) gresult = g(x);
  else if (num==2) hresult = h(x);
}
result = fresult + gresult + hresult;
```

The first thing we want to do is create a team of threads. This is done with a *parallel region*. Here is a very simple example:

206

```
// hello.c
#pragma omp parallel
  {
    int t = omp_get_thread_num();
    printf("Hello world from %d!\n",t);
  }
```

or in Fortran

```
// hellocount.F90
!$omp parallel
  nthreads = omp_get_num_threads()
  mythread = omp_get_thread_num()
  write(*,'("Hello from",i3," out of",i3)') mythread,nthreads
!$omp end parallel
```

This code corresponds to the model we just discussed:

- Immediately preceding the parallel block, one thread will be executing the code. In the main program this is the *initial thread*.
- At the start of the block, a new *team of threads* is created, and the thread that was active before the block becomes the *master thread* of that team.
- After the block only the master thread is active.
- Inside the block there is team of threads: each thread in the team executes the body of the block, and it will have access to all variables of the surrounding environment. How many threads there are can be determined in a number of ways; we will get to that later.

Exercise 17.1.   Make a full program based on this fragment. Insert different print statements before, inside, and after the parallel region. Run this example. How many times is each print statement executed?

You see that the `parallel` directive

- Is preceded by a special marker: a `#pragma omp` for C/C++, and the `!$OMP` *sentinel* for Fortran;
- Is followed by a single statement or a block in C/C++, or followed by a block in Fortran which is delimited by an `!$omp end` directive.

Directives look like *cpp directives*, but they are actually handled by the compiler, not the preprocessor.

Exercise 17.2.   Take the 'hello world' program above, and modify it so that you get multiple messages to you screen, saying

```
            Hello from thread 0 out of 4!
            Hello from thread 1 out of 4!
```

and so on. (The messages may very well appear out of sequence.)
What happens if you set your number of threads larger than the available cores on your computer?

Exercise 17.3. What happens if you call `omp_get_thread_num` and
`omp_get_num_threads` outside a parallel region?

```
omp_get_thread_limit
```

`OMP_WAIT_POLICY` values: `ACTIVE,PASSIVE`

17.1 Nested parallelism

What happens if you call a function from inside a parallel region, and that function itself contains a parallel region?

```
int main() {
  ...
#pragma omp parallel
  {
  ...
  func(...)
  ...
  }
} // end of main
void func(...) {
#pragma omp parallel
  {
  ...
  }
}
```

By default, the nested parallel region will have only one thread. To allow nested thread creation, set

```
OMP_NESTED=true
 or
omp_set_nested(1)
```

Exercise 17.4. Test nested parallelism by writing an OpenMP program as follows:
1. Write a subprogram that contains a parallel region.
2. Write a main program with a parallel region; call the subprogram both inside and outside the parallel region.
3. Insert print statements
    (a) in the main program outside the parallel region,
    (b) in the parallel region in the main program,
    (c) in the subprogram outside the parallel region,
    (d) in the parallel region inside the subprogram.
Run your program and count how many print statements of each type you get.

Writing subprograms that are called in a parallel region illustrates the following point: directives are evaluation with respect to the *dynamic scope* of the parallel region, not just the lexical scope. In the following example:

```
#pragma omp parallel
{
  f();
}
void f() {
#pragma omp for
  for ( .... ) {
    ...
  }
}
```

the body of the function f falls in the dynamic scope of the parallel region, so the for loop will be parallelized.

If the function may be called both from inside and outside parallel regions, you can test which is the case with omp_in_parallel.

The amount of nested parallelism can be set:

```
OMP_NUM_THREADS=4,2
```

means that initially a parallel region will have four threads, and each thread can create two more threads.

```
OMP_MAX_ACTIVE_LEVELS=123

omp_set_max_active_levels( n )
n = omp_get_max_active_levels()

OMP_THREAD_LIMIT=123

n = omp_get_thread_limit()

omp_set_max_active_levels
omp_get_max_active_levels
omp_get_level
omp_get_active_level
omp_get_ancestor_thread_num

omp_get_team_size(level)
```

Chapter 18

OpenMP topic: Loop parallelism

18.1 Loop parallelism

Loop parallelism is a very common type of parallelism in scientific codes, so OpenMP has an easy mechanism for it. OpenMP parallel loops are a first example of OpenMP 'worksharing' constructs (see section 19 for the full list): constructs that take an amount of work and distribute it over the available threads in a parallel region.

The parallel execution of a loop can be handled a number of different ways. For instance, you can create a parallel region around the loop, and adjust the loop bounds:

```
#pragma omp parallel
{
  int threadnum = omp_get_thread_num(),
    numthreads = omp_get_num_threads();
  int low = N*threadnum/numthreads,
    high = N*(threadnum+1)/numthreads;
  for (i=low; i<high; i++)
    // do something with i
}
```

A more natural option is to use the `parallel for` pragma:

```
#pragma omp parallel
#pragma omp for
for (i=0; i<N; i++) {
  // do something with i
}
```

This has several advantages. For one, you don't have to calculate the loop bounds for the threads yourself, but you can also tell OpenMP to assign the loop iterations according to different schedules (section 18.2).

Figure 18.1 shows the execution on four threads of

210

```
#pragma omp parallel
{
  code1();
#pragma omp for
  for (i=1; i<=4*N; i++) {
    code2();
  }
  code3();
}
```

The code before and after the loop is executed identically in each thread; the loop iterations are spread over the four threads.

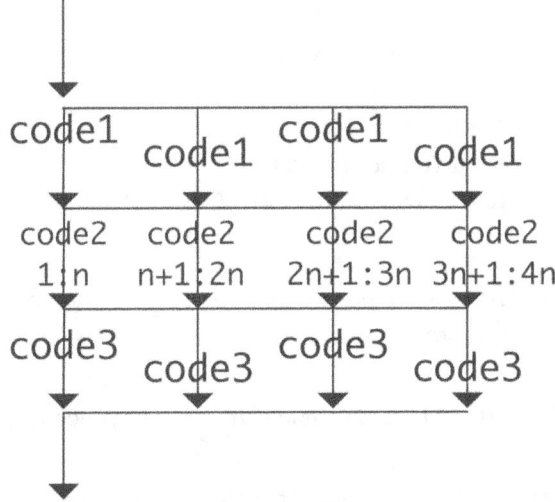

Figure 18.1: Execution of parallel code inside and outside a loop

Note that the `parallel do` and `parallel for` pragmas do not create a team of threads: they take the team of threads that is active, and divide the loop iterations over them.

This means that the `omp for` or `omp do` directive needs to be inside a parallel region. It is also possible to have a combined `omp parallel for` or `omp parallel do` directive.

If your parallel region only contains a loop, you can combine the pragmas for the parallel region and distribution of the loop iterations:

```
#pragma omp parallel for
  for (i=0; .....
```

Exercise 18.1. Compute π by *numerical integration*. We use the fact that π is the area of the unit circle, and we approximate this by computing the area of a quarter circle using *Riemann sums*.

- Let $f(x) = \sqrt{1 - x^2}$ be the function that describes the quarter circle for $x = 0 \ldots 1$;
- Then we compute

$$\pi/4 \approx \sum_{i=0}^{N-1} \Delta x f(x_i) \qquad \text{where } x_i = i\Delta x \text{ and } \Delta x = 1/N$$

Write a program for this, and parallelize it using OpenMP parallel for directives.

1. Put a `parallel` directive around your loop. Does it still compute the right result? Does the time go down with the number of threads? (The answers should be no and no.)
2. Change the `parallel` to `parallel for` (or `parallel do`). Now is the result correct? Does execution speed up? (The answers should now be no and yes.)
3. Put a `critical` directive in front of the update. (Yes and very much no.)
4. Remove the `critical` and add a clause `reduction(+:quarterpi)` to the `for` directive. Now it should be correct and efficient.

Use different numbers of cores and compute the speedup you attain over the sequential computation. Is there a performance difference between the OpenMP code with 1 thread and the sequential code?

Remark 2 *In this exercise you may have seen the runtime go up a couple of times where you weren't expecting it. The issue here is* false sharing; *see HPSC-3.3.7 for more explanation.*

There are some restrictions on the loop: basically, OpenMP needs to be able to determine in advance how many iterations there will be.

- The loop can not contains `break`, `return`, `exit` statements, or `goto` to a label outside the loop.
- The `continue` (C) or `cycle` (F) statement is allowed.
- The index update has to be an increment (or decrement) by a fixed amount.
- The loop index variable is automatically private, and not changes to it inside the loop are allowed.

18.2   Loop schedules

Usually you will have many more iterations in a loop than there are threads. Thus, there are several ways you can assign your loop iterations to the threads. OpenMP lets you specify this with the `schedule` clause.

```
#pragma omp for schedule(....)
```

The first distinction we now have to make is between static and dynamic schedules. With static schedules, the iterations are assigned purely based on the number of iterations and the number of threads (and the `chunk` parameter; see later). In dynamic schedules, on the other hand, iterations are assigned to threads that are unoccupied. Dynamic schedules are a good idea if iterations take an unpredictable amount of time, so that *load balancing* is needed.

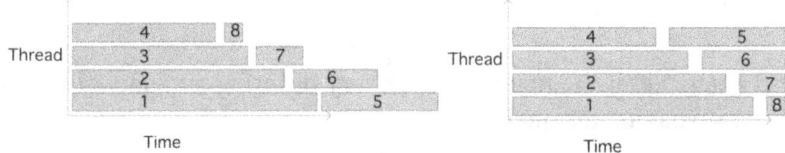

Figure 18.2: Illustration static round-robin scheduling versus dynamic

Figure 18.2 illustrates this: assume that each core gets assigned two (blocks of) iterations and these blocks take gradually less and less time. You see from the left picture that thread 1 gets two fairly long blocks, where as thread 4 gets two short blocks, thus finishing much earlier. (This phenomenon of threads having unequal amounts of work is known as *load imbalance*.) On the other hand, in the right figure thread 4 gets block 5, since it finishes the first set of blocks early. The effect is a perfect load balancing.

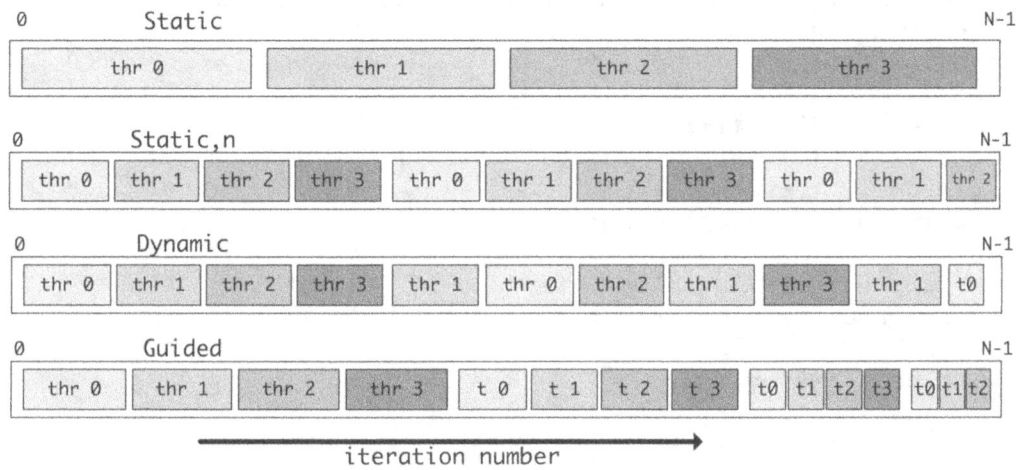

Figure 18.3: Illustration of the scheduling strategies of loop iterations

The default static schedule is to assign one consecutive block of iterations to each thread. If you want different sized blocks you can defined a `chunk` size:

```
#pragma omp for schedule(static[,chunk])
```

(where the square brackets indicate an optional argument). With static scheduling, the compiler will split up the loop iterations at compile time, so, provided the iterations take roughly the same amount of time, this is the most efficient at runtime.

The choice of a chunk size is often a balance between the low overhead of having only a few chunks, versus the load balancing effect of having smaller chunks.

Exercise 18.2. Why is a chunk size of 1 typically a bad idea? (Hint: think about cache lines, and read HPSC-1.4.1.2.)

In dynamic scheduling OpenMP will put blocks of iterations (the default chunk size is 1) in a task queue, and the threads take one of these tasks whenever they are finished with the previous.

```
#pragma omp for schedule(static[,chunk])
```

While this schedule may give good load balancing if the iterations take very differing amounts of time to execute, it does carry runtime overhead for managing the queue of iteration tasks.

Finally, there is the `guided` schedule, which gradually decreases the chunk size. The thinking here is that large chunks carry the least overhead, but smaller chunks are better for load balancing. The various schedules are illustrated in figure 18.3.

If you don't want to decide on a schedule in your code, you can specify the `runtime` schedule. The actual schedule will then at runtime be read from the `OMP_SCHEDULE` environment variable. You can even just leave it to the runtime library by specifying `auto`

Exercise 18.3. We continue with exercise 18.1. We add 'adaptive integration': where needed, the program refines the step size[1]. This means that the iterations no longer take a predictable amount of time.

```
for (i=0; i<nsteps; i++) {
  double
    x = i*h,x2 = (i+1)*h,
    y = sqrt(1-x*x),y2 = sqrt(1-x2*x2),
    slope = (y-y2)/h;
  if (slope>15) slope = 15;
  int
    samples = 1+(int)slope, is;
  for (is=0; is<samples; is++) {
    double
      hs = h/samples,
      xs = x+ is*hs,
      ys = sqrt(1-xs*xs);
    quarterpi += hs*ys;
    nsamples++;
  }
}
pi = 4*quarterpi;
```

1. Use the `omp parallel for` construct to parallelize the loop. As in the previous lab, you may at first see an incorrect result. Use the `reduction` clause to fix this.
2. Your code should now see a decent speedup, using up to 8 cores. However, it is possible to get completely linear speedup. For this you need to adjust the schedule.
   Start by using `schedule(static,$n$)`. Experiment with values for n.
   When can you get a better speedup? Explain this.

---

1. It doesn't actually do this in a mathematically sophisticated way, so this code is more for the sake of the example.

3. Since this code is somewhat dynamic, try `schedule(dynamic)`. This will actually give a fairly bad result. Why? Use `schedule(dynamic, $n$)` instead, and experiment with values for n.

4. Finally, use `schedule(guided)`, where OpenMP uses a heuristic. What results does that give?

Exercise 18.4. Program the *LU factorization* algorithm without pivoting.

```
for k=1,n:
  A[k,k] = 1./A[k,k]
  for i=k+1,n:
    A[i,k] = A[i,k]/A[k,k]
    for j=k+1,n:
      A[i,j] = A[i,j] - A[i,k]*A[k,j]
```

1. Argue that it is not possible to parallelize the outer loop.
2. Argue that it is possible to parallelize both the i and j loops.
3. Parallelize the algorithm by focusing on the i loop. Why is the algorithm as given here best for a matrix on row-storage? What would you do if the matrix was on column storage?
4. Argue that with the default schedule, if a row is updated by one thread in one iteration, it may very well be updated by another thread in another. Can you find a way to schedule loop iterations so that this does not happen? What practical reason is there for doing so?

The schedule can be declared explicitly, set at runtime through the `OMP_SCHEDULE` environment variable, or left up to the runtime system by specifying `auto`. Especially in the last two cases you may want to enquire what schedule is currently being used with `omp_get_schedule`.

```
int omp_get_schedule(omp_sched_t * kind, int * modifier );
```

Its mirror call is `omp_set_schedule`, which sets the value that is used when schedule value `runtime` is used. It is in effect equivalent to setting the environment variable `OMP_SCHEDULE`.

```
void omp_set_schedule (omp_sched_t kind, int modifier);
```

Type	environment variable OMP_SCHEDULE=	clause schedule(...)	modifier default
static	static[,n]	static[,n]	$N/nthreads$
dynamic	dynamic[,n]	dynamic[,n]	1
guided	guided[,n]	guided[,n]	

Here are the various schedules you can set with the `schedule` clause:

affinity Set by using value `omp_sched_affinity`

auto The schedule is left up to the implementation. Set by using value `omp_sched_auto`

dynamic value: 2. The modifier parameter is the *chunk* size; default 1. Set by using value `omp_sched_dynamic`

guided Value: 3. The modifier parameter is the `chunk` size. Set by using value `omp_sched_guided`

runtime Use the value of the `OMP_SCHEDULE` environment variable. Set by using value `omp_sched_`
    `runtime`

static value: 1. The modifier parameter is the *chunk* size. Set by using value `omp_sched_static`

18.3 Reductions

So far we have focused on loops with independent iterations. Reductions are a common type of loop with dependencies. There is an extended discussion of reductions in section 21.

18.4 Collapsing nested loops

In general, the more work there is to divide over a number of threads, the more efficient the parallelization will be. In the context of parallel loops, it is possible to increase the amount of work by parallelizing all levels of loops instead of just the outer one.

Example: in

```
for ( i=0; i<N; i++ )
  for ( j=0; j<N; j++ )
    A[i][j] = B[i][j] + C[i][j]
```

all N^2 iterations are independent, but a regular `omp for` directive will only parallelize one level. The `collapse` clause will parallelize more than one level:

```
#pragma omp for collapse(2)
for ( i=0; i<N; i++ )
  for ( j=0; j<N; j++ )
    A[i][j] = B[i][j] + C[i][j]
```

It is only possible to collapse perfectly nested loops, that is, the loop body of the outer loop can consist only of the inner loop; there can be no statements before or after the inner loop in the loop body of the outer loop. That is, the two loops in

```
for (i=0; i<N; i++) {
  y[i] = 0.;
  for (j=0; j<N; j++)
    y[i] + A[i][j] * x[j]
}
```

can not be collapsed.

Exercise 18.5.   Can you rewrite the preceding code example so that it can be collapsed? Do
        timing tests to see if you can notice the improvement from collapsing.

18.5   Ordered iterations

Iterations in a parallel loop that are execution in parallel do not execute in lockstep. That means that in

```
#pragma omp parallel for
for ( ... i ... ) {
  ... f(i) ...
  printf("something with %d\n",i);
}
```

it is not true that all function evaluations happen more or less at the same time, followed by all print statements. The print statements can really happen in any order. The ordered clause coupled with the ordered directive can force execution in the right order:

```
#pragma omp parallel for ordered
for ( ... i ... ) {
  ... f(i) ...
#pragma omp ordered
  printf("something with %d\n",i);
}
```

Example code structure:

```
#pragma omp parallel for shared(y) ordered
for ( ... i ... ) {
  int x = f(i)
#pragma omp ordered
  y[i] += f(x)
  z[i] = g(y[i])
}
```

There is a limitation: each iteration can encounter only one ordered directive.

18.6   `nowait`

The implicit barrier at the end of a work sharing construct can be cancelled with a nowait clause. This has the effect that threads that are finished can continue with the next code in the parallel region:

```
#pragma omp parallel
{
#pragma omp for nowait
  for (i=0; i<N; i++) { ... }
  // more parallel code
}
```

In the following example, threads that are finished with the first loop can start on the second. Note that this requires both loops to have the same schedule.

```
#pragma omp parallel
{
  x = local_computation()
#pragma omp for nowait
  for (i=0; i<N; i++) {
    x[i] = ...
  }
#pragma omp for
  for (i=0; i<N; i++) {
    y[i] = ... x[i] ...
  }
}
```

18.7 While loops

OpenMP can only handle 'for' loops: *while loops* can not be parallelized. So you have to find a way around that. While loops are for instance used to search through data:

```
while ( a[i]!=0 && i<imax ) {
 i++; }
// now i is the first index for which \n{a[i]} is zero.
```

We replace the while loop by a for loop that examines all locations:

```
result = -1;
#pragma omp parallel for
for (i=0; i<imax; i++) {
  if (a[i]!=0 && result<0) result = i;
}
```

Exercise 18.6.   Show that this code has a race condition.

You can fix the race condition by making the condition into a critical section; section 22.2.1. In this particular example, with a very small amount of work per iteration, that is likely to be inefficient in this case (why?). A more efficient solution uses the `lastprivate` pragma:

```
result = -1;
#pragma omp parallel for lastprivate(result)
for (i=0; i<imax; i++) {
  if (a[i]!=0) result = i;
}
```

You have now solved a slightly different problem: the result variable contains the *last* location where a[i] is zero.

Chapter 19

OpenMP topic: Work sharing

The declaration of a *parallel region* establishes a team of threads. This offers the possibility of parallelism, but to actually get meaningful parallel activity you need something more. OpenMP uses the concept of a *work sharing construct*: a way of dividing parallelizable work over a team of threads. The work sharing constructs are:

- `for/do` The threads divide up the loop iterations among themselves; see 18.1.
- `sections` The threads divide a fixed number of sections between themselves; see section 19.1.
- `single` The section is executed by a single thread; section 19.2.
- `task` See section 23.
- `workshare` Can parallelize Fortran array syntax; section 19.3.

19.1   Sections

A parallel loop is an example of independent work units that are numbered. If you have a pre-determined number of independent work units, the `sections` is more appropriate. In a `sections` construct can be any number of `section` constructs. These need to be independent, and they can be execute by any available thread in the current team, including having multiple sections done by the same thread.

```
#pragma omp sections
{
#pragma omp section
  // one calculation
#pragma omp section
  // another calculation
}
```

This construct can be used to divide large blocks of independent work. Suppose that in the following line, both `f(x)` and `g(x)` are big calculations:

```
y = f(x) + g(x)
```

You could then write

```
double y1,y2;
#pragma omp sections
{
#pragma omp section
  y1 = f(x)
#pragma omp section
  y2 = g(x)
}
y = y1+y2;
```

Instead of using two temporaries, you could also use a critical section; see section 22.2.1. However, the best solution is have a `reduction` clause on the `sections` directive:

```
y = f(x) + g(x)
```

You could then write

```
y = 0;
#pragma omp sections reduction(+:y)
{
#pragma omp section
  y += f(x)
#pragma omp section
  y += g(x)
}
```

19.2   Single/master

The `single` and `master` pragma limit the execution of a block to a single thread. This can for instance be used to print tracing information or doing *I/O* operations.

```
#pragma omp parallel
{
#pragma omp single
  printf("We are starting this section!\n");
  // parallel stuff
}
```

Another use of `single` is to perform initializations in a parallel region:

```
int a;
#pragma omp parallel
{
    #pragma omp single
```

```
        a = f(); // some computation
    #pragma omp sections
        // various different computations using a
}
```

The point of the single directive in this last example is that the computation needs to be done only once, because of the shared memory. Since it's a work sharing construct there is an *implicit barrier* after it, which guarantees that all threads have the correct value in their local memory (see section 25.3.

Exercise 19.1. What is the difference between this approach and how the same computation would be parallelized in MPI?

The master directive, also enforces execution on a single thread, specifically the master thread of the team, but it does not have the synchronization through the implicit barrier.

Exercise 19.2. Modify the above code to read:

```
        int a;
        #pragma omp parallel
        {
          #pragma omp master
            a = f(); // some computation
          #pragma omp sections
            // various different computations using a
        }
```

This code is no longer correct. Explain.

Above we motivated the single directive as a way of initializing shared variables. It is also possible to use single to initialize private variables. In that case you add the copyprivate clause. This is a good solution if setting the variable takes I/O.

Exercise 19.3. Give two other ways to initialize a private variable, with all threads receiving the same value. Can you give scenarios where each of the three strategies would be preferable?

19.3   Fortran array syntax parallelization

The parallel do directive is used to parallelize loops, and this applies to both C and Fortran. However, Fortran also has implied loops in its *array syntax*. To parallelize array syntax you can use the workshare directive.

The workshare directive exists only in Fortran. It can be used to parallelize the implied loops in *array syntax*, as well as *forall* loops.

Chapter 20

OpenMP topic: Controlling thread data

In a parallel region there are two types of data: private and shared. In this sections we will see the various way you can control what category your data falls under; for private data items we also discuss how their values relate to shared data.

20.1   Shared data

In a parallel region, any data declared outside it will be shared: any thread using a variable x will access the same memory location associated with that variable.

Example:

```
    int x = 5;
#pragma omp parallel
    {
      x = x+1;
      printf("shared: x is %d\n",x);
    }
```

All threads increment the same variable, so after the loop it will have a value of five plus the number of threads; or maybe less because of the data races involved. See HPSC-2.6.1.5 for an explanation of the issues involved; see 22.2.1 for a solution in OpenMP.

Sometimes this global update is what you want; in other cases the variable is intended only for intermediate results in a computation. In that case there are various ways of creating data that is local to a thread, and therefore invisible to other threads.

20.2   Private data

In the C/C++ language it is possible to declare variables inside a *lexical scope*; roughly: inside curly braces. This concept extends to OpenMP parallel regions and directives: any variable declared in a block following an OpenMP directive will be local to the executing thread.

Example:

```
      int x = 5;
#pragma omp parallel
   {
      int x; x = 3;
      printf("local: x is %d\n",x);
   }
```

After the parallel region the outer variable x will still have the value 5: there is no *storage association* between the private variable and global one.

The Fortran language does not have this concept of scope, so you have to use a `private` clause:

```
   !$OMP parallel private(x)
```

The `private` directive declares data to have a separate copy in the memory of each thread. Such private variables are initialized as they would be in a main program. Any computed value goes away at the end of the parallel region. (However, see below.) Thus, you should not rely on any initial value, or on the value of the outer variable after the region.

```
      int x = 5;
#pragma omp parallel private(x)
   {
      x = x+1; // dangerous
      printf("private: x is %d\n",x);
   }
   printf("after: x is %d\n",x); // also dangerous
```

Data that is declared private with the `private` directive is put on a separate *stack per thread*. The OpenMP standard does not dictate the size of these stacks, but beware of *stack overflow*. A typical default is a few megabyte; you can control it with the environment variable `OMP_STACKSIZE`. Its values can be literal or with suffixes:

```
123 456k 567K 678m 789M 246g 357G
```

A normal *Unix process* also has a stack, but this is independent of the OpenMP stacks for private data. You can query or set the Unix stack with `ulimit`:

```
[] ulimit -s
64000
[] ulimit -s 8192
[] ulimit -s
8192
```

The Unix stack can grow dynamically as space is needed. This does not hold for the OpenMP stacks: they are immediately allocated at their requested size. Thus it is important not too make them too large.

20.3   Data in dynamic scope

Functions that are called from a parallel region fall in the *dynamic scope* of that parallel region. The rules for variables in that function are as follows:

- Any variables locally defined to the function are private.
- `static` variables in C and `save` variables in Fortran are shared.
- The function arguments inherit their status from the calling environment.

20.4   Temporary variables in a loop

It is common to have a variable that is set and used in each loop iteration:

```
#pragma omp parallel for
for ( ... i ... ) {
  x = i*h;
  s = sin(x); c = cos(x);
  a[i] = s+c;
  b[i] = s-c;
}
```

By the above rules, the variables x, s, c are all shared variables. However, the values they receive in one iteration are not used in a next iteration, so they behave in fact like private variables to each iteration.

- In both C and Fortran you can declare these variables private in the parallel for directive.
- In C, you can also redefine the variables inside the loop.

Sometimes, even if you forget to declare these temporaries as private, the code may still give the correct output. That is because the compiler can sometimes eliminate them from the loop body, since it detects that their values are not otherwise used.

20.5   Default

- Loop variables in an `omp for` are private;
- Local variables in the parallel region are private.

You can alter this default behaviour with the `default` clause:

```
#pragma omp parallel default(shared) private(x)
{ ... }
#pragma omp parallel default(private) shared(matrix)
{ ... }
```

and if you want to play it safe:

```
#pragma omp parallel default(none) private(x) shared(matrix)
{ ... }
```

- The `shared` clause means that all variables from the outer scope are shared in the parallel region; any private variables need to be declared explicitly. This is the default behaviour.
- The `private` clause means that all outer variables become private in the parallel region. They are not initialized; see the next option. Any shared variables in the parallel region need to be declared explicitly. This value is not available in C.
- The `firstprivate` clause means all outer variables are private in the parallel region, and initialized with their outer value. Any shared variables need to be declared explicitly. This value is not available in C.
- The `none` option is good for debugging, because it forces you to specify for each variable in the parallel region whether it's private or shared. Also, if your code behaves differently in parallel from sequential there is probably a data race. Specifying the status of every variable is a good way to debug this.

20.6   Array data

The rules for arrays are slightly different from those for scalar data:

1. Statically allocated data, that is with a syntax like
   ```
   int array[100];
   integer,dimension(:) :: array(100}
   ```

   can be shared or private, depending on the clause you use.
2. Dynamically allocated data, that is, created with `malloc` or `allocate`, can only be shared.

Example of the first type: in
```
// alloc3.c
int array[nthreads];
{
  int t = 2;
  array += t;
  array[0] = t;
}
```

each thread gets a private copy of the array, properly initialized.

On the other hand, in
```
// alloc1.c
int *array = (int*) malloc(nthreads*sizeof(int));
#pragma omp parallel firstprivate(array)
{
  int t = omp_get_thread_num();
  array += t;
  array[0] = t;
}
```

each thread gets a private pointer, but all pointers point to the same object.

20.7 First and last private

Above, you saw that private variables are completely separate from any variables by the same name in the surrounding scope. However, there are two cases where you may want some *storage association* between a private variable and a global counterpart.

First of all, private variables are created with an undefined value. You can force their initialization with firstprivate.

```
    int t=2;
#pragma omp parallel firstprivate(t)
    {
      t += f( omp_get_thread_num() );
      g(t);
    }
```

The variable t behaves like a private variable, except that it is initialized to the outside value.

Secondly, you may want a private value to be preserved to the environment outside the parallel region. This really only makes sense in one case, where you preserve a private variable from the last iteration of a parallel loop, or the last section in an sections construct. This is done with lastprivate:

```
#pragma omp parallel for \
        lastprivate(tmp)
for (i=0; i<N; i+) {
  tmp = ......
  x[i] = .... tmp ....
}
..... tmp ....
```

20.8 Persistent data through threadprivate

Most data in OpenMP parallel regions is either inherited from the master thread and therefore shared, or temporary within the scope of the region and fully private. There is also a mechanism for *thread-private data*, which is not limited in lifetime to one parallel region. The threadprivate pragma is used to declare that each thread is to have a private copy of a variable:

```
#pragma omp threadprivate(var)
```

The variable needs be:

- a file or static variable in C,
- a static class member in C++, or
- a program variable or common block in Fortran.

20.8.1 Thread private initialization

If each thread needs a different value in its threadprivate variable, the initialization needs to happen in a parallel region.

In the following example a team of 7 threads is created, all of which set their thread-private variable. Later, this variable is read by a larger team: the variables that have not been set are undefined, though often simply zero:

```
// threadprivate.c
#include <stdlib.h>
#include <stdio.h>
#include <omp.h>

static int tp;

int main(int argc, char **argv) {

#pragma omp threadprivate(tp)

#pragma omp parallel num_threads(7)
  tp = omp_get_thread_num();

#pragma omp parallel num_threads(9)
  printf("Thread %d has %d\n", omp_get_thread_num(), tp);

  return 0;
}
```

On the other hand, if the thread private data starts out identical in all threads, the `copyin` clause can be used:

```
#pragma omp threadprivate(private_var)

private_var = 1;
#pragma omp parallel copyin(private_var)
  private_var += omp_get_thread_num()
```

If one thread needs to set all thread private data to its value, the `copyprivate` clause can be used:

```
#pragma omp parallel
{
  ...
#pragma omp single copyprivate(private_var)
  private_var = read_data();
  ...
```

```
}
```

20.8.2 Thread private example

The typical application for thread-private variables is in *random number generation*. A random number generator needs saved state, since it computes each next value from the current one. To have a parallel generator, each thread will create and initialize a private 'current value' variable. This will persist even when the execution is not in a parallel region; it gets updated only in a parallel region.

Exercise 20.1.   Calculate the area of the *Mandelbrot set* by random sampling. Initialize the random number generator separately for each thread; then use a parallel loop to evaluate the points. Explore performance implications of the different loop scheduling strategies.

Fortran note Named common blocks can be made thread-private with the syntax
```
$!OMP threadprivate( /blockname/ )
```

Threadprivate variables require `OMP_DYNAMIC` to be switched off.

Chapter 21

OpenMP topic: Reductions

Parallel tasks often produce some quantity that needs to be summed or otherwise combined. In section 17 you saw an example, and it was stated that the solution given there was not very good.

The problem in that example was the *race condition* involving the `result` variable. The simplest solution is to eliminate the race condition by declaring a *critical section*:

```
double result = 0;
#pragma omp parallel
{
  double local_result;
  int num = omp_get_thread_num();
  if (num==0)      local_result = f(x);
  else if (num==1) local_result = g(x);
  else if (num==2) local_result = h(x);
#pragma omp critical
  result += local_result;
}
```

This is a good solution if the amount of serialization in the critical section is small compared to computing the functions f, g, h. On the other hand, you may not want to do that in a loop:

```
double result = 0;
#pragma omp parallel
{
  double local_result;
#pragma omp for
  for (i=0; i<N; i++) {
    local_result = f(x,i);
#pragma omp critical
    result += local_result;
  } // end of for loop
}
```

Exercise 21.1. Can you think of a small modification of this code, that still uses a critical section, that is more efficient? Time both codes.

The easiest way to effect a reduction is of course to use the `reduction` clause. Adding this to an `omp for` or an `omp sections` construct has the following effect:

- OpenMP will make a copy of the reduction variable per thread, initialized to the identity of the reduction operator, for instance 1 for multiplication.
- Each thread will then reduce into its local variable;
- At the end of the loop, the local results are combined, again using the reduction operator, into the global variable.

This is one of those cases where the parallel execution can have a slightly different value from the one that is computed sequentially, because floating point operations are not associative. See HPSC-3.3.7 for more explanation.

If your code can not be easily structure as a reduction, you can realize the above scheme by hand by 'duplicating' the global variable and gather the contributions later. This example presumes three threads, and gives each a location of their own to store the result computed on that thread:

```
double result,local_results[3];
#pragma omp parallel
{
  int num = omp_get_thread_num();
  if (num==0)        local_results[num] = f(x)
  else if (num==1) local_results[num] = g(x)
  else if (num==2) local_results[num] = h(x)
}
result = local_results[0]+local_results[1]+local_results[2]
```

While this code is correct, it may be inefficient because of a phenomemon called *false sharing*. Even though the threads write to separate variables, those variables are likely to be on the same *cacheline* (see HPSC-1.4.1.2 for an explanation). This means that the cores will be wasting a lot of time and bandwidth updating each other's copy of this cacheline.

False sharing can be prevent by giving each thread its own cacheline:

```
double result,local_results[3][8];
#pragma omp parallel
{
  int num = omp_get_thread_num();
  if (num==0)        local_results[num][1] = f(x)
// et cetera
}
```

A more elegant solution gives each thread a true local variable, and uses a critical section to sum these, at the very end:

```
double result = 0;
#pragma omp parallel
{
  double local_result;
  local_result = .....
#pragam omp critical
  result += local_result;
}
```

21.1   Built-in reduction operators

Arithmetic reductions: $+, *, -, \max, \min$

Logical operator reductions in C: `& && | || ^`

Logical operator reductions in Fortran: `.and. .or. .eqv. .neqv. .iand. .ior. .ieor.`

Exercise 21.2.   The maximum and minimum reductions were not added to OpenMP until
version 3.1. Write a parallel loop that computes the maximum and minimum values
in an array. Discuss the various options. Do timings to evaluate the speedup that is
attained and to find the best option.

21.2   Initial value for reductions

The treatment of initial values in reductions is slightly involved.

```
x = init_x
#pragma omp parallel for reduction(min:x)
  for (int i=0; i<N; i++)
    x = min(x,data[i]);
```

Each thread does a partial reduction, but its initial value is not the user-supplied `init_x` value, but a value
dependent on the operator. In the end, the partial results will then be combined with the user initial value.
The initialization values are mostly self-evident, such as zero for addition and one for multiplication. For
min and max they are respectively the maximal and minimal representable value of the result type.

Figure 21.1 illustrates this, where `1,2,3,4` are four data items, `i` is the OpenMP initialization, and `u` is
the user initialization; each `p` stands for a partial reduction value. The figure is based on execution using
two threads.

Exercise 21.3.   Write a program to test the fact that the partial results are initialized to the unit
of the reduction operator.

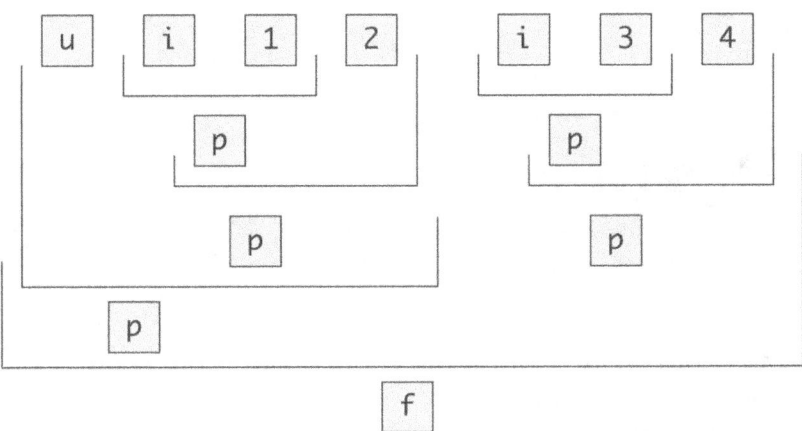

Figure 21.1: Reduction of four items on two threads, taking into account initial values.

21.3 User-defined reductions

With *user-defined reductions*, the programmer specifies the function that does the elementwise comparison. This takes two steps.

1. You need a function of two arguments that returns the result of the comparison. You can do this yourself, but, especially with the C++ standard library, you can use functions such as `std::vector::insert`.
2. Specifying how this function operates on two variables `omp_out` and `omp_in`, corresponding to the partially reduced result and the new operand respectively. The new partial result should be left in `omp_out`.
3. Optionally, you can specify the value to which the reduction should be initialized.

This is the syntax of the definition of the reduction, which can then be used in multiple `reduction` clauses.

```
#pragma omp declare reduction
    ( identifier : typelist : combiner )
    [initializer(initializer-expression)]
```

where:

identifier is a name; this can be overloaded for different types, and redefined in inner scopes.
typelist is a list of types.
combiner is an expression that updates the internal variable `omp_out` as function of itself and `omp_in`.
initializer sets `omp_priv` to the identity of the reduction; this can be an expression or a brace initializer.

For instance, recreating the maximum reduction would look like this:

```
// ireduct.c
int mymax(int r,int n) {
  // r is the already reduced value
```

```
// n is the new value
int m;
if (n>r) {
  m = n;
} else {
  m = r;
}
return m;
}
#pragma omp declare reduction \
  (rwz:int:omp_out=mymax(omp_out,omp_in)) \
  initializer(omp_priv=INT_MIN)
  m = INT_MIN;
#pragma omp parallel for reduction(rwz:m)
  for (int idata=0; idata<ndata; idata++)
    m = mymax(m,data[idata]);
```

Exercise 21.4. Write a reduction routine that operates on an array of non-negative integers, finding the smallest nonzero one. If the array has size zero, or entirely consists of zeros, return -1.

21.4 Reductions and floating-point math

The mechanisms that OpenMP uses to make a reduction parallel go against the strict rules for floating point expression evaluation in C; see HPSC-3.4. OpenMP ignores this issue: it is the programmer's job to ensure proper rounding behaviour.

Chapter 22

OpenMP topic: Synchronization

In the constructs for declaring parallel regions above, you had little control over in what order threads executed the work they were assigned. This section will discuss *synchronization* constructs: ways of telling threads to bring a certain order to the sequence in which they do things.

- `critical`: a section of code can only be executed by one thread at a time; see 22.2.1.
- `atomic` Update of a single memory location. Only certain specified syntax pattterns are supported. This was added in order to be able to use hardware support for atomic updates.
- `barrier`: section 22.1.
- `ordered`: section 18.5.
- locks: section **??**.
- `flush`: section 25.3.
- `nowait`: section 18.6.

22.1   Barrier

A barrier defines a point in the code where all active threads will stop until all threads have arrived at that point. With this, you can guarantee that certain calculations are finished. For instance, in this code snippet, computation of y can not proceed until another thread has computed its value of x.

```
#pragma omp parallel
{
  int mytid = omp_get_thread_num();
  x[mytid] = some_calculation();
  y[mytid] = x[mytid]+x[mytid+1];
}
```

This can be guaranteed with a `barrier` pragma:

```
#pragma omp parallel
{
  int mytid = omp_get_thread_num();
  x[mytid] = some_calculation();
```

```
#pragma omp barrier
  y[mytid] = x[mytid]+x[mytid+1];
}
```

Apart from the barrier directive, which inserts an explicit barrier, OpenMP has *implicit barriers* after a load sharing construct. Thus the following code is well defined:

```
#pragma omp parallel
{
#pragma omp for
  for (int mytid=0; mytid<number_of_threads; mytid++)
    x[mytid] = some_calculation();
#pragma omp for
  for (int mytid=0; mytid<number_of_threads-1; mytid++)
    y[mytid] = x[mytid]+x[mytid+1];
}
```

You can also put each parallel loop in a parallel region of its own, but there is some overhead associated with creating and deleting the team of threads in between the regions.

22.1.1   Implicit barriers

At the end of a parallel region the team of threads is dissolved and only the master thread continues. Therefore, there is an *implicit barrier at the end of a parallel region*.

There is some *barrier behaviour* associated with omp for loops and other *worksharing constructs* (see section **??**). For instance, there is an *implicit barrier* at the end of the loop. This barrier behaviour can be cancelled with the nowait clause.

You will often see the idiom

```
#pragma omp parallel
{
#pragma omp for nowait
  for (i=0; i<N; i++)
    a[i] = // some expression
#pragma omp for
  for (i=0; i<N; i++)
    b[i] = ...... a[i] ......
```

Here the nowait clause implies that threads can start on the second loop while other threads are still working on the first. Since the two loops use the same schedule here, an iteration that uses a[i] can indeed rely on it that that value has been computed.

22.2 Mutual exclusion

Sometimes it is necessary to let only one thread execute a piece of code. Such a piece of code is called a *critical section*, and OpenMP has several mechanisms for realizing this.

The most common use of critical sections is to update a variable. Since updating involves reading the old value, and writing back the new, this has the possibility for a *race condition*: another thread reads the current value before the first can update it; the second thread the updates to the wrong value.

Critical sections are an easy way to turn an existing code into a correct parallel code. However, there are disadvantages to this, and sometimes a more drastic rewrite is called for.

22.2.1 critical and atomic

There are two pragmas for critical sections: `critical` and `atomic`. The second one is more limited but has performance advantages.

The typical application of a critical section is to update a variable:

```
#pragma omp parallel
{
  int mytid = omp_get_thread_num();
  double tmp = some_function(mytid);
#pragma omp critical
  sum += tmp;
}
```

Exercise 22.1.   Consider a loop where each iteration updates a variable.
```
#pragma omp parallel for shared(result)
  for ( i ) {
        result += some_function_of(i);
  }
```

Discuss qualitatively the difference between:
  • turning the update statement into a critical section, versus
  • letting the threads accumulate into a private variable `tmp` as above, and
    summing these after the loop.
Do an Ahmdal-style quantitative analysis of the first case, assuming that you do n
iterations on p threads, and each iteration has a critical section that takes a fraction f.
Assume the number of iterations n is a multiple of the number of threads p. Also
assume the default static distribution of loop iterations over the threads.

A `critical` section works by acquiring a lock, which carries a substantial overhead. Furthermore, if your code has multiple critical sections, they are all mutually exclusive: if a thread is in one critical section, the other ones are all blocked.

On the other hand, the syntax for `atomic` sections is limited to the update of a single memory location, but such sections are not exclusive and they can be more efficient, since they assume that there is a hardware mechanism for making them critical.

The problem with `critical` sections being mutually exclusive can be mitigated by naming them:

```
#pragma omp critical (optional_name_in_parens)
```

22.3   Locks

lock—(textbf

OpenMP also has the traditional mechanism of a *lock*. A lock is somewhat similar to a critical section: it guarantees that some instructions can only be performed by one process at a time. However, a critical section is indeed about code; a lock is about data. With a lock you make sure that some data elements can only be touched by one process at a time.

One simple example of the use of locks is generation of a *histogram*. A histogram consists of a number of bins, that get updated depending on some data. Here is the basic structure of such a code:

```
int count[100];
float x = some_function();
int ix = (int)x;
if (ix>=100)
  error();
else
  count[ix]++;
```

It would be possible to guard the last line:

```
#pragma omp critical
  count[ix]++;
```

but that is unnecessarily restrictive. If there are enough bins in the histogram, and if the `some_function` takes enough time, there are unlikely to be conflicting writes. The solution then is to create an array of locks, with one lock for each `count` location.

Create/destroy:

```
void omp_init_lock(omp_lock_t *lock);
void omp_destroy_lock(omp_lock_t *lock);
```

Set and release:

```
void omp_set_lock(omp_lock_t *lock);
void omp_unset_lock(omp_lock_t *lock);
```

Since the set call is blocking, there is also

```
omp_test_lock();
```

Unsetting a lock needs to be done by the thread that set it.

Lock operations implicitly have a `flush`.

Exercise 22.2.   In the following code, one process sets array A and then uses it to update B;
          the other process sets array B and then uses it to update A. Argue that this code can
          deadlock. How could you fix this?

```
#pragma omp parallel shared(a, b, nthreads, locka, lockb)
  #pragma omp sections nowait
    {
    #pragma omp section
      {
      omp_set_lock(&locka);
      for (i=0; i<N; i++)
        a[i] = ..

      omp_set_lock(&lockb);
      for (i=0; i<N; i++)
        b[i] = .. a[i] ..
      omp_unset_lock(&lockb);
      omp_unset_lock(&locka);
      }

    #pragma omp section
      {
      omp_set_lock(&lockb);
      for (i=0; i<N; i++)
        b[i] = ...

      omp_set_lock(&locka);
      for (i=0; i<N; i++)
        a[i] = .. b[i] ..
      omp_unset_lock(&locka);
      omp_unset_lock(&lockb);
      }
    }  /* end of sections */
  }  /* end of parallel region */
```

22.3.1   Nested locks

A lock as explained above can not be locked if it is already locked. A *nested lock* can be locked multiple times by the same thread before being unlocked.

- `omp_init_nest_lock`
- `omp_destroy_nest_lock`
- `omp_set_nest_lock`
- `omp_unset_nest_lock`
- `omp_test_nest_lock`

lock—)

22.4   Example: Fibonacci computation

The *Fibonacci sequence* is recursively defined as

$$F(0) = 1, \qquad F(1) = 1, \qquad F(n) = F(n-1) + F(n-2) \text{ for } n \geq 2.$$

We start by sketching the basic single-threaded solution. The naive code looks like:

```
int main() {
  value = new int[nmax+1];
  value[0] = 1;
  value[1] = 1;
  fib(10);
}

int fib(int n) {
  int i, j, result;
  if (n>=2) {
    i=fib(n-1); j=fib(n-2);
    value[n] = i+j;
  }
  return value[n];
}
```

Howver, this is inefficienty, since most intermediate values will be computed more than once. We solve this by keeping track of which results are known:

```
  ...
  done = new int[nmax+1];
  for (i=0; i<=nmax; i++)
    done[i] = 0;
  done[0] = 1;
  done[1] = 1;
  ...
int fib(int n) {
  int i, j;
  if (!done[n]) {
```

```
    i = fib(n-1); j = fib(n-2);
    value[n] = i+j; done[n] = 1;
  }
  return value[n];
}
```

The OpenMP parallel solution calls for two different ideas. First of all, we parallelize the recursion by using tasks (section 23:

```
int fib(int n) {
  int i, j;
  if (n>=2) {
#pragma omp task shared(i) firstprivate(n)
    i=fib(n-1);
#pragma omp task shared(j) firstprivate(n)
    j=fib(n-2);
#pragma omp taskwait
    value[n] = i+j;
  }
  return value[n];
}
```

This computes the right solution, but, as in the naive single-threaded solution, it recomputes many of the intermediate values.

A naive addition of the done array leads to data races, and probably an incorrect solution:

```
int fib(int n) {
  int i, j, result;
  if (!done[n]) {
#pragma omp task shared(i) firstprivate(n)
    i=fib(n-1);
#pragma omp task shared(i) firstprivate(n)
    j=fib(n-2);
#pragma omp taskwait
    value[n] = i+j;
    done[n] = 1;
  }
  return value[n];
}
```

For instance, there is no guarantee that the done array is updated later than the value array, so a thread can think that done[n-1] is true, but value[n-1] does not have the right value yet.

One solution to this problem is to use a lock, and make sure that, for a given index n, the values done[n] and value[n] are never touched by more than one thread at a time:

```
int fib(int n)
{
  int i, j;
  omp_set_lock( &(dolock[n]) );
  if (!done[n]) {
#pragma omp task shared(i) firstprivate(n)
    i = fib(n-1);
#pragma omp task shared(j) firstprivate(n)
    j = fib(n-2);
#pragma omp taskwait
    value[n] = i+j;
    done[n] = 1;
  }
  omp_unset_lock( &(dolock[n]) );
  return value[n];
}
```

This solution is correct, optimally efficient in the sense that it does not recompute anything, and it uses tasks to obtain a parallel execution.

However, the efficiency of this solution is only up to a constant. A lock is still being set, even if a value is already computed and therefore will only be read. This can be solved with a complicated use of critical sections, but we will forego this.

Chapter 23

OpenMP topic: Tasks

Tasks are a mechanism that OpenMP uses under the cover: if you specify something as being parallel, OpenMP will create a 'block of work': a section of code plus the data environment in which it occurred. This block is set aside for execution at some later point.

Let's look at a simple example using the `task` directive.

Code	Execution
`x = f();`	the variable x gets a value
`#pragma omp task` `{ y = g(x); }`	a task is created with the current value of x
`z = h();`	the variable z gets a value

The thread that executes this code segment creates a task, which will later be executed, probably by a different thread. The exact timing of the execution of the task is up to a *task scheduler*, which operates invisible to the user.

The task mechanism allows you to do things that are hard or impossible with the loop and section constructs. For instance, a *while loop* traversing a *linked list* can be implemented with tasks:

Code	Execution
`p = head_of_list();`	one thread traverses the list
`while (!end_of_list(p)) {`	
`#pragma omp task`	a task is created,
`  process( p );`	one for each element
`  p = next_element(p);`	the generating thread goes on without waiting
`}`	the tasks are executed while more are being generated.

The way tasks and threads interact is different from the worksharing constructs you've seen so far. Typically, one thread will generate the tasks, adding them to a queue, from which all threads can take and execute them. This leads to the following idiom:

```
#pragma omp parallel
#pragma omp single
{
  ...
#pragma omp task
```

```
    { ... }
    ...
}
```

1. A parallel region creates a team of threads;
2. a single thread then creates the tasks, adding them to a queue that belongs to the team,
3. and all the threads in that team (possibly including the one that generated the tasks)

With tasks it becomes possible to parallelize processes that did not fit the earlier OpenMP constructs. For instance, if a certain operation needs to be applied to all elements of a linked list, you can have one thread go down the list, generating a task for each element of the list.

Another concept that was hard to parallelize earlier is the 'while loop'. This does not fit the requirement for OpenMP parallel loops that the loop bound needs to be known before the loop executes.

Exercise 23.1. Use tasks to find the smallest factor of a large number (using $2999 \cdot 3001$ as test case): generate a task for each trial factor. Start with this code:

```
int factor=0;
#pragma omp parallel
#pragma omp single
  for (int f=2; f<4000; f++) {
    { // see if 'f' is a factor
      if (N%f==0) { // found factor!
        factor = f;
      }
    }
    if (factor>0)
      break;
  }
  if (factor>0)
    printf("Found a factor: %d\n",factor);
```

- Turn the factor finding block into a task.
- Run your program a number of times:

```
for i in `seq 1 1000` ; do ./taskfactor ; done | grep -v 2999
```

  Does it find the wrong factor? Why? Try to fix this.
- Once a factor has been found, you should stop generating tasks. Let tasks that should not have been generated, meaning that they test a candidate larger than the factor found, print out a message.

23.1 Task data

Treatment of data in a task is somewhat subtle. The basic problem is that a task gets created at one time, and executed at another. Thus, if shared data is accessed, does the task see the value at creation time or at execution time? In fact, both possibilities make sense depending on the application, so we need to discuss the rules when which possibility applies.

The first rule is that shared data is shared in the task, but private data becomes `firstprivate`. To see the distinction, consider two code fragments. In the first example:

```
int count = 100;
#pragma omp parallel
#pragma omp single
{
  while (count>0) {
#pragma omp task
    {
      int countcopy = count;
      if (count==50) {
        sleep(1);
        printf("%d,%d\n",count,countcopy);
      } // end if
    }     // end task
    count--;
  }       // end while
}         // end single
```

the variable `count` is declared outside the parallel region and is therefore shared. When the print statement is executed, all tasks will have been generated, and so `count` will be zero. Thus, the output will likely be `0,50`.

In the second example:

```
#pragma omp parallel
#pragma omp single
{
  int count = 100;
  while (count>0) {
#pragma omp task
    {
      int countcopy = count;
      if (count==50) {
        sleep(1);
        printf("%d,%d\n",count,countcopy);
      } // end if
    }     // end task
    count--;
  }       // end while
}         // end single
```

the `count` variable is private to the thread creating the tasks, and so it will be `firstprivate` in the task, preserving the value that was current when the task was created.

23.2   Task synchronization

Even though the above segment looks like a linear set of statements, it is impossible to say when the code after the `task` directive will be executed. This means that the following code is incorrect:

```
x = f();
#pragma omp task
  { y = g(x); }
z = h(y);
```

Explanation: when the statement computing `z` is executed, the task computing `y` has only been scheduled; it has not necessarily been executed yet.

In order to have a guarantee that a task is finished, you need the `taskwait` directive. The following creates two tasks, which can be executed in parallel, and then waits for the results:

Code	Execution
`x = f();`	the variable x gets a value

`#pragma omp task`
`  { y1 = g1(x); }`
`#pragma omp task`
`  { y2 = g2(x); }`
	two tasks are created with the current value of x

`#pragma omp taskwait`	the thread waits until the tasks are finished
`z = h(y1)+h(y2);`	the variable z is computed using the task results

The `task` pragma is followed by a structured block. Each time the structured block is encountered, a new task is generated. On the other hand `taskwait` is a standalone directive; the code that follows is just code, it is not a structured block belonging to the directive.

Another aspect of the distinction between generating tasks and executing them: usually the tasks are generated by one thread, but executed by many threads. Thus, the typical idiom is:

```
#pragma omp parallel
#pragma omp single
{
  // code that generates tasks
}
```

This makes it possible to execute loops in parallel that do not have the right kind of iteration structure for a `omp parallel for`. As an example, you could traverse and process a linked list:

```
#pragma omp parallel
#pragma omp single
{
```

```
   while (!tail(p)) {
      p = p->next();
#pragma omp task
      process(p)
   }
#pragma omp taskwait
   }
```

One task traverses the linked list creating an independent task for each element in the list. These tasks are then executed in parallel; their assignment to threads is done by the task scheduler.

You can indicate task dependencies in several ways:

1. Using the 'task wait' directive you can explicitly indicate the *join* of the *forked* tasks. The instruction after the wait directive will therefore be dependent on the spawned tasks.
2. The `taskgroup` directive, followed by a structured block, ensures completion of all tasks created in the block, even if recursively created.
3. Each OpenMP task can have a `depend` clause, indicating what *data dependency* of the task. By indicating what data is produced or absorbed by the tasks, the scheduler can construct the dependency graph for you.

Another mechanism for dealing with tasks is the `taskgroup`: a task group is a code block that can contain `task` directives; all these tasks need to be finished before any statement after the block is executed.

A task group is somewhat similar to having a `taskwait` directive after the block. The big difference is that that `taskwait` directive does not wait for tasks that are recursively generated, while a `taskgroup` does.

23.3   Task dependencies

It is possible to put a partial ordering on tasks through use of the `depend` clause. For example, in

```
#pragma omp task
   x = f()
#pragma omp task
   y = g(x)
```

it is conceivable that the second task is executed before the first, possibly leading to an incorrect result. This is remedied by specifying:

```
#pragma omp task depend(out:x)
   x = f()
#pragma omp task depend(in:x)
   y = g(x)
```

Exercise 23.2.   Consider the following code:

```
for i in [1:N]:
    x[0,i] = some_function_of(i)
    x[i,0] = some_function_of(i)

for i in [1:N]:
    for j in [1:N]:
        x[i,j] = x[i-1,j]+x[i,j-1]
```

- Observe that the second loop nest is not amenable to OpenMP loop parallelism.
- Can you think of a way to realize the computation with OpenMP loop parallelism? Hint: you need to rewrite the code so that the same operations are done in a different order.
- Use tasks with dependencies to make this code parallel without any rewriting: the only change is to add OpenMP directives.

Tasks dependencies are used to indicated how two uses of one data item relate to each other. Since either use can be a read or a write, there are four types of dependencies.

RaW (Read after Write) The second task reads an item that the first task writes. The second task has to be executed after the first:

```
... omp task depend(OUT:x)
  foo(x)
... omp task depend( IN:x)
  foo(x)
```

WaR (Write after Read) The first task reads and item, and the second task overwrites it. The second task has to be executed second to prevent overwriting the initial value:

```
... omp task depend( IN:x)
  foo(x)
... omp task depend(OUT:x)
  foo(x)
```

WaW (Write after Write) Both tasks set the same variable. Since the variable can be used by an intermediate task, the two writes have to be executed in this order.

```
... omp task depend(OUT:x)
  foo(x)
... omp task depend(OUT:x)
  foo(x)
```

RaR (Read after Read) Both tasks read a variable. Since neither tasks has an 'out' declaration, they can run in either order.

```
... omp task depend(IN:x)
  foo(x)
... omp task depend(IN:x)
  foo(x)
```

23.4 More

23.4.1 Scheduling points

Normally, a task stays tied to the thread that first executes it. However, at a *task scheduling point* the thread may switch to the execution of another task created by the same team.

- There is a scheduling point after explicit task creation. This means that, in the above examples, the thread creating the tasks can also participate in executing them.
- There is a scheduling point at `taskwait` and `taskyield`.

On the other hand a task created with them `untied` clause on the task pragma is never tied to one thread. This means that after suspension at a scheduling point any thread can resume execution of the task. If you do this, beware that the value of a thread-id does not stay fixed. Also locks become a problem.

Example: if a thread is waiting for a lock, with a scheduling point it can suspend the task and work on another task.

```
while (!omp_test_lock(lock))
#pragma omp taskyield
    ;
```

23.4.2 Task cancelling

It is possible (in *OpenMP version 4*) to cancel tasks. This is useful when tasks are used to perform a search: the task that finds the result first can cancel any outstanding search tasks.

The directive `cancel` takes an argument of the surrounding construct (`parallel, for, sections, taskgroup`) in which the tasks are cancelled.

Exercise 23.3. Modify the prime finding example.

23.5 Examples

23.5.1 Fibonacci

As an example of the use of tasks, consider computing an array of Fibonacci values:

```
// taskgroup0.c
for (int i=2; i<N; i++)
  {
    fibo_values[i] = fibo_values[i-1]+fibo_values[i-2];
  }
```

If you simply turn each calculation into a task, results will be unpredictable (confirm this!) since tasks can be executed in any sequence. To solve this, we put dependencies on the tasks:

```
// taskgroup2.c
for (int i=2; i<N; i++)
#pragma omp task \
depend(out:fibo_values[i]) \
depend(in:fibo_values[i-1],fibo_values[i-2])
  {
     fibo_values[i] = fibo_values[i-1]+fibo_values[i-2];
  }
```

23.5.2   Binomial coefficients

Exercise 23.4.   An array of binomial coefficients can be computed as follows:

```
// binomial1.c
for (int row=1; row<=n; row++)
  for (int col=1; col<=row; col++)
     if (row==1 || col==1 || col==row)
array[row][col] = 1;
     else
array[row][col] = array[row-1][col-1] + array[row-1][col];
```

Putting a single task group around the double loop, and use depend clauses to make the execution satisfy the proper dependencies.

23.5.3   Tree traversal

OpenMP tasks are a great way of handling trees.

23.5.3.1   Post-order traversal

In *post-order tree traversal* you visit the subtrees before visiting the root. This is the traversal that you use to find summary information about a tree, for instance the sum of all nodes, and the sums of nodes of all subtrees:

for *all children c* **do**
    compute the sum s_c

$s \leftarrow \sum_c s_c$

Another example is matrix factorization:

$$S = A_{33} - A_{31}A_{11}^{-1}A_{13} - A_{32}A_{22}^{-1}A_{23}$$

where the two inverses A_{11}^{-1}, A_{22}^{-1} can be computed indepedently and recursively.

23.5.3.2 Pre-order traversal

If a property needs to propagate from the root to all subtrees and nodes, you can use *pre-order tree traversal*:

Update node value s

for *all children c* **do**
    update c with the new value s

Chapter 24

OpenMP topic: Affinity

24.1 OpenMP thread affinity control

The matter of thread affinity becomes important on *multi-socket nodes*; see the example in section 24.2.

Thread placement can be controlled with two environment variables:

- the environment variable `OMP_PROC_BIND` describes how threads are bound to *OpenMP places*; while
- the variable `OMP_PLACES` describes these places in terms of the available hardware.
- When you're experimenting with these variables it is a good idea to set `OMP_DISPLAY_ENV` to true, so that OpenMP will print out at runtime how it has interpreted your specification. The examples in the following sections will display this output.

24.1.1 Thread binding

The variable `OMP_PLACES` defines a series of places to which the threads are assigned.

Example: if you have two sockets and you define

```
OMP_PLACES=sockets
```

then

- thread 0 goes to socket 0,
- thread 1 goes to socket 1,
- thread 2 goes to socket 0 again,
- and so on.

On the other hand, if the two sockets have a total of sixteen cores and you define

```
OMP_PLACES=cores
OMP_PROC_BIND=close
```

then

- thread 0 goes to core 0, which is on socket 0,
- thread 1 goes to core 1, which is on socket 0,

- thread 2 goes to core 2, which is on socket 0,
- and so on, until thread 7 goes to core 7 on socket 0, and
- thread 8 goes to core 8, which is on socket 1,
- et cetera.

The value `OMP_PROC_BIND=close` means that the assignment goes successively through the available places. The variable `OMP_PROC_BIND` can also be set to `spread`, which spreads the threads over the places. With

```
OMP_PLACES=cores
OMP_PROC_BIND=spread
```

you find that

- thread 0 goes to core 0, which is on socket 0,
- thread 1 goes to core 8, which is on socket 1,
- thread 2 goes to core 1, which is on socket 0,
- thread 3 goes to core 9, which is on socket 1,
- and so on, until thread 14 goes to core 7 on socket 0, and
- thread 15 goes to core 15, which is on socket 1.

So you see that `OMP_PLACES=cores` and `OMP_PROC_BIND=spread` very similar to `OMP_PLACES=sockets`. The difference is that the latter choice does not bind a thread to a specific core, so the operating system can move threads about, and it can put more than one thread on the same core, even if there is another core still unused.

The value `OMP_PROC_BIND=master` puts the threads in the same place as the master of the team. This is convenient if you create teams recursively. In that case you would use the `proc_bind` clause rather than the environment variable, set to `spread` for the initial team, and to `master` for the recursively created team.

24.1.2 Effects of thread binding

Let's consider two example program. First we consider the program for computing π, which is purely compute-bound.

#threads	close/cores	spread/sockets	spread/cores
1	0.359	0.354	0.353
2	0.177	0.177	0.177
4	0.088	0.088	0.088
6	0.059	0.059	0.059
8	0.044	0.044	0.044
12	0.029	0.045	0.029
16	0.022	0.050	0.022

We see pretty much perfect speedup for the `OMP_PLACES=cores` strategy; with `OMP_PLACES=sockets` we probably get occasional collisions where two threads wind up on the same core.

Next we take a program for computing the time evolution of the *heat equation*:

$$t = 0, 1, 2, \ldots : \forall_i : x_i^{(t+1)} = 2x_i^{(t)} - x_{i-1}^{(t)} - x_{i+1}^{(t)}$$

This is a bandwidth-bound operation because the amount of computation per data item is low.

#threads	close/cores	spread/sockets	spread/cores
1	2.88	2.89	2.88
2	1.71	1.41	1.42
4	1.11	0.74	0.74
6	1.09	0.57	0.57
8	1.12	0.57	0.53
12	0.72	0.53	0.52
16	0.52	0.61	0.53

Again we see that `OMP_PLACES=sockets` gives worse performance for high core counts, probably because of threads winding up on the same core. The thing to observe in this example is that with 6 or 8 cores the `OMP_PROC_BIND=spread` strategy gives twice the performance of `OMP_PROC_BIND=close`.

The reason for this is that a single socket does not have enough bandwidth for all eight cores on the socket. Therefore, dividing the eight threads over two sockets gives each thread a higher available bandwidth than putting all threads on one socket.

24.1.3 Place definition

There are three predefined values for the `OMP_PLACES` variable: `sockets, cores, threads`. You have already seen the first two; the `threads` value becomes relevant on processors that have hardware threads. In that case, `OMP_PLACES=cores` does not tie a thread to a specific hardware thread, leading again to possible collisions as in the above example. Setting `OMP_PLACES=threads` ties each OpenMP thread to a specific hardware thread.

There is also a very general syntax for defining places that uses a

> `location:number:stride`

syntax. Examples:

- `OMP_PLACES="{0:8:1},{8:8:1}"`

  is equivalent to `sockets` on a two-socket design with eight cores per socket: it defines two places, each having eight consecutive cores. The threads are then places alternating between the two places, but not further specified inside the place.
- The setting `cores` is equivalent to
  `OMP_PLACES="{0},{1},{2},...,{15}"`

- On a four-socket design, the specification
  `OMP_PLACES="{0:4:8}:4:1"`

states that the place 0, 8, 16, 24 needs to be repeated four times, with a stride of one. In other words, thread 0 winds up on core 0 of some socket, the thread 1 winds up on core 1 of some socket, et cetera.

24.1.4 Binding possibilities

Values for OMP_PROC_BIND are: false, true, master, close, spread.

- false: set no binding
- true: lock threads to a core
- master: collocate threads with the master thread
- close: place threads close to the master in the places list
- spread: spread out threads as much as possible

This effect can be made local by giving the proc_bind clause in the parallel directive.

A safe default setting is

```
export OMP_PROC_BIND=true
```

which prevents the operating system from *migrating a thread*. This prevents many scaling problems.

Good examples of *thread placement* on the *Intel Knight's Landing*: https://software.intel.com/en-us/articles/process-and-thread-affinity-for-intel-xeon-phi-processors-x200

24.2 First-touch

The affinity issue shows up in the *first-touch* phenomemon. Memory allocated with malloc and like routines is not actually allocated; that only happens when data is written to it. In light of this, consider the following OpenMP code:

```
double *x = (double*) malloc(N*sizeof(double));

for (i=0; i<N; i++)
  x[i] = 0;

#pragma omp parallel for
for (i=0; i<N; i++)
  .... something with x[i] ...
```

Since the initialization loop is not parallel it is executed by the master thread, making all the memory associated with the socket of that thread. Subsequent access by the other socket will then access data from memory not attached to that socket.

Exercise 24.1.   Finish the following fragment and run it with first all the cores of one socket, then all cores of both sockets. (If you know how to do explicit placement, you can also try fewer cores.)

```
        for (int i=0; i<nlocal+2; i++)
          in[i] = 1.;
        for (int i=0; i<nlocal; i++)
          out[i] = 0.;

        for (int step=0; step<nsteps; step++) {
    #pragma omp parallel for schedule(static)
          for (int i=0; i<nlocal; i++) {
            out[i] = ( in[i]+in[i+1]+in[i+2] )/3.;
          }
    #pragma omp parallel for schedule(static)
          for (int i=0; i<nlocal; i++)
            in[i+1] = out[i];
          in[0] = 0; in[nlocal+1] = 1;
        }
```

Exercise 24.2. How do the OpenMP dynamic schedules relate to this?

C++ `valarray` does initialization, so it will allocate memory on thread 0.

You could move pages with `move_pages`.

By regarding affinity, in effect you are adopting an SPMD style of programming. You could make this explicit by having each thread allocate its part of the arrays separately, and storing a private pointer as `threadprivate` [ ]. However, this makes it impossible for threads to access each other's parts of the distributed array, so this is only suitable for total *data parallel* or *embarrassingly parallel* applications.

24.3   Affinity control outside OpenMP

There are various utilities to control process and thread placement.

Process placement can be controlled on the Operating system level by `numactl` (the TACC utility `tacc_affinity` is a wrapper around this) on Linux (also `taskset`); Windows `start/affinity`.

Corresponding system calls: `pbing` on Solaris, `sched_setaffinity` on Linux, `SetThreadAffinityMask` on Windows.

Corresponding environment variables: `SUNW_MP_PROCBIND` on Solaris, `KMP_AFFINITY` on Intel.

The *Intel compiler* has an environment variable for affinity control:

```
        export KMP_AFFINITY=verbose,scatter
```

values: `none,scatter,compact`

For *gcc*:

```
export GOMP_CPU_AFFINITY=0,8,1,9
```

For the *Sun compiler*:

```
SUNW_MP_PROCBIND
```

Chapter 25

OpenMP tocic: Memory model

25.1   Thread synchronization

Let's do a *producer-consumer* model[1]. This can be implemented with sections, where one section, the producer, sets a flag when data is available, and the other, the consumer, waits until the flag is set.

```
#pragma omp parallel sections
{
  // the producer
  #pragma omp section
  {
    ... do some producing work ...
    flag = 1;
  }
  // the consumer
  #pragma omp section
  {
    while (flag==0) { }
    ... do some consuming work ...
  }
}
```

One reason this doesn't work, is that the compiler will see that the flag is never used in the producing section, and that is never changed in the consuming section, so it may optimize these statements, to the point of optimizing them away.

The producer then needs to do:

```
    ... do some producing work ...
#pragma omp flush
#pragma atomic write
  flag = 1;
#pragma omp flush(flag)
```

---

1.   This example is from Intel's excellent OMP course by Tim Mattson

258

and the consumer does:

```
#pragma omp flush(flag)
while (flag==0) {
   #pragma omp flush(flag)
}
#pragma omp flush
```

This code strictly speaking has a *race condition* on the flag variable. It is better to use an atomic pragma here: the producer has

```
#pragma atomic write
   flag = 1;
```

and the consumer:

```
while (1) {
   #pragma omp flush(flag)
   #pragma omp atomic read
     flag_read = flag
   if (flag_read==1) break;
}
```

25.2 Data races

OpenMP, being based on shared memory, has a potential for *race conditions*. These happen when two threads access the same data item. The problem with race conditions is that programmer convenience runs counter to efficient execution. For this reason, OpenMP simply does not allow some things that would be desirable.

The basic rule about multiple-thread access of a single data item is:

> Any memory location that is *written* by one thread, can not be *read* by another thread
> in the same parallel region, if no synchronization is done.

To start with that last clause: any workshare construct ends with an *implicit barrier*, so data written before that barrier can safely be read after it.

As an illustration of a possible problem:

```
c = d = 0;
#pragma omp sections
{
#pragma omp section
  { a = 1; c = b; }
```

```
#pragma omp section
  { b = 1; d = a; }
}
```

Under any reasonable interpretation of parallel execution, the possible values for c, d are $1, 1 \ 0, 1$ or $1, 0$. This is known as *sequential consistency*: the parallel outcome is consistent with a sequential execution that interleaves the parallel computations, respecting their local statement orderings. (See also HPSC-2.6.1.6.)

However, without synchronization, threads are allowed to maintain a value for a variable locally that is not the same as the stored value. In this example, that means that the thread executing the first section need not write its value of a to memory, and likewise b in the second thread, so $0, 0$ is in fact a possible outcome.

In order to resolve multiple accesses:

1. Thread one reads the variable.
2. Thread one flushes the variable.
3. Thread two flushes the variable.
4. Thread two reads the variable.

25.3   Relaxed memory model

flush

- There is an implicit flush of all variables at the start and end of a *parallel region*.
- There is a flush at each barrier, whether explicit or implicit, such as at the end of a *work sharing*.
- At entry and exit of a *critical section*
- When a *lock* is set or unset.

Chapter 26

OpenMP tocic: SIMD processing

You can declare a loop to be executable with *vector instructions* with `simd`

The `simd` pragma has the following clauses:

- `safelen(n)`: limits the number of iterations in a SIMD chunk. Presumably useful if you combine `parallel for simd`.
- `linear`: lists variables that have a linear relation to the iteration parameter.
- `aligned`: specifies alignment of variables.

If your SIMD loop includes a function call, you can declare that the function can be turned into vector instructions with `declare simd`

If a loop is both multi-threadable and vectorizable, you can combine directives as `pragma omp parallel for simd`.

Compilers can be made to report whether a loop was vectorized:

```
LOOP BEGIN at simdf.c(61,15)
    remark #15301: OpenMP SIMD LOOP WAS VECTORIZED
LOOP END
```

with such options as `-Qvec-report=3` for the Intel compiler.

Performance improvements of these directives need not be immediately obvious. In cases where the operation is bandwidth-limited, using `simd` parallelism may give the same or worse performance as thread parallelism.

The following function can be vectorized:

```
// tools.c
#pragma omp declare simd
double cs(double x1,double x2,double y1,double y2) {
  double
    inprod = x1*x2+y1*y2,
    xnorm = sqrt(x1*x1 + x2*x2),
    ynorm = sqrt(y1*y1 + y2*y2);
  return inprod / (xnorm*ynorm);
```

```
        }
        #pragma omp declare simd uniform(x1,x2,y1,y2) linear(i)
        double csa(double *x1,double *x2,double *y1,double *y2, int i) {
          double
            inprod = x1[i]*x2[i]+y1[i]*y2[i],
            xnorm = sqrt(x1[i]*x1[i] + x2[i]*x2[i]),
            ynorm = sqrt(y1[i]*y1[i] + y2[i]*y2[i]);
          return inprod / (xnorm*ynorm);
        }
```

Compiling this the regular way

```
        # parameter 1(x1): %xmm0
        # parameter 2(x2): %xmm1
        # parameter 3(y1): %xmm2
        # parameter 4(y2): %xmm3


        movaps     %xmm0, %xmm5    5 <- x1
        movaps     %xmm2, %xmm4    4 <- y1
        mulsd      %xmm1, %xmm5    5 <- 5 * x2 = x1 * x2
        mulsd      %xmm3, %xmm4    4 <- 4 * y2 = y1 * y2
        mulsd      %xmm0, %xmm0    0 <- 0 * 0 = x1 * x1
        mulsd      %xmm1, %xmm1    1 <- 1 * 1 = x2 * x2
        addsd      %xmm4, %xmm5    5 <- 5 + 4 = x1*x2 + y1*y2
        mulsd      %xmm2, %xmm2    2 <- 2 * 2 = y1 * y1
        mulsd      %xmm3, %xmm3    3 <- 3 * 3 = y2 * y2
        addsd      %xmm1, %xmm0    0 <- 0 + 1 = x1*x1 + x2*x2
        addsd      %xmm3, %xmm2    2 <- 2 + 3 = y1*y1 + y2*y2
        sqrtsd     %xmm0, %xmm0    0 <- sqrt(0) = sqrt( x1*x1 + x2*x2 )
        sqrtsd     %xmm2, %xmm2    2 <- sqrt(2) = sqrt( y1*y1 + y2*y2 )
```

which uses the scalar instruction `mulsd`: multiply scalar double precision.

With a `declare simd` directive:

```
        movaps     %xmm0, %xmm7
        movaps     %xmm2, %xmm4
        mulpd      %xmm1, %xmm7
        mulpd      %xmm3, %xmm4
```

which uses the vector instruction `mulpd`: multiply packed double precision, operating on 128-bit *SSE2 registers*.

Compiling for the *Intel Knight's Landing* gives more complicated code:

```
        # parameter 1(x1): %xmm0
```

```
# parameter 2(x2): %xmm1
# parameter 3(y1): %xmm2
# parameter 4(y2): %xmm3

vmulpd      %xmm3, %xmm2, %xmm4                                      4 <- y1*y2
vmulpd      %xmm1, %xmm1, %xmm5                                      5 <- x1*x2
vbroadcastsd .L_2il0floatpacket.0(%rip), %zmm21
movl        $3, %eax                                                set accumulator EAX
vbroadcastsd .L_2il0floatpacket.5(%rip), %zmm24
kmovw       %eax, %k3                                               set mask k3
vmulpd      %xmm3, %xmm3, %xmm6                                      6 <-y1*y1 (stall)
vfmadd231pd %xmm0, %xmm1, %xmm4                                      4 <- 4 + x1*x2 (no
vfmadd213pd %xmm5, %xmm0, %xmm0                                      0 <- 0 + 0*5 = x1 +
vmovaps     %zmm21, %zmm18                                          #25.26 c7
vmovapd     %zmm0, %zmm3{%k3}{z}                                    #25.26 c11
vfmadd213pd %xmm6, %xmm2, %xmm2                                     #24.29 c13
vpcmpgtq    %zmm0, %zmm21, %k1{%k3}                                 #25.26 c13
vscalefpd   .L_2il0floatpacket.1(%rip){1to8}, %zmm0, %zmm3{%k1} #25.26 c15
vmovaps     %zmm4, %zmm26                                          #25.26 c15
vmovapd     %zmm2, %zmm7{%k3}{z}                                   #25.26 c17
vpcmpgtq    %zmm2, %zmm21, %k2{%k3}                                #25.26 c17
vscalefpd   .L_2il0floatpacket.1(%rip){1to8}, %zmm2, %zmm7{%k2} #25.26 c19
vrsqrt28pd  %zmm3, %zmm16{%k3}{z}                                  #25.26 c19
vpxorq      %zmm4, %zmm4, %zmm26{%k3}                              #25.26 c19
vrsqrt28pd  %zmm7, %zmm20{%k3}{z}                                  #25.26 c21
vmulpd      {rn-sae}, %zmm3, %zmm16, %zmm19{%k3}{z}                #25.26 c27 stall 2
vscalefpd   .L_2il0floatpacket.2(%rip){1to8}, %zmm16, %zmm17{%k3}{z} #25.26 c
vmulpd      {rn-sae}, %zmm7, %zmm20, %zmm23{%k3}{z}                #25.26 c29
vscalefpd   .L_2il0floatpacket.2(%rip){1to8}, %zmm20, %zmm22{%k3}{z} #25.26 c
vfnmadd231pd {rn-sae}, %zmm17, %zmm19, %zmm18{%k3}              #25.26 c33 stall 1
vfnmadd231pd {rn-sae}, %zmm22, %zmm23, %zmm21{%k3}             #25.26 c35
vfmadd231pd {rn-sae}, %zmm19, %zmm18, %zmm19{%k3}              #25.26 c39 stall 1
vfmadd231pd {rn-sae}, %zmm23, %zmm21, %zmm23{%k3}              #25.26 c41
vfmadd213pd {rn-sae}, %zmm17, %zmm17, %zmm18{%k3}              #25.26 c45 stall 1
vfnmadd231pd {rn-sae}, %zmm19, %zmm19, %zmm3{%k3}              #25.26 c47
vfmadd213pd {rn-sae}, %zmm22, %zmm22, %zmm21{%k3}             #25.26 c51 stall 1
vfnmadd231pd {rn-sae}, %zmm23, %zmm23, %zmm7{%k3}             #25.26 c53
vfmadd213pd %zmm19, %zmm18, %zmm3{%k3}                         #25.26 c57 stall 1
vfmadd213pd %zmm23, %zmm21, %zmm7{%k3}                         #25.26 c59
vscalefpd   .L_2il0floatpacket.3(%rip){1to8}, %zmm3, %zmm3{%k1} #25.26 c63 st
vscalefpd   .L_2il0floatpacket.3(%rip){1to8}, %zmm7, %zmm7{%k2} #25.26 c65
vfixupimmpd $112, .L_2il0floatpacket.4(%rip){1to8}, %zmm0, %zmm3{%k3} #25.2
vfixupimmpd $112, .L_2il0floatpacket.4(%rip){1to8}, %zmm2, %zmm7{%k3} #25.2
```

```
vmulpd      %xmm7, %xmm3, %xmm0                              #25.26 c71
vmovaps     %zmm0, %zmm27                                   #25.26 c79
vmovaps     %zmm0, %zmm25                                   #25.26 c79
vrcp28pd    {sae}, %zmm0, %zmm27{%k3}                       #25.26 c81
vfnmadd213pd {rn-sae}, %zmm24, %zmm27, %zmm25{%k3}          #25.26 c89 stal
vfmadd213pd {rn-sae}, %zmm27, %zmm25, %zmm27{%k3}           #25.26 c95 stal
vcmppd      $8, %zmm26, %zmm27, %k1{%k3}                    #25.26 c101 sta
vmulpd      %zmm27, %zmm4, %zmm1{%k3}{z}                    #25.26 c101
kortestw    %k1, %k1                                        #25.26 c103
je          ..B1.3          # Prob 25%                      #25.26 c105
vdivpd      %zmm0, %zmm4, %zmm1{%k1}                        #25.26 c3 stall
vmovaps     %xmm1, %xmm0                                    #25.26 c77
ret                                                         #25.26 c79
```

```
#pragma omp declare simd uniform(op1) linear(k) notinbranch
  double SqrtMul(double *op1, double op2, int k) {
    return (sqrt(op1[k]) * sqrt(op2));
  }
```

Chapter 27

OpenMP remaining topics

27.1   Runtime functions and internal control variables

OpenMP has a number of settings that can be set through *environment variables*, and both queried and set through *library routines*. These settings are called *Internal Control Variables (ICVs)*: an OpenMP implementation behaves as if there is an internal variable storing this setting.

The runtime functions are:

- `omp_set_num_threads`
- `omp_get_num_threads`
- `omp_get_max_threads`
- `omp_get_thread_num`
- `omp_get_num_procs`
- `omp_in_parallel`
- `omp_set_dynamic`
- `omp_get_dynamic`
- `omp_set_nested`
- `omp_get_nested`
- `omp_get_wtime`
- `omp_get_wtick`
- `omp_set_schedule`
- `omp_get_schedule`
- `omp_set_max_active_levels`
- `omp_get_max_active_levels`
- `omp_get_thread_limit`
- `omp_get_level`
- `omp_get_active_level`
- `omp_get_ancestor_thread_num`
- `omp_get_team_size`

Here are the OpenMP *environment variables*:

- `OMP_CANCELLATION` Set whether cancellation is activated
- `OMP_DISPLAY_ENV` Show OpenMP version and environment variables

- `OMP_DEFAULT_DEVICE` Set the device used in target regions
- `OMP_DYNAMIC` Dynamic adjustment of threads
- `OMP_MAX_ACTIVE_LEVELS` Set the maximum number of nested parallel regions
- `OMP_MAX_TASK_PRIORITY` Set the maximum task priority value
- `OMP_NESTED` Nested parallel regions
- `OMP_NUM_THREADS` Specifies the number of threads to use
- `OMP_PROC_BIND` Whether theads may be moved between CPUs
- `OMP_PLACES` Specifies on which CPUs the theads should be placed
- `OMP_STACKSIZE` Set default thread stack size
- `OMP_SCHEDULE` How threads are scheduled
- `OMP_THREAD_LIMIT` Set the maximum number of threads
- `OMP_WAIT_POLICY` How waiting threads are handled

There are 4 ICVs that behave as if each thread has its own copy of them. The default is implementation-defined unless otherwise noted.

- It may be possible to adjust dynamically the number of threads for a parallel region. Variable: `OMP_DYNAMIC`; routines: `omp_set_dynamic`, `omp_get_dynamic`.
- If a code contains *nested parallel regions*, the inner regions may create new teams, or they may be executed by the single thread that encounters them. Variable: `OMP_NESTED`; routines `omp_set_nested`, `omp_get_nested`. Allowed values are `TRUE` and `FALSE`; the default is false.
- The number of threads used for an encountered parallel region can be controlled. Variable: `OMP_NUM_THREADS`; routines `omp_set_num_threads`, `omp_get_max_threads`.
- The schedule for a parallel loop can be set. Variable: `OMP_SCHEDULE`; routines `omp_set_schedule`, `omp_get_schedule`.

Non-obvious syntax:

```
export OMP_SCHEDULE="static,100"
```

Other settings:

- `omp_get_num_threads`: query the number of threads active at the current place in the code; this can be lower than what was set with `omp_set_num_threads`. For a meaningful answer, this should be done in a parallel region.
- `omp_get_thread_num`
- `omp_in_parallel`: test if you are in a parallel region (see for instance section 17).
- `omp_get_num_procs`: query the physical number of cores available.

Other environment variables:

- `OMP_STACKSIZE` controls the amount of space that is allocated as per-thread *stack*; the space for private variables.
- `OMP_WAIT_POLICY` determines the behaviour of threads that wait, for instance for *critical section*:
    - `ACTIVE` puts the thread in a *spin-lock*, where it actively checks whether it can continue;
    - `PASSIVE` puts the thread to sleep until the Operating System (OS) wakes it up.

The 'active' strategy uses CPU while the thread is waiting; on the other hand, activating it after the wait is instantaneous. With the 'passive' strategy, the thread does not use any CPU while waiting, but activating it again is expensive. Thus, the passive strategy only makes sense if threads will be waiting for a (relatively) long time.

- OMP_PROC_BIND with values TRUE and FALSE can bind threads to a processor. On the one hand, doing so can minimize data movement; on the other hand, it may increase load imbalance.

27.2 Timing

OpenMP has a wall clock timer routine omp_get_wtime

```
double omp_get_wtime(void);
```

The starting point is arbitrary and is different for each program run; however, in one run it is identical for all threads. This timer has a resolution given by omp_get_wtick.

Exercise 27.1.   Use the timing routines to demonstrate speedup from using multiple threads.
- Write a code segment that takes a measurable amount of time, that is, it should take a multiple of the tick time.
- Write a parallel loop and measure the speedup. You can for instance do this

```
for (int use_threads=1; use_threads<=nthreads; use_threads++) {
#pragma omp parallel for num_threads(use_threads)
    for (int i=0; i<nthreads; i++) {
        .....
    }
    if (use_threads==1)
      time1 = tend-tstart;
    else // compute speedup
```

- In order to prevent the compiler from optimizing your loop away, let the body compute a result and use a reduction to preserve these results.

27.3 Dependency analysis

If two statements refer to the same data item, we say that there is a *data dependency* between the statements. Such dependencies limit the extent to which the execution of the statements can be rearranged. The study of this topic probably started in the 1960s, when processors could execute statements *out of order* to increase throughput. The re-ordering of statements was limited by the fact that the execution had to obey the *program order* semantics: the result had to be as if the statements were executed strictly in the order in which they appear in the program.

These issues of statement ordering, and therefore of data dependencies, arise in OpenMP in two main ways:

1. When a loop is parallelized, the iterations are no longer executed in their program order, so we have to check for dependencies.

2. The introduction of tasks also means that parts of a program can be executed in a different order from in which they appear in a sequential execution.

The easiest case of dependency analysis is that of detecting that loop iterations can be executed independently. Iterations are of course independent if a data item is read in two different iterations, but if the same item is read in one iteration and written in another, or written in two different iterations, we need to do further analysis.

Analysis of *data dependencies* can be performed by a compiler, but compilers take, of necessity, a conservative approach. This means that iterations may be independent, but can not be recognized as such by a compiler. Therefore, OpenMP shifts this responsibility to the programmer; see for instance section 18.5.

The three types of dependencies are:

- flow dependencies, or 'read-after-write';
- anti dependencies, or 'write-after-read'; and
- output dependencies, or 'write-after-write'.

```
for (i) {
  y[i] = t;
  x[i+1] = y[i+1];
  t = x[i];
}
```

27.3.1   Flow dependencies

Flow dependencies, or read-afer-write, are not a problem if the read and write occur in the same loop iteration:

```
for (i=0; i<N; i++) {
  x[i] = .... ;
  .... = ... x[i] ... ;
}
```

On the other hand, if the read happens in a later iteration, there is no simple way to parallelize the loop:

```
for (i=0; i<N; i++) {
  .... = ... x[i] ... ;
  x[i+1] = .... ;
}
```

This usually requires rewriting the code.

27.3.2   Anti dependencies

The simplest case of write-after-read is a reduction:

```
for (i=0; i<N; i++) {
  t = t + .....
}
```

This can be dealt with by explicit declaring the loop to be a reduction, or to use any of the other strategies in section 21.

If the read and write are on an array the situation is more complicated. The iterations in this fragment

```
for (i=0; i<N; i++) {
  x[i] = ... x[i+1] ... ;
}
```

can not be executed in arbitrary order as such. However, conceptually there is no dependency. We can solve this by introducing a temporary array:

```
for (i=0; i<N; i++)
  xtmp[i] = x[i];
for (i=0; i<N; i++) {
  x[i] = ... xtmp[i+1] ... ;
}
```

This is an example of a transformation that a compiler is unlikely to perform, since it can greatly affect the memory demands of the program. Thus, this is left to the programmer.

27.3.3   Output dependencies

The case of write-after-write does not occur by itself: if a variable is written twice in sequence without an intervening read, the first write can be removed without changing the meaning of the program. Thus, this case reduces to a flow dependency.

Other output dependencies can easily be removed. In the following code, t can be declared private, thereby removing the dependency.

```
for (i=0; i<N; i++) {
  t = f(i)
  s += t*t;
}
```

If the final value of t is wanted, the lastprivate can be used.

27.4   Thread safety

With OpenMP it is relatively easy to take existing code and make it parallel by introducing parallel sections. If you're careful to declare the appropriate variables shared and private, this may work fine. However, your code may include calls to library routines that include a *race condition*; such code is said not to be *thread-safe*.

For example a routine

```
static int isave;
int next_one() {
 int i = isave;
 isave += 1;
 return i;
}


...
for ( .... ) {
  int ivalue = next_one();
}
```

has a clear race condition, as the iterations of the loop may get different `next_one` values, as they are supposed to, or not. This can be solved by using an `critical` pragma for the `next_one` call; another solution is to use an `threadprivate` declaration for `isave`. This is for instance the right solution if the `next_one` routine implements a *random number generator*.

27.5   Performance and tuning

The performance of an OpenMP code can be influenced by the following.

Amdahl effects Your code needs to have enough parts that are parallel (see HPSC-2.2.3). Sequential parts may be sped up by having them executed redundantly on each thread, since that keeps data locally.

Dynamism Creating a thread team takes time. In practice, a team is not created and deleted for each parallel region, but creating teams of different sizes, or recursize thread creation, may introduce overhead.

Load imbalance Even if your program is parallel, you need to worry about load balance. In the case of a parallel loop you can set the `schedule` clause to `dynamic`, which evens out the work, but may cause increased communication.

Communication Cache coherence causes communication. Threads should, as much as possible, refer to their own data.

- Threads are likely to read from each other's data. That is largely unavoidable.
- Threads writing to each other's data should be avoided: it may require synchronization, and it causes coherence traffic.
- If threads can migrate, data that was local at one time is no longer local after migration.
- Reading data from one socket that was allocated on another socket is inefficient; see section 24.2.

Affinity Both data and execution threads can be bound to a specific locale to some extent. Using local data is more efficient than remote data, so you want to use local data, and minimize the extent to which data or execution can move.

- See the above points about phenomena that cause communication.
- Section 24.1.1 describes how you can specify the binding of threads to places. There can, but does not need, to be an effect on affinity. For instance, if an OpenMP thread can migrate between hardware threads, cached data will stay local. Leaving an OpenMP thread completely free to migrate can be advantageous for load balancing, but you should only do that if data affinity is of lesser importance.
- Static loop schedules have a higher chance of using data that has affinity with the place of execution, but they are worse for load balancing. On the other hand, the `nowait` clause can aleviate some of the problems with static loop schedules.

Binding You can choose to put OpenMP threads close together or to spread them apart. Having them close together makes sense if they use lots of shared data. Spreading them apart may increase bandwidth. (See the examples in section 24.1.2.)

Synchronization Barriers are a form of synchronization. They are expensive by themselves, and they expose load imbalance. Implicit barriers happen at the end of worksharing constructs; they can be removed with `nowait`.

Critical sections imply a loss of parallelism, but they are also slow as they are realized through *operating system* functions. These are often quite costly, taking many thousands of cycles. Critical sections should be used only if the parallel work far outweighs it.

27.6 Accelerators

In OpenMP 4.0 there is support for offloading work to an *accelerator* or *co-processor*:

```
#pragma omp target [clauses]
```

with clauses such as

- `data`: place data
- `update`: make data consistent between host and device

Chapter 28

OpenMP Review

28.1 Concepts review

28.1.1 Basic concepts

- process / thread / thread team
- threads / cores / tasks
- directives / library functions / environment variables

28.1.2 Parallel regions

execution by a team

28.1.3 Work sharing

- loop / sections / single / workshare
- implied barrier
- loop scheduling, reduction
- sections
- single vs master
- (F) workshare

28.1.4 Data scope

- shared vs private, C vs F
- loop variables and reduction variables
- default declaration
- firstprivate, lastprivate

28.1.5 Synchronization

- barriers, implied and explicit
- nowait
- critical sections
- locks, difference with critical

28.1.6 Tasks

- generation vs execution
- dependencies

28.2 Review questions

28.2.1 Directives

What do the following program output?

```c
int main() {
  printf("procs_%d\n",
    omp_get_num_procs());
  printf("threads_%d\n",
    omp_get_num_threads());
  printf("num_%d\n",
    omp_get_thread_num());
  return 0;
}
```

```c
int main() {
#pragma omp parallel
  {
  printf("procs_%d\n",
    omp_get_num_procs());
  printf("threads_%d\n",
    omp_get_num_threads());
  printf("num_%d\n",
    omp_get_thread_num());
  }
  return 0;
}
```

```fortran
Program main
  use omp_lib
  print *,"Procs:",&
    omp_get_num_procs()
  print *,"Threads:",&
    omp_get_num_threads()
  print *,"Num:",&
    omp_get_thread_num()
End Program
```

```fortran
Program main
  use omp_lib
!$OMP parallel
  print *,"Procs:",&
    omp_get_num_procs()
  print *,"Threads:",&
    omp_get_num_threads()
  print *,"Num:",&
    omp_get_thread_num()
!$OMP end parallel
End Program
```

28.2.2 Parallelism

Can the following loops be parallelized? If so, how? (Assume that all arrays are already filled in, and that there are no out-of-bounds errors.)

```
// variant #1
for (i=0; i<N; i++) {
  x[i] = a[i]+b[i+1];
  a[i] = 2*x[i] + c[i+1];
}
```

```
// variant #3
for (i=1; i<N; i++) {
  x[i] = a[i]+b[i+1];
  a[i] = 2*x[i-1] + c[i+1];
}
```

```
// variant #2
for (i=0; i<N; i++) {
  x[i] = a[i]+b[i+1];
  a[i] = 2*x[i+1] + c[i+1];
}
```

```
// variant #4
for (i=1; i<N; i++) {
  x[i] = a[i]+b[i+1];
  a[i+1] = 2*x[i-1] + c[i+1];
}
```

```
! variant #1
do i=1,N
  x(i) = a(i)+b(i+1)
  a(i) = 2*x(i) + c(i+1)
end do
```

```
! variant #3
do i=2,N
  x(i) = a(i)+b(i+1)
  a(i) = 2*x(i-1) + c(i+1)
end do
```

```
! variant #2
do i=1,N
  x(i) = a(i)+b(i+1)
  a(i) = 2*x(i+1) + c(i+1)
end do
```

```
! variant #3
do i=2,N
  x(i) = a(i)+b(i+1)
  a(i+1) = 2*x(i-1) + c(i+1)
end do
```

28.2.3 Data and synchronization

28.2.3.1

What is the output of the following fragments? Assume that there are four threads.

```
// variant #1
int nt;
#pragma omp parallel
  {
    nt = omp_get_thread_num();
    printf("thread_number:_%d\n",nt);
  }
```

```
// variant #2
int nt;
#pragma omp parallel private(nt)
  {
    nt = omp_get_thread_num();
    printf("thread_number:_%d\n",nt);
  }
```

```
// variant #3
int nt;
#pragma omp parallel
  {
#pragma omp single
    {
      nt = omp_get_thread_num();
      printf("thread_number:_%d\n",nt);
    }
  }
```

```
// variant #4
int nt;
#pragma omp parallel
  {
#pragma omp master
    {
      nt = omp_get_thread_num();
      printf("thread_number:_%d\n",nt);
    }
  }
```

```
// variant #5
int nt;
#pragma omp parallel
  {
#pragma omp critical
    {
      nt = omp_get_thread_num();
      printf("thread_number:_%d\n",nt);
    }
  }
```

```
! variant #1
  integer nt
!$OMP parallel
  nt = omp_get_thread_num()
  print *,"thread_number:",nt
!$OMP end parallel
```

```
! variant #2
  integer nt
!$OMP parallel private(nt)
  nt = omp_get_thread_num()
  print *,"thread_number:",nt
!$OMP end parallel
```

```
! variant #3
  integer nt
!$OMP parallel
!$OMP single
  nt = omp_get_thread_num()
  print *,"thread_number:",nt
!$OMP end single
!$OMP end parallel
```

```
! variant #4
  integer nt
!$OMP parallel
!$OMP master
    nt = omp_get_thread_num ()
    print *,"thread_number:",nt
!$OMP end master
!$OMP end parallel
```

```
! variant #5
  integer nt
!$OMP parallel
!$OMP critical
    nt = omp_get_thread_num ()
    print *,"thread_number:",nt
!$OMP end critical
!$OMP end parallel
```

28.2.3.2

The following is an attempt to parallelize a serial code. Assume that all variables and arrays are defined. What errors and potential problems do you see in this code? How would you fix them?

```
#pragma omp parallel
{
   x = f ();
   #pragma omp for
   for ( i=0; i<N; i++)
     y[i] = g(x,i);
   z = h(y);
}
```

```
!$OMP parallel
   x = f ()
!$OMP do
   do i=1,N
     y(i) = g(x,i)
   end do
!$OMP end do
   z = h(y)
!$OMP end parallel
```

28.2.3.3

Assume two threads. What does the following program output?

```
int a;
#pragma omp parallel private(a) {
  ...
  a = 0;
  #pragma omp for
  for (int i = 0; i < 10; i++)
  {
    #pragma omp atomic
    a++; }
  #pragma omp single
    printf("a=%e\n",a);
}
```

28.2.4   Reductions

28.2.4.1

Is the following code correct? Is it efficient? If not, can you improve it?

```
#pragma omp parallel shared(r)
{
  int x;
  x = f(omp_get_thread_num());
#pragma omp critical
  r += f(x);
}
```

28.2.4.2

Compare two fragments:

```
// variant 1
#pragma omp parallel reduction(+:s)
#pragma omp for
  for (i=0; i<N; i++)
    s += f(i);
```

```
// variant 2
#pragma omp parallel
#pragma omp for reduction(+:s)
  for (i=0; i<N; i++)
    s += f(i);
```

```
! variant 1                        ! variant 2
!$OMP parallel reduction(+:s)      !$OMP parallel
!$OMP do                           !$OMP do reduction(+:s)
  do i=1,N                           do i=1,N
    s += f(i);                         s += f(i);
  end do                             end do
!$OMP end do                       !$OMP end do
!$OMP end parallel                 !$OMP end parallel
```

Do they compute the same thing?

28.2.5 Barriers

Are the following two code fragments well defined?

```
#pragma omp parallel
{
#pragma omp for
for (mytid=0; mytid<nthreads; mytid++)
    x[mytid] = some_calculation();
#pragma omp for
for (mytid=0; mytid<nthreads-1; mytid++)
    y[mytid] = x[mytid]+x[mytid+1];
}
```

```
#pragma omp parallel
{
#pragma omp for
for (mytid=0; mytid<nthreads; mytid++)
    x[mytid] = some_calculation();
#pragma omp for nowait
for (mytid=0; mytid<nthreads-1; mytid++)
    y[mytid] = x[mytid]+x[mytid+1];
}
```

28.2.6 Data scope

The following program is supposed to initialize as many rows of the array as there are threads.

```
int main() {
  int i,icount,iarray[100][100];
  icount = -1;
#pragma omp parallel private(i)
  {
#pragma omp critical
    { icount++; }
    for (i=0; i<100; i++)
      iarray[icount][i] = 1;
  }
  return 0;
}
```

```
Program main
  integer :: i,icount,iarray(100,100)
  icount = 0
!$OMP parallel private(i)
!$OMP critical
    icount = icount + 1
!$OMP end critical
    do i=1,100
      iarray(icount,i) = 1
    end do
!$OMP end parallel
End program
```

Describe the behaviour of the program, with argumentation,

- as given;
- if you add a clause private(icount) to the parallel directive;
- if you add a clause firstprivate(icount).

What do you think of this solution:

```
#pragma omp parallel private(i) shared(icount)
  {
#pragma omp critical
    { icount++;
      for (i=0; i<100; i++)
        iarray[icount][i] = 1;
    }
  }
  return 0;
```

```
}
```

```
!$OMP parallel private(i) shared(icount)
!$OMP critical
    icount = icount+1
    do i=1,100
      iarray(icount,i) = 1
    end do
!$OMP critical
!$OMP end parallel
```

28.2.7   Tasks

Fix two things in the following example:

```
#pragma omp parallel
#pragma omp single
{
  int x,y,z;
#pragma omp task
  x = f();
#pragma omp task
  y = g();
#pragma omp task
  z = h();
  printf("sum=%d\n",x+y+z);
}
```

```
    integer :: x,y,z
!$OMP parallel
!$OMP single

!$OMP task
  x = f()
!$OMP end task

!$OMP task
  y = g()
!$OMP end task

!$OMP task
  z = h()
!$OMP end task

  print *,"sum=",x+y+z
!$OMP end single
!$OMP end parallel
```

28.2.8   Scheduling

Compare these two fragments. Do they compute the same result? What can you say about their efficiency?

```
#pragma omp parallel
#pragma omp single
  {
    for (i=0; i<N; i++) {
    #pragma omp task
      x[i] = f(i)
```

```
    }
    #pragma omp taskwait
}
```

```
#pragma omp parallel                        x[i] = f(i)
#pragma omp for schedule(dynamic)         }
  {                                       }
    for (i=0; i<N; i++) {
```

How would you make the second loop more efficient? Can you do something similar for the first loop?

PART III

PETSC

Chapter 29

PETSc basics

29.1 Startup

```
ierr = PetscInitialize(&Argc,&Args,PETSC_NULL,PETSC_NULL);
MPI_Comm comm = PETSC_COMM_WORLD;

MPI_Comm_rank(comm,&mytid);
MPI_Comm_size(comm,&ntids);
```

Python note The following works if you don't need commandline options.
```
from petsc4py import PETSc
```

To pass commandline arguments to PETSc, do:
```
import sys
from petsc4py import init
init(sys.argv)
from petsc4py import PETSc
```

```
comm = PETSc.COMM_WORLD
nprocs = comm.getSize(self)
procno = comm.getRank(self)
```

29.2 Commandline options

See section 29.1 about passing the commandline options.

Python note In Python, do not specify the initial hyphen of an option name.
```
hasn = PETSc.Options().hasName("n")
```

29.3 Printing

Printing screen output in parallel is tricky. If two processes execute a print statement at more or less the same time there is no guarantee as to in what order they may appear on screen. (Even attempts to have them print one after the other may not result in the right ordering.) Furthermore, lines from multi-line print actions on two processes may wind up on the screen interleaved.

PETSc has two routines that fix this problem. First of all, often the information printed is the same on all processes, so it is enough if only one process, for instance process 0, prints it.

```
C:
PetscErrorCode   PetscPrintf(MPI_Comm comm,const char format[],...)

Fortran:
PetscPrintf(MPI_Comm, character(*), PetscErrorCode ierr)

Python:
PETSc.Sys.Print(type cls, *args, **kwargs)
kwargs:
comm : communicator object
```

How to read routine prototypes: 1.5.4.

If all processes need to print, there is a routine that forces the output to appear in process order.

```
C:
PetscErrorCode   PetscSynchronizedPrintf(
    MPI_Comm comm,const char format[],...)

Fortran:
PetscSynchronizedPrintf(MPI_Comm, character(*), PetscErrorCode ierr)

python:
PETSc.Sys.syncPrint(type cls, *args, **kargs)
kwargs:
comm : communicator object
flush : if True, do synchronizedFlush
other keyword args as for python3 print function
```

How to read routine prototypes: 1.5.4.

To make sure that output is properly flushed from all system buffers use a flush routine:

```
C:
PetscErrorCode   PetscSynchronizedFlush(MPI_Comm comm,FILE *fd)
fd : output file pointer, needs to be valid on process zero

python:
PETSc.Sys.syncFlush(type cls, comm=None)
```

How to read routine prototypes: 1.5.4.

where for ordinary screen output you would use stdout for the file.

Python note Since the print routines use the python `print` call, they automatically include the trailing newline. You don't have to specify it as in the C calls.

Chapter 30

PETSc objects

30.1 Vectors

Create a vector:

```
C:
PetscErrorCode VecCreate(MPI_Comm comm,Vec *v);

Python:
vec = PETSc.Vec()
vec.create()
# or:
vec = PETSc.Vec().create()
```

How to read routine prototypes: 1.5.4.

Python note In python, PETSc.Vec() creates an object with null handle, so a subsequent create() call is needed.

In C and Fortran, the vector type is a keyword; in Python it is a member of PETSc.Vec.Type.

You can set both local and global size, or set one and let the other be derived:

```
C:
#include "petscvec.h"
PetscErrorCode  VecSetSizes(Vec v, PetscInt n, PetscInt N)
Collective on Vec

Input Parameters
v :the vector
n : the local size (or PETSC_DECIDE to have it set)
N : the global size (or PETSC_DECIDE)

Python:
PETSc.Vec.setSizes(self, size, bsize=None)
size is a tuple of local/global
```

How to read routine prototypes: 1.5.4.

To query the sizes:

```
C:
#include "petscvec.h"
PetscErrorCode  VecGetSize(Vec x,PetscInt *size)

Input Parameter
x -the vector

Output Parameters
size -the global length of the vector

PetscErrorCode  VecGetLocalSize(Vec x,PetscInt *size)

Input Parameter
x -the vector

Output Parameter
size -the length of the local piece of the vector

Python:
PETSc.Vec.getLocalSize(self)
PETSc.Vec.getSize(self)
PETSc.Vec.getSizes(self)
```

How to read routine prototypes: 1.5.4.

There are many routines operating on vectors.

```
C:
#include "petscvec.h"
PetscErrorCode  VecNorm(Vec x,NormType type,PetscReal *val)
where type is
    NORM_1, NORM_2, NORM_FROBENIUS, NORM_INFINITY

Python:
PETSc.Vec.norm(self, norm_type=None)

where norm is variable in PETSc.NormType:
    NORM_1, NORM_2, NORM_FROBENIUS, NORM_INFINITY or
    N1, N2, FRB, INF
```

How to read routine prototypes: 1.5.4.

The VecView routine can be used to display vectors on screen as ascii output

```
C:
#include "petscvec.h"
PetscErrorCode  VecView(Vec vec,PetscViewer viewer)
```

```
for ascii output use:
PETSC_VIEWER_STDOUT_WORLD

Python:
PETSc.Vec.view(self, Viewer viewer=None)

ascii output is default or use:
PETSc.Viewer.STDOUT(type cls, comm=None)
```

How to read routine prototypes: 1.5.4.

but the routine call also use more general `Viewer` objects.

For most operations on vectors you don't need the actual data. But should you need it, here are the routines:

```
C:
#include "petscvec.h"
PetscErrorCode VecGetArray(Vec x,PetscScalar **a)

Input Parameter
x : the vector

Output Parameter
a : location to put pointer to the array

PetscErrorCode VecRestoreArray(Vec x,PetscScalar **a)

Input Parameters
x : the vector
a : location of pointer to array obtained from VecGetArray()

Fortran:
VecGetArrayF90(Vec x,{Scalar, pointer :: xx_v(:)},integer ierr)
(there is a Fortran77 version)

Input Parameter
x : vector

Output Parameters
xx_v- the Fortran90 pointer to the array
ierr- error code

VecRestoreArrayF90(Vec x,{Scalar, pointer :: xx_v(:)},integer ierr)

Input Parameters
x : vector
xx_v : the Fortran90 pointer to the array

Output Parameter
ierr : error code
```

```
Python:
PETSc.Vec.getArray(self, readonly=False)
?? PETSc.Vec.resetArray(self, force=False)
```

How to read routine prototypes: 1.5.4.

30.2   Matrices

Create a matrix:

```
C:
PetscErrorCode MatCreate(MPI_Comm comm,Mat *v);

Python:
mat = PETSc.Mat()
mat.create()
# or:
mat = PETSc.Mat().create()
```

How to read routine prototypes: 1.5.4.

Just as with vectors, there is a local and global size; except that that now applies to rows and columns.

```
C:
#include "petscmat.h"
PetscErrorCode MatSetSizes(Mat A,
    PetscInt m, PetscInt n, PetscInt M, PetscInt N)

Input Parameters
A : the matrix
m : number of local rows (or PETSC_DECIDE)
n : number of local columns (or PETSC_DECIDE)
M : number of global rows (or PETSC_DETERMINE)
N : number of global columns (or PETSC_DETERMINE)

Python:
PETSc.Mat.setSizes(self, size, bsize=None)
where 'size' is a tuple of 2 global sizes
or a tuple of 2 local/global pairs
```

How to read routine prototypes: 1.5.4.

```
C:
#include "petscmat.h"
PetscErrorCode MatGetSize(Mat mat,PetscInt *m,PetscInt *n)
PetscErrorCode MatGetLocalSize(Mat mat,PetscInt *m,PetscInt *n)

Python:
PETSc.Mat.getSize(self) # tuple of global sizes
```

```
PETSc.Mat.getLocalSize(self) # tuple of local sizes
PETSc.Mat.getSizes(self) # tuple of local/global size tuples
```

How to read routine prototypes: 1.5.4.

You can set a single matrix element, or a block of them, where you supply a set of i and j indices:

```
C:
#include <petscmat.h>
PetscErrorCode MatSetValue(
    Mat m,PetscInt row,PetscInt col,PetscScalar value,InsertMode mode)

Input Parameters
m : the matrix
row : the row location of the entry
col : the column location of the entry
value : the value to insert
mode : either INSERT_VALUES or ADD_VALUES

Python:
PETSc.Mat.setValue(self, row, col, value, addv=None)
also supported:
A[row,col] = value
```

How to read routine prototypes: 1.5.4.

After setting matrix elements, the matrix needs to be assembled. This is where PETSc moves matrix elements to the right processor, if they were specified elsewhere.

```
C:
#include "petscmat.h"
PetscErrorCode MatAssemblyBegin(Mat mat,MatAssemblyType type)
PetscErrorCode MatAssemblyEnd(Mat mat,MatAssemblyType type)

Input Parameters
mat- the matrix
type- type of assembly, either MAT_FLUSH_ASSEMBLY
    or MAT_FINAL_ASSEMBLY

Python:
assemble(self, assembly=None)
assemblyBegin(self, assembly=None)
assemblyEnd(self, assembly=None)

there is a class PETSc.Mat.AssemblyType:
FINAL = FINAL_ASSEMBLY = 0
FLUSH = FLUSH_ASSEMBLY = 1
```

How to read routine prototypes: 1.5.4.

PETSc sparse matrices are very flexible: you can create them empty and then start adding elements. However, this is very inefficient in execution since the OS needs to reallocate the matrix every time it grows a little. Therefore, PETSc has calls for the user to indicate how many elements the matrix will ultimately contain.

```
#include "petscmat.h"
PetscErrorCode  MatSeqAIJSetPreallocation
  (Mat B,PetscInt nz,const PetscInt nnz[])
PetscErrorCode  MatMPIAIJSetPreallocation
  (Mat B,PetscInt d_nz,const PetscInt d_nnz[],
   PetscInt o_nz,const PetscInt o_nnz[])

Input Parameters

B - the matrix
nz/d_nz/o_nz - number of nonzeros per row in matrix or
    diagonal/off-diagonal portion of local submatrix
nnz/d_nnz/o_nnz - array containing the number of nonzeros in the various rows
    the sequential matrix / diagonal / offdiagonal part of the local submatrix
    or NULL (PETSC_NULL_INTEGER in Fortran) if nz/d_nz/o_nz is used.

Python:
PETSc.Mat.setPreallocationNNZ(self, nnz)
PETSc.Mat.setPreallocationCSR(self, csr)
PETSc.Mat.setPreallocationDense(self, array)
```

How to read routine prototypes: 1.5.4.

```
MatSetOption(A, MAT_NEW_NONZERO_ALLOCATION_ERR, PETSC_FALSE)
```

30.3   KSP: iterative solvers

Create a KSP object:

```
C:
PetscErrorCode KSPCreate(MPI_Comm comm,KSP *v);

Python:
ksp = PETSc.KSP()
ksp.create()
# or:
ksp = PETSc.KSP().create()
```

How to read routine prototypes: 1.5.4.

Get the reason `KSPSolve` stopped:

```
C:
PetscErrorCode KSPGetConvergedReason
    (KSP ksp,KSPConvergedReason *reason)
```

Not Collective

Input Parameter
ksp -the KSP context

Output Parameter
reason -negative value indicates diverged, positive value converged,
see KSPConvergedReason

Python:
r = KSP.getConvergedReason(self)
where r in PETSc.KSP.ConvergedReason

How to read routine prototypes: 1.5.4.

30.4 DMDA: distributed arrays

```
#include "petscdmda.h"
PetscErrorCode  DMDACreate2d(MPI_Comm comm,
    DMBoundaryType bx,DMBoundaryType by,DMDAStencilType stencil_type,
    PetscInt M,PetscInt N,PetscInt m,PetscInt n,PetscInt dof,
    PetscInt s,const PetscInt lx[],const PetscInt ly[],
    DM *da)
```

Input Parameters

comm - MPI communicator
bx,by - type of ghost nodes: DM_BOUNDARY_NONE, DM_BOUNDARY_GHOSTED, DM_BOUNDARY_PE
stencil_type - stencil type: DMDA_STENCIL_BOX or DMDA_STENCIL_STAR.
M,N - global dimension in each direction of
m,n - corresponding number of processors in each dimension (or PETSC_DECIDE)
dof - number of degrees of freedom per node
s - stencil width
lx, ly - arrays containing the number of
    nodes in each cell along the x and y coordinates, or NULL.

Output Parameter

da -the resulting distributed array object

How to read routine prototypes: 1.5.4.

Chapter 31

PETSc topics

31.1 Communicators

PETSc has a 'world' communicator, which by default equals `MPI_COMM_WORLD`. If you want to run PETSc on a subset of processes, you can assign a subcommunicator to the variable `PETSC_COMM_WORLD` in between the calls to `MPI_Init` and `PetscInitialize`.

```
C:
#include <petscsys.h>
F:
#include "petsc/finclude.petscsys.h"

PETSC_COMM_WORLD
PETSC_COMM_SELF
variables of type MPI_Comm

Python:
PETSc.COMM_WORLD
PETSc.COMM_SELF
PETSc.COMM_NULL
```

How to read routine prototypes: 1.5.4.

PART IV

THE REST

Chapter 32

Process and thread affinity

In the preceeding chapters we mostly considered all MPI nodes or OpenMP thread as being in one flat pool. However, for high performance you need to worry about *affinity*: the question of which process or thread is placed where, and how efficiently they can interact.

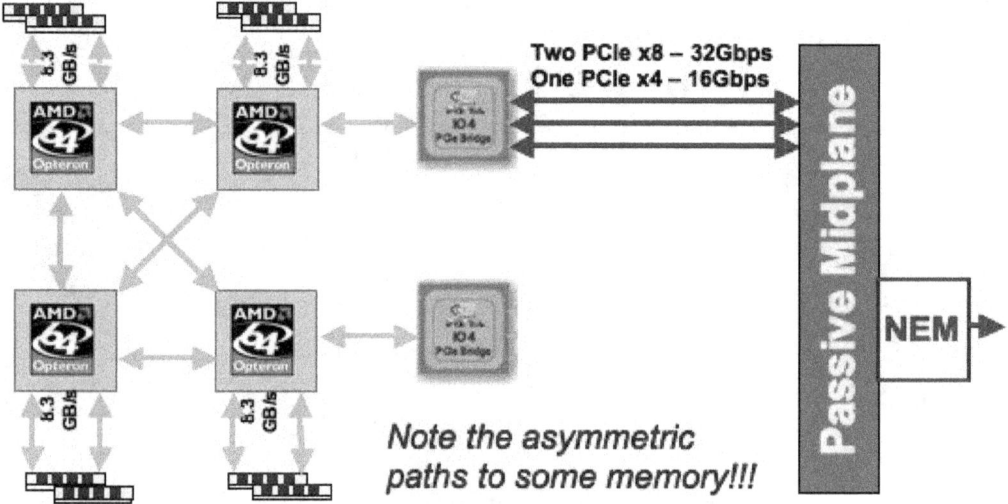

Figure 32.1: The NUMA structure of a Ranger node

Here are some situations where you affinity becomes a concern.

- In pure MPI mode processes that are on the same node can typically communicate faster than processes on different nodes. Since processes are typically placed sequentially, this means that a scheme where process p interacts mostly with $p + 1$ will be efficient, while communication with large jumps will be less so.
- If the cluster network has a structure (*processor grid* as opposed to *fat-tree*), placement of processes has an effect on program efficiency. MPI tries to address this with *graph topology*; section **??**.
- Even on a single node there can be asymmetries. Figure 32.1 illustrates the structure of the four sockets of the *Ranger* supercomputer (no longer in production). Two cores have no direct connection.

This asymmetry affects both MPI processes and threads on that node.

- Another problem with multi-socket designs is that each socket has memory attached to it. While every socket can address all the memory on the node, its local memory is faster to access. This asymmetry becomes quite visible in the *first-touch* phenomemon; section 24.2.
- If a node has fewer MPI processes than there are cores, you want to be in control of their placement. Also, the operating system can migrate processes, which is detrimental to performance since it negates data locality. For this reason, utilities such as `numactl` (and at TACC `tacc_affinity`) can be used to *pin a thread* or process to a specific core.
- Processors with *hyperthreading* or *hardware threads* introduce another level or worry about where threads go.

32.1 What does the hardware look like?

If you want to optimize affinity, you should first know what the hardware looks like. The `hwloc` utility is valuable here [ ] (`https://www.open-mpi.org/projects/hwloc/`).

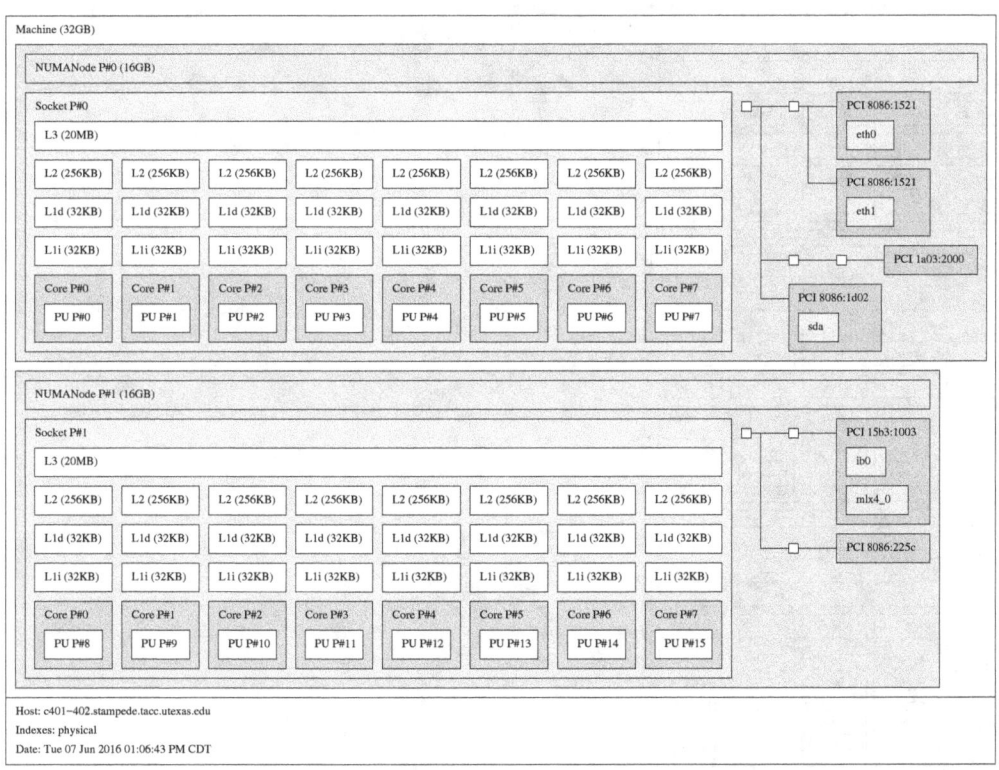

Figure 32.2: Structure of a Stampede compute node

Figure 32.2 depicts a *Stampede compute node*, which is a two-socket *Intel SandyBridge* design; figure 32.3 shows a *Stampede largemem node*, which is a four-socket design. Finally, figure 32.4 shows a *Lonestar5* compute node, a two-socket design with 12-core *Intel Haswell* processors with two hardware threads each.

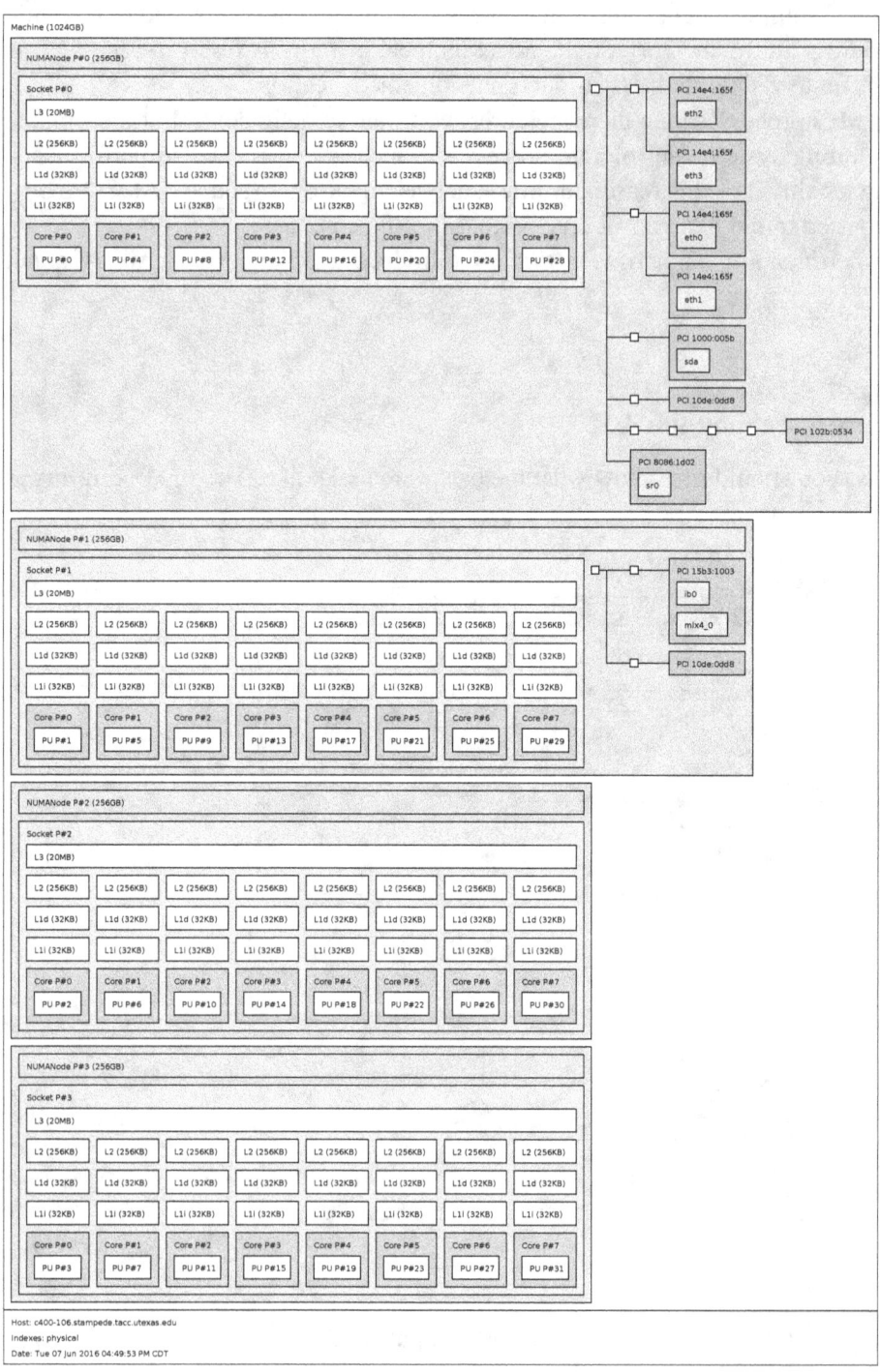

Figure 32.3: Structure of a Stampede largemem four-socket compute node

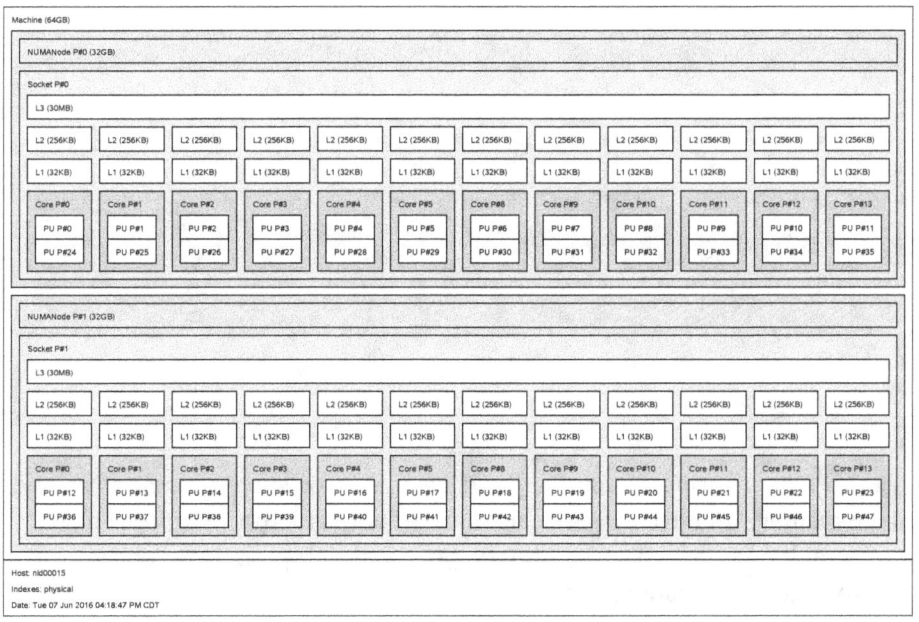

Figure 32.4: Structure of a Lonestar5 compute node

32.2   Affinity control

See chapter 24 for OpenMP affinity control.

Chapter 33

Hybrid computing

So far, you have learned to use MPI for distributed memory and OpenMP for shared memory parallel programming. However, distribute memory architectures actually have a shared memory component, since each cluster node is typically of a multicore design. Accordingly, you could program your cluster using MPI for inter-node and OpenMP for intra-node parallelism.

Say you use 100 cluster nodes, each with 16 cores. You could then start 1600 MPI processes, one for each core, but you could also start 100 processes, and give each access to 16 OpenMP threads.

In your slurm scripts, the first scenario would be specified -N 100 -n 1600, and the second as

```
#$ SBATCH -N 100
#$ SBATCH -n 100

export OMP_NUM_THREADS=16
```

There is a third choice, in between these extremes, that makes sense. A cluster node often has more than one socket, so you could put one MPI process on each *socket*, and use a number of threads equal to the number of cores per socket.

The script for this would be:

```
#$ SBATCH -N 100
#$ SBATCH -n 200

export OMP_NUM_THREADS=8
ibrun tacc_affinity yourprogram
```

The tacc_affinity script unsets the following variables:

```
export MV2_USE_AFFINITY=0
export MV2_ENABLE_AFFINITY=0
export VIADEV_USE_AFFINITY=0
export VIADEV_ENABLE_AFFINITY=0
```

If you don't use `tacc_affinity` you may want to do this by hand, otherwise `mvapich2` will use its own affinity rules.

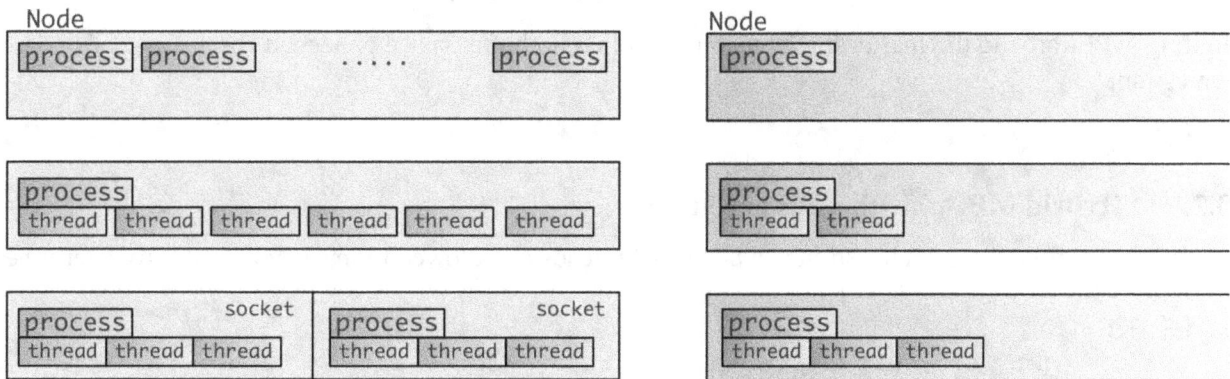

Figure 33.1: Three modes of MPI/OpenMP usage on a multi-core cluster

Figure 33.1 illustrates these three modes: pure MPI with no threads used; one MPI process per node and full multi-threading; two MPI processes per node, one per socket, and multiple threads on each socket.

33.1 Discussion

The performance implications of the pure MPI strategy versus hybrid are subtle.

- First of all, we note that there is no obvious speedup: in a well balanced MPI application all cores are busy all the time, so using threading can give no immediate improvement.
- Both MPI and OpenMP are subject to Amdahl's law that quantifies the influence of sequential code; in hybrid computing there is a new version of this law regarding the amount of code that is MPI-parallel, but not OpenMP-parallel.
- MPI processes run unsynchronized, so small variations in load or in processor behaviour can be tolerated. The frequent barriers in OpenMP constructs make a hybrid code more tightly synchronized, so load balancing becomes more critical.
- On the other hand, in OpenMP codes it is easier to divide the work into more tasks than there are threads, so statistically a certain amount of load balancing happens automatically.
- Each MPI process has its own buffers, so hybrid takes less buffer overhead.

Exercise 33.1.   Review the scalability argument for 1D versus 2D matrix decomposition in HPSC-6.2. Would you get scalable performance from doing a 1D decomposition (for instance, of the rows) over MPI processes, and decomposing the other directions (the columns) over OpenMP threads?

Another performance argument we need to consider concerns message traffic. If let all threads make MPI calls (see section 33.2) there is going to be little difference. However, in one popular hybrid computing strategy we would keep MPI calls out of the OpenMP regions and have them in effect done by the master thread. In that case there are only MPI messages between nodes, instead of between cores. This leads to a decrease in message traffic, though this is hard to quantify. The number of messages goes down approximately by the number of cores per node, so this is an advantage if the average message size is small. On the other hand, the amount of data sent is only reduced if there is overlap in content between the messages.

Limiting MPI traffic to the master thread also means that no buffer space is needed for the on-node communication.

33.2 Hybrid MPI-plus-threads execution

In hybrid execution, the main question is whether all threads are allowed to make MPI calls. To determine this, replace the `MPI_Init` call by

```
C:
int MPI_Init_thread(int *argc, char ***argv, int required, int *provided)

Fortran:
MPI_Init_thread(required, provided, ierror)
INTEGER, INTENT(IN) :: required
INTEGER, INTENT(OUT) :: provided
INTEGER, OPTIONAL, INTENT(OUT) :: ierror
```

How to read routine prototypes: 1.5.4.

Here the `required` and `provided` parameters can take the following values:

MPI_THREAD_SINGLE Only a single thread will execute.

MPI_THREAD_FUNNELLED The program may use multiple threads, but only the main thread will make MPI calls.

> The main thread is usually the one selected by the `master` directive, but technically it is the only that executes `MPI_Init_thread`. If you call this routine in a parallel region, the main thread may be different from the master.

MPI_THREAD_SERIAL The program may use multiple threads, all of which may make MPI calls, but there will never be simultaneous MPI calls in more than one thread.

MPI_THREAD_MULTIPLE Multiple threads may issue MPI calls, without restrictions.

The *mvapich* implementation of MPI does have the required threading support, but you need to set this environment variable:

```
export MV2_ENABLE_AFFINITY=0
```

Another solution is to run your code like this:

```
ibrun tacc_affinity <my_multithreaded_mpi_executable
```

The *mpirun* program usually propagates *environment variables*, so the value of `OMP_NUM_THREADS` when you call `mpirun` will be seen by each MPI process.

- It is possible to use blocking sends in threads, and let the threads block. This does away with the need for polling.

- You can not send to a thread number: use the MPI *message tag* to send to a specific thread.

Exercise 33.2. Consider the 2D heat equation and explore the mix of MPI/OpenMP parallelism:

- Give each node one MPI process that is fully multi-threaded.
- Give each core an MPI process and don't use multi-threading.

Discuss theoretically why the former can give higher performance. Implement both schemes as special cases of the general hybrid case, and run tests to find the optimal mix.

Chapter 34

Random number generation

Here is how you initialize the random number generator uniquely on each process:

```
C:
```

```
// Initialize the random number generator
srand((int)(mytid*(double)RAND_MAX/ntids));
// compute a random number
randomfraction = (rand() / (double)RAND_MAX);
```

```
Fortran:
```

```
  integer :: randsize
  integer,allocatable,dimension(:) :: randseed
  real :: random_value

  call random_seed(size=randsize)
  allocate(randseed(randsize))
  do i=1,randsize
     randseed(i) = 1023*mytid
  end do
  call random_seed(put=randseed)
```

Chapter 35

Parallel I/O

Parallel I/O is a tricky subject. You can try to let all processors jointly write one file, or to write a file per process and combine them later. With the standard mechanisms of your programming language there are the following considerations:

- On clusters where the processes have individual file systems, the only way to write a single file is to let it be generated by a single processor.
- Writing one file per process is easy to do, but
    - You need a post-processing script;
    - if the files are not on a shared file system (such as *Lustre*), it takes additional effort to bring them together;
    - if the files *are* on a shared file system, writing many files may be a burden on the metadata server.
- On a shared file system it is possible for all files to open the same file and set the file pointer individually. This can be difficult if the amount of data per process is not uniform.

Illustrating the last point:

```
// pseek.c
FILE *pfile;
pfile = fopen("pseek.dat","w");
fseek(pfile,procid*sizeof(int),SEEK_CUR);
fseek(pfile,procid*sizeof(char),SEEK_CUR);
fprintf(pfile,"%d\n",procid);
fclose(pfile);
```

MPI also has its own portable I/O: *MPI I/O*, for which see chapter 9.

Alternatively, one could use a library such as *hdf5*.

Chapter 36

Support libraries

ParaMesh

Global Arrays

PETSc

Hdf5 and Silo

PART V

TUTORIALS

here are some tutorials

36.1 Debugging

When a program misbehaves, *debugging* is the process of finding out *why*. There are various strategies of finding errors in a program. The crudest one is debugging by print statements. If you have a notion of where in your code the error arises, you can edit your code to insert print statements, recompile, rerun, and see if the output gives you any suggestions. There are several problems with this:

- The edit/compile/run cycle is time consuming, especially since
- often the error will be caused by an earlier section of code, requiring you to edit, compile, and rerun repeatedly. Furthermore,
- the amount of data produced by your program can be too large to display and inspect effectively, and
- if your program is parallel, you probably need to print out data from all proccessors, making the inspection process very tedious.

For these reasons, the best way to debug is by the use of an interactive *debugger*, a program that allows you to monitor and control the behaviour of a running program. In this section you will familiarize yourself with *gdb*, which is the open source debugger of the *GNU* project. Other debuggers are proprietary, and typically come with a compiler suite. Another distinction is that gdb is a commandline debugger; there are graphical debuggers such as *ddd* (a frontend to gdb) or *DDT* and *TotalView* (debuggers for parallel codes). We limit ourselves to gdb, since it incorporates the basic concepts common to all debuggers.

In this tutorial you will debug a number of simple programs with gdb and valgrind. The files can be downloaded from `http://tinyurl.com/ISTC-debug-tutorial`.

36.1.1 Step 0: compiling for debug

You often need to recompile your code before you can debug it. A first reason for this is that the binary code typically knows nothing about what variable names corresponded to what memory locations, or what lines in the source to what instructions. In order to make the binary executable know this, you have to include the *symbol table* in it, which is done by adding the `-g` option to the compiler line.

Usually, you also need to lower the *compiler optimization level*: a production code will often be compiled with flags such as `-O2` or `-Xhost` that try to make the code as fast as possible, but for debugging you need to replace this by `-O0` ('oh-zero'). The reason is that higher levels will reorganize your code, making it hard to relate the execution to the source[1].

36.1.2 Invoking `gdb`

There are three ways of using gdb: using it to start a program, attaching it to an already running program, or using it to inspect a *core dump*. We will only consider the first possibility.

Here is an exaple of how to start gdb with program that has no arguments (Fortran users, use `hello.F`):

tutorials/gdb/c/hello.c

---

1.   Typically, actual code motion is done by `-O3`, but at level `-O2` the compiler will inline functions and make other simplifications.

```
%% cc -g -o hello hello.c
# regular invocation:
%% ./hello
hello world
# invocation from gdb:
%% gdb hello
GNU gdb 6.3.50-20050815 # ..... version info
Copyright 2004 Free Software Foundation, Inc. .... copyright info ....
(gdb) run
Starting program: /home/eijkhout/tutorials/gdb/hello
Reading symbols for shared libraries +. done
hello world

Program exited normally.
(gdb) quit
%%
```

Important note: the program was compiled with the *debug flag* -g. This causes the *symbol table* (that is, the translation from machine address to program variables) and other debug information to be included in the binary. This will make your binary larger than strictly necessary, but it will also make it slower, for instance because the compiler will not perform certain optimizations[2].

To illustrate the presence of the symbol table do

```
%% cc -g -o hello hello.c
%% gdb hello
GNU gdb 6.3.50-20050815 # ..... version info
(gdb) list
```

and compare it with leaving out the -g flag:

```
%% cc -o hello hello.c
%% gdb hello
GNU gdb 6.3.50-20050815 # ..... version info
(gdb) list
```

For a program with commandline input we give the arguments to the run command (Fortran users use say.F):

tutorials/gdb/c/say.c

```
%% cc -o say -g say.c
%% ./say 2
```

---

2.   Compiler optimizations are not supposed to change the semantics of a program, but sometimes do. This can lead to the nightmare scenario where a program crashes or gives incorrect results, but magically works correctly with compiled with debug and run in a debugger.

```
hello world
hello world
%% gdb say
.... the usual messages ...
(gdb) run 2
Starting program: /home/eijkhout/tutorials/gdb/c/say 2
Reading symbols for shared libraries +. done
hello world
hello world

Program exited normally.
```

36.1.3 Finding errors

Let us now consider some programs with errors.

36.1.3.1 C programs

tutorials/gdb/c/square.c

```
%% cc -g -o square square.c
 %% ./square
5000
Segmentation fault
```

The *segmentation fault* (other messages are possible too) indicates that we are accessing memory that we are not allowed to, making the program abort. A debugger will quickly tell us where this happens:

```
%% gdb square
(gdb) run
50000

Program received signal EXC_BAD_ACCESS, Could not access memory.
Reason: KERN_INVALID_ADDRESS at address: 0x000000000000eb4a
0x00007fff824295ca in __svfscanf_l ()
```

Apparently the error occurred in a function `__svfscanf_l`, which is not one of ours, but a system function. Using the `backtrace` (or `bt`, also `where` or `w`) command we quickly find out how this came to be called:

```
(gdb) backtrace
#0  0x00007fff824295ca in __svfscanf_l ()
#1  0x00007fff8244011b in fscanf ()
#2  0x0000000100000e89 in main (argc=1, argv=0x7fff5fbfc7c0) at square.c:7
```

We take a close look at line 7, and see that we need to change `nmax` to `&nmax`.

There is still an error in our program:

```
(gdb) run
50000

Program received signal EXC_BAD_ACCESS, Could not access memory.
Reason: KERN_PROTECTION_FAILURE at address: 0x000000010000f000
0x0000000100000ebe in main (argc=2, argv=0x7fff5fbfc7a8) at square1.c:9
9               squares[i] = 1./(i*i); sum += squares[i];
```

We investigate further:

```
(gdb) print i
$1 = 11237
(gdb) print squares[i]
Cannot access memory at address 0x10000f000
```

and we quickly see that we forgot to allocate `squares`.

By the way, we were lucky here: this sort of memory errors is not always detected. Starting our programm with a smaller input does not lead to an error:

```
(gdb) run
50
Sum: 1.625133e+00

Program exited normally.
```

36.1.3.2   Fortran programs

Compile and run the following program:

| tutorials/gdb/f/square.F | It should abort with a message such as 'Illegal instruction'. Running the program in gdb quickly tells you where the problem lies:

```
(gdb) run
Starting program: tutorials/gdb//fsquare
Reading symbols for shared libraries ++++. done

Program received signal EXC_BAD_INSTRUCTION, Illegal instruction/operan
0x0000000100000da3 in square () at square.F:7
7                    sum = sum + squares(i)
```

We take a close look at the code and see that we did not allocate `squares` properly.

36.1.4   Memory debugging with Valgrind

Insert the following allocation of `squares` in your program:

```
squares = (float *) malloc( nmax*sizeof(float) );
```

Compile and run your program. The output will likely be correct, although the program is not. Can you see the problem?

To find such subtle memory errors you need a different tool: a memory debugging tool. A popular (because open source) one is *valgrind*; a common commercial tool is *purify*.

`tutorials/gdb/c/square1.c`   Compile this program with `cc -o square1 square1.c` and run it with `valgrind square1` (you need to type the input value). You will lots of output, starting with:

```
%% valgrind square1
==53695== Memcheck, a memory error detector
==53695== Copyright (C) 2002-2010, and GNU GPL'd, by Julian Seward et al.
==53695== Using Valgrind-3.6.1 and LibVEX; rerun with -h for copyright info
==53695== Command: a.out
==53695==
10
==53695== Invalid write of size 4
==53695==    at 0x100000EB0: main (square1.c:10)
==53695==  Address 0x10027e148 is 0 bytes after a block of size 40 alloc'd
==53695==    at 0x1000101EF: malloc (vg_replace_malloc.c:236)
==53695==    by 0x100000E77: main (square1.c:8)
==53695==
==53695== Invalid read of size 4
==53695==    at 0x100000EC1: main (square1.c:11)
==53695==  Address 0x10027e148 is 0 bytes after a block of size 40 alloc'd
==53695==    at 0x1000101EF: malloc (vg_replace_malloc.c:236)
==53695==    by 0x100000E77: main (square1.c:8)
```

Valgrind is informative but cryptic, since it works on the bare memory, not on variables. Thus, these error messages take some exegesis. They state that a line 10 writes a 4-byte object immediately after a block of 40 bytes that was allocated. In other words: the code is writing outside the bounds of an allocated array. Do you see what the problem in the code is?

Note that valgrind also reports at the end of the program run how much memory is still in use, meaning not properly `freed`.

If you fix the array bounds and recompile and rerun the program, valgrind still complains:

```
==53785== Conditional jump or move depends on uninitialised value(s)
==53785==    at 0x10006FC68: __dtoa (in /usr/lib/libSystem.B.dylib)
==53785==    by 0x10003199F: __vfprintf (in /usr/lib/libSystem.B.dylib)
==53785==    by 0x1000738AA: vfprintf_l (in /usr/lib/libSystem.B.dylib)
==53785==    by 0x1000A1006: printf (in /usr/lib/libSystem.B.dylib)
==53785==    by 0x100000EF3: main (in ./square2)
```

Although no line number is given, the mention of `printf` gives an indication where the problem lies. The reference to an 'uninitialized value' is again cryptic: the only value being output is `sum`, and that is not uninitialized: it has been added to several times. Do you see why valgrind calls is uninitialized all the same?

36.1.5   Stepping through a program

Often the error in a program is sufficiently obscure that you need to investigate the program run in detail. Compile the following program

tutorials/gdb/c/roots.c   and run it:

```
%% ./roots
sum: nan
```

Start it in gdb as follows:

```
%% gdb roots
GNU gdb 6.3.50-20050815 (Apple version gdb-1469) (Wed May  5 04:36:56 U1
Copyright 2004 Free Software Foundation, Inc.
....
(gdb) break main
Breakpoint 1 at 0x100000ea6: file root.c, line 14.
(gdb) run
Starting program: tutorials/gdb/c/roots
Reading symbols for shared libraries +. done

Breakpoint 1, main () at roots.c:14
14          float x=0;
```

Here you have done the following:

- Before calling `run` you set a *breakpoint* at the main program, meaning that the execution will stop when it reaches the main program.
- You then call `run` and the program execution starts;
- The execution stops at the first instruction in main.

If execution is stopped at a breakpoint, you can do various things, such as issuing the `step` command:

```
Breakpoint 1, main () at roots.c:14
14          float x=0;
(gdb) step
15          for (i=100; i>-100; i--)
(gdb)
16              x += root(i);
(gdb)
```

(if you just hit return, the previously issued command is repeated). Do a number of `steps` in a row by hitting return. What do you notice about the function and the loop?

Switch from doing `step` to doing `next`. Now what do you notice about the loop and the function?

Set another breakpoint: `break 17` and do `cont`. What happens?

Rerun the program after you set a breakpoint on the line with the `sqrt` call. When the execution stops there do `where` and `list`.

- If you set many breakpoints, you can find out what they are with `info breakpoints`.
- You can remove breakpoints with `delete n` where n is the number of the breakpoint.
- If you restart your program with `run` without leaving gdb, the breakpoints stay in effect.
- If you leave gdb, the breakpoints are cleared but you can save them: `save breakpoints <file>`. Use `source <file>` to read them in on the next gdb run.

36.1.6 Inspecting values

Run the previous program again in gdb: set a breakpoint at the line that does the `sqrt` call before you actually call `run`. When the program gets to line 8 you can do `print n`. Do `cont`. Where does the program stop?

If you want to repair a variable, you can do `set var=value`. Change the variable n and confirm that the square root of the new value is computed. Which commands do you do?

If a problem occurs in a loop, it can be tedious keep typing `cont` and inspecting the variable with `print`. Instead you can add a condition to an existing breakpoint: the following:

```
condition 1 if (n<0)
```

or set the condition when you define the breakpoint:

```
break 8 if (n<0)
```

Another possibility is to use `ignore 1 50`, which will not stop at breakpoint 1 the next 50 times.

Remove the existing breakpoint, redefine it with the condition n<0 and rerun your program. When the program breaks, find for what value of the loop variable it happened. What is the sequence of commands you use?

36.1.7 Parallel debugging

Debugging parallel programs is harder than than sequential programs, because every sequential bug may show up, plus a number of new types, caused by the interaction of the various processes.

Here are a few possible parallel bugs:

- Processes can *deadlock* because they are waiting for a message that never comes. This typically happens with blocking send/receive calls due to an error in program logic.
- If an incoming message is unexpectedly larger than anticipated, a memory error can occur.

- A collective call will hang if somehow one of the processes does not call the routine.

There are few low-budget solutions to parallel debugging. The main one is to create an xterm for each process. We will describe this next. There are also commercial packages such as *DDT* and *TotalView*, that offer a GUI. They are very convenient but also expensive. The *Eclipse* project has a parallel package, *Eclipse PTP*, that includes a graphic debugger.

36.1.7.1 MPI debugging with gdb

You can not run parallel programs in gdb, but you can start multiple gdb processes that behave just like MPI processes! The command

```
mpirun -np <NP> xterm -e gdb ./program
```

create a number of `xterm` windows, each of which execute the commandline `gdb ./program`. And because these xterms have been started with `mpirun`, they actually form a communicator.

36.1.8   Further reading

A good tutorial: http://www.dirac.org/linux/gdb/.

Reference manual: http://www.ofb.net/gnu/gdb/gdb_toc.html.

36.2 Tracing

36.2.1 TAU profiling and tracing

TAU http://www.cs.uoregon.edu/Research/tau/home.php is a utility for profiling and tracing your parallel programs. Profiling is the gathering and displaying of bulk statistics, for instance showing you which routines take the most time, or whether communication takes a large portion of your runtime. When you get concerned about performance, a good profiling tool is indispensible.

Tracing is the construction and displaying of time-dependent information on your program run, for instance showing you if one process lags behind others. For understanding a program's behaviour, and the reasons behind profiling statistics, a tracing tool can be very insightful.

TAU works by adding *instrumentation* to your code: in effect it is a source-to-source translator that takes your code and turns it into one that generates run-time statistics. Doing this instrumentation is fortunately simple: start by having this code fragment in your makefile:

```
ifdef TACC_TAU_DIR
  CC = tau_cc.sh
else
  CC = mpicc
endif

% : %.c
${CC} -o $@ $^
```

PART VI

PROJECTS, INDEX

Chapter 37

Class projects

37.1   A Style Guide to Project Submissions

Here are some guidelines for how to submit assignments and projects. As a general rule, consider programming as an experimental science, and your writeup as a report on some tests you have done: explain the problem you're addressing, your strategy, your results.

Structure of your writeup   Most of the exercises in this book test whether you are able to code the solution to a certain problem. That does not mean that turning in the code is sufficient, nor code plus sample output. Turn in a writeup in pdf form that was generated from a text processing program such as Word or (preferably) LaTeX (for a tutorial, see HPSC-28). Your writeup should have

- The relevant fragments of your code,
- an explanation of your algorithms or solution strategy,
- a discussion of what you observed,
- graphs of runtimes and TAU plots; see 36.2.

Observe, measure, hypothesize, deduce   In most applications of computing machinery we care about the efficiency with which we find the solution. Thus, make sure that you do measurements. In general, make observations that allow you to judge whether your program behaves the way you would expect it to.

Quite often your program will display unexpected behaviour. It is important to observe this, and hypothesize what the reason might be for your observed behaviour.

Including code   If you include code samples in your writeup, make sure they look good. For starters, use a mono-spaced font. In LaTeX, you can use the `verbatim` environment or the `verbatiminput` command. In that section option the source is included automatically, rather than cut and pasted. This is to be preferred, since your writeup will stay current after you edit the source file.

Including whole source files makes for a long and boring writeup. The code samples in this book were generated as follows. In the source files, the relevant snippet was marked as

```
... boring stuff
#pragma samplex
   .. interesting! ..
#pragma end
... more boring stuff
```

The files were then processed with the following command line (actually, included in a makefile, which requires doubling the dollar signs):

```
for f in *.{c,cxx,h} ; do
  cat $x | awk 'BEGIN {f=0}
                    /#pragma end/ {f=0}
                    f==1 {print $0 > file}
                    /pragma/ {f=1; file=$2 }
              '
done
```

which gives (in this example) a file `samplex`. Other solutions are of course possible.

Code formatting   Code without proper indentation is very hard to read. Fortunately, most editors have some knowledge of the syntax of the most popular languages. The *emacs* editor will, most of the time, automatically activate the appropriate mode based on the file extension. If this does not happen, you can activate a mode by `ESC x fortran-mode` et cetera, or by putting the string `-*- fortran -*-` in a comment on the first line of your file.

The *vi* editor also has syntax support: use the commands `:synxtax on` to get syntax colouring, and `:set cindent` to get automatic indentation while you're entering text. Some of the more common questions are addressed in `http://stackoverflow.com/questions/97694/auto-indent-spaces-with-c-`

Running your code   A single run doesn't prove anything. For a good report, you need to run your code for more than one input dataset (if available) and in more than one processor configuration. When you choose problem sizes, be aware that an average processor can do a billion operations per second: you need to make your problem large enough for the timings to rise above the level of random variations and startup phenomena.

When you run a code in parallel, beware that on clusters the behaviour of a parallel code will always be different between one node and multiple nodes. On a single node the MPI implementation is likely optimized to use the shared memory. This means that results obtained from a single node run will be unrepresentative. In fact, in timing and scaling tests you will often see a drop in (relative) performance going from one node to two. Therefore you need to run your code in a variety of scenarios, using more than one node.

Reporting scaling   If you do a scaling analysis, a graph reporting runtimes should not have a linear time axis: a logarithmic graph is much easier to read. A speedup graph can also be informative.

Some algorithms are mathematically equivalent in their sequential and parallel versions. Others, such as iterative processes, can take more operations in parallel than sequentially, for instance because the number of iterations goes up. In this case, report both the speedup of a single iteration, and the total improvement of running the full algorithm in parallel.

Repository organization   If you submit your work through a repository, make sure you organize your submissions in subdirectories, and that you give a clear name to all files. Object files and binaries should not be in a repository since they are dependent on hardware and things like compilers.

37.2 Warmup Exercises

We start with some simple exercises.

37.2.1 Hello world

The exercises in this section are about the routines introduced in section 2.3; for the reference information see section ??.

First of all we need to make sure that you have a working setup for parallel jobs. The example program `helloworld.c` does the following:

```
// helloworld.c
MPI_Init(&argc,&argv);
MPI_Comm_size(MPI_COMM_WORLD,&ntids);
MPI_Comm_rank(MPI_COMM_WORLD,&mytid);
printf("Hello, this is processor %d out of %d\n",mytid,ntids);
MPI_Finalize();
```

Compile this program and run it in parallel. Make sure that the processors do *not* all say that they are `processor 0 out of 1`!

37.2.2 Collectives

It is a good idea to be able to collect statistics, so before we do anything interesting, we will look at MPI collectives; section **??**.

Take a look at `time_max.cxx`. This program sleeps for a random number of seconds:

```
// time_max.cxx
wait = (int) ( 6.*rand() / (double)RAND_MAX );
tstart = MPI_Wtime();
sleep(wait);
tstop = MPI_Wtime();
jitter = tstop-tstart-wait;
```

and measures how long the sleep actually was:

```
if (mytid==0)
  sendbuf = MPI_IN_PLACE;
else sendbuf = (void*)&jitter;
MPI_Reduce(sendbuf,(void*)&jitter,1,MPI_DOUBLE,MPI_MAX,0,comm);
```

In the code, this quantity is called 'jitter', which is a term for random deviations in a system.

Exercise 37.1.   Change this program to compute the average jitter by changing the reduction operator.

Exercise 37.2. Now compute the standard deviation

$$\sigma = \sqrt{\frac{\sum_i (x_i - m)^2}{n}}$$

where m is the average value you computed in the previous exercise.

- Solve this exercise twice: once by following the reduce by a broadcast operation and once by using an `Allreduce`.
- Run your code both on a single cluster node and on multiple nodes, and inspect the TAU trace. Some MPI implementations are optimized for shared memory, so the trace on a single node may not look as expected.
- Can you see from the trace how the allreduce is implemented?

Exercise 37.3. Finally, use a gather call to collect all the values on processor zero, and print them out. Is there any process that behaves very differently from the others?

37.2.3 Linear arrays of processors

In this section you are going to write a number of variations on a very simple operation: all processors pass a data item to the processor with the next higher number.

- In the file `linear-serial.c` you will find an implementation using blocking send and receive calls.
- You will change this code to use non-blocking sends and receives; they require an `MPI_Wait` call to finalize them.
- Next, you will use `MPI_Sendrecv` to arrive at a synchronous, but deadlock-free implementation.
- Finally, you will use two different one-sided scenarios.

In the reference code `linear-serial.c`, each process defines two buffers:

```
// linear-serial.c
int my_number = mytid, other_number=-1.;
```

where `other_number` is the location where the data from the left neighbour is going to be stored.

To check the correctness of the program, there is a gather operation on processor zero:

```
int *gather_buffer=NULL;
if (mytid==0) {
  gather_buffer = (int*) malloc(ntids*sizeof(int));
  if (!gather_buffer) MPI_Abort(comm,1);
}
MPI_Gather(&other_number,1,MPI_INT,
           gather_buffer,1,MPI_INT, 0,comm);
if (mytid==0) {
  int i,error=0;
  for (i=0; i<ntids; i++)
```

```
        if (gather_buffer[i]!=i-1) {
          printf("Processor %d was incorrect: %d should be %d\n",
                 i,gather_buffer[i],i-1);
          error =1;
        }
      if (!error) printf("Success!\n");
      free(gather_buffer);
    }
```

37.2.3.1 Coding with blocking calls

Passing data to a neighbouring processor should be a very parallel operation. However, if we code this naively, with `MPI_Send` and `MPI_Recv`, we get an unexpected serial behaviour, as was explained in section 4.2.2.

```
      if (mytid<ntids-1)
        MPI_Ssend( /* data: */ &my_number,1,MPI_INT,
                   /* to: */ mytid+1, /* tag: */ 0, comm);
      if (mytid>0)
        MPI_Recv( /* data: */ &other_number,1,MPI_INT,
                   /* from: */ mytid-1, 0, comm, &status);
```

(Note that this uses an `Ssend`; see section 12.11 for the explanation why.)

Exercise 37.4.   Compile and run this code, and generate a TAU trace file. Confirm that the execution is serial. Does replacing the `Ssend` by `Send` change this?

Let's clean up the code a little.

Exercise 37.5.   First write this code more elegantly by using `MPI_PROC_NULL`.

37.2.3.2 A better blocking solution

The easiest way to prevent the serialization problem of the previous exercises is to use the `MPI_Sendrecv` call. This routine acknowledges that often a processor will have a receive call whenever there is a send. For border cases where a send or receive is unmatched you can use `MPI_PROC_NULL`.

Exercise 37.6.   Rewrite the code using `MPI_Sendrecv`. Confirm with a TAU trace that execution is no longer serial.

Note that the `Sendrecv` call itself is still blocking, but at least the ordering of its constituent send and recv are no longer ordered in time.

37.2.3.3 Non-blocking calls

The other way around the blocking behaviour is to use `Isend` and `Irecv` calls, which do not block. Of course, now you need a guarantee that these send and receive actions are concluded; in this case, use `MPI_Waitall`.

Exercise 37.7. Implement a fully parallel version by using `MPI_Isend` and `MPI_Irecv`.

37.2.3.4 One-sided communication

Another way to have non-blocking behaviour is to use one-sided communication. During a `Put` or `Get` operation, execution will only block while the data is being transferred out of or into the origin process, but it is not blocked by the target. Again, you need a guarantee that the transfer is concluded; here use `MPI_Win_fence`.

Exercise 37.8. Write two versions of the code: one using `MPI_Put` and one with `MPI_Get`. Make TAU traces.

Investigate blocking behaviour through TAU visualizations.

Exercise 37.9. If you transfer a large amount of data, and the target processor is occupied, can you see any effect on the origin? Are the fences synchronized?

37.3 Mandelbrot set

If you've never heard the name *Mandelbrot set*, you probably recognize the picture; figure 37.1 Its formal

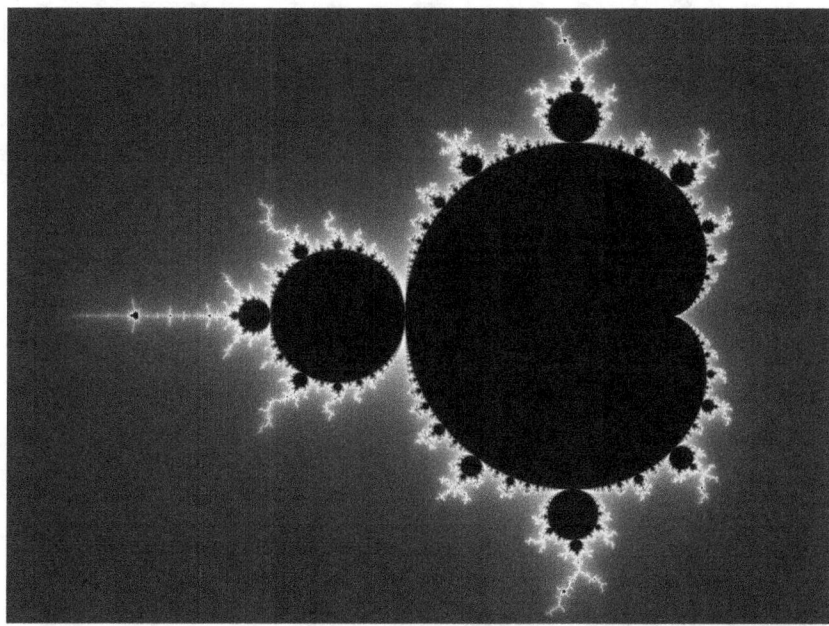

Figure 37.1: The Mandelbrot set

definition is as follows:

A point c in the complex plane is part of the Mandelbrot set if the series x_n defined by

$$\begin{cases} x_0 = 0 \\ x_{n+1} = x_n^2 + c \end{cases}$$

satisfies

$$\forall_n : |x_n| \leq 2.$$

It is easy to see that only points c in the bounding circle $|c| < 2$ qualify, but apart from that it's hard to say much without a lot more thinking. Or computing; and that's what we're going to do.

In this set of exercises you are going to take an example program `mandel_main.cxx` and extend it to use a variety of MPI programming constructs. This program has been set up as a *master-worker* model: there is one master processor (for a change this is the last processor, rather than zero) which gives out work to, and accepts results from, the worker processors. It then takes the results and constructs an image file from them.

37.3.1 Invocation

The `mandel_main` program is called as

```
mpirun -np 123 mandel_main steps 456 iters 789
```

where the `steps` parameter indicates how many steps in x, y direction there are in the image, and `iters` gives the maximum number of iterations in the `belong` test.

If you forget the parameter, you can call the program with

```
mandel_serial -h
```

and it will print out the usage information.

37.3.2   Tools

The driver part of the Mandelbrot program is simple. There is a circle object that can generate coordinates

```
// mandel.h
class circle {
 public :
   circle(int pxls,int bound,int bs);
   void next_coordinate(struct coordinate& xy);
   int is_valid_coordinate(struct coordinate xy);
   void invalid_coordinate(struct coordinate& xy);
```

and a global routine that tests whether a coordinate is in the set, at least up to an iteration bound. It returns zero if the series from the given starting point has not diverged, or the iteration number in which it diverged if it did so.

```
int belongs(struct coordinate xy,int itbound) {
double x=xy.x, y=xy.y; int it;
for (it=0; it<itbound; it++) {
  double xx,yy;
  xx = x*x - y*y + xy.x;
  yy = 2*x*y + xy.y;
  x = xx; y = yy;
  if (x*x+y*y>4.) {
    return it;
  }
}
return 0;
}
```

In the former case, the point could be in the Mandelbrot set, and we colour it black, in the latter case we give it a colour depending on the iteration number.

```
if (iteration==0)
  memset(colour,0,3*sizeof(float));
```

```
else {
  float rfloat = ((float) iteration) / workcircle->infty;
  colour[0] = rfloat;
  colour[1] = MAX((float)0,(float)(1-2*rfloat));
  colour[2] = MAX((float)0,(float)(2*(rfloat-.5)));
}
```

We use a fairly simple code for the worker processes: they execute a loop in which they wait for input, process it, return the result.

```
void queue::wait_for_work(MPI_Comm comm,circle *workcircle) {
MPI_Status status; int ntids;
MPI_Comm_size(comm,&ntids);
int stop = 0;

while (!stop) {
  struct coordinate xy;
  int res;

  MPI_Recv(&xy,1,coordinate_type,ntids-1,0, comm,&status);
  stop = !workcircle->is_valid_coordinate(xy);
  if (stop) break; //res = 0;
  else {
    res = belongs(xy,workcircle->infty);
  }
  MPI_Send(&res,1,MPI_INT,ntids-1,0, comm);
}
return;
}
```

A very simple solution using blocking sends on the master is given:

```
// mandel_serial.cxx
class serialqueue : public queue {
private :
  int free_processor;
public :
  serialqueue(MPI_Comm queue_comm,circle *workcircle)
    : queue(queue_comm,workcircle) {
    free_processor=0;
  };
  /**
      The 'addtask' routine adds a task to the queue. In this
      simple case it immediately sends the task to a worker
      and waits for the result, which is added to the image.
```

```
            This routine is only called with valid coordinates;
            the calling environment will stop the process once
            an invalid coordinate is encountered.
      */
      int addtask(struct coordinate xy) {
        MPI_Status status; int contribution, err;

        err = MPI_Send(&xy,1,coordinate_type,
          free_processor,0,comm); CHK(err);
        err = MPI_Recv(&contribution,1,MPI_INT,
          free_processor,0,comm, &status); CHK(err);

        coordinate_to_image(xy,contribution);
        total_tasks++;
        free_processor = (free_processor+1)%(ntids-1);

        return 0;
      };
```

Exercise 37.10.   Explain why this solution is very inefficient. Make a trace of its execution that bears this out.

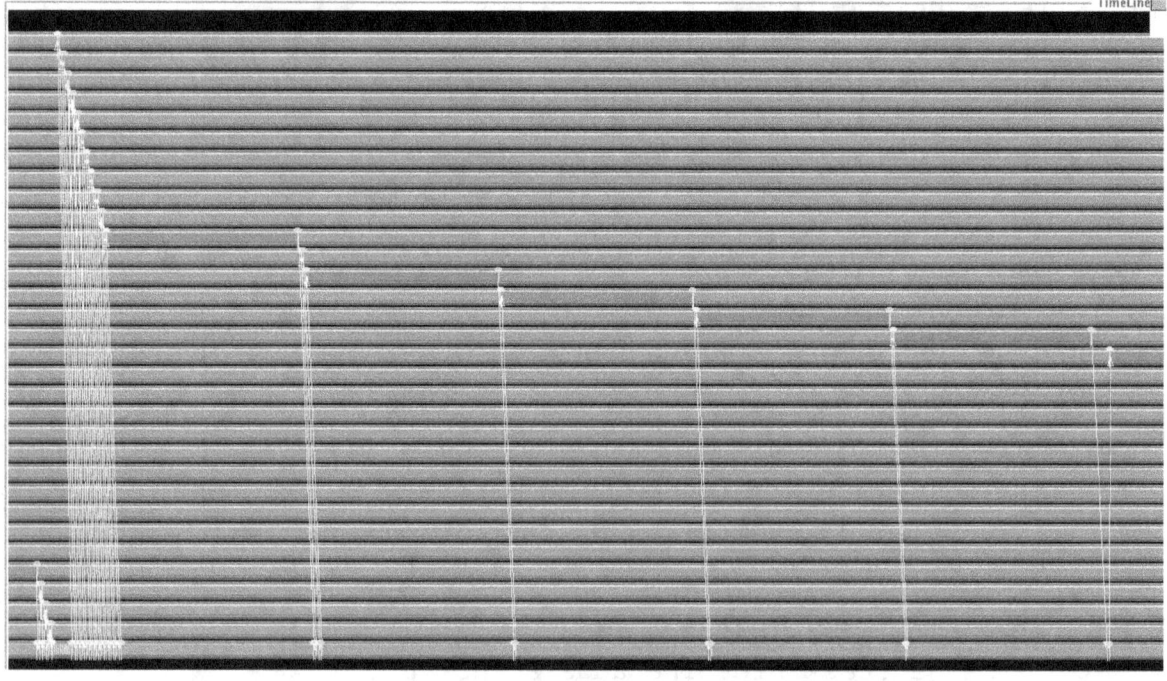

Figure 37.2: Trace of a serial Mandelbrot calculation

37.3.3 Bulk task scheduling

The previous section showed a very inefficient solution, but that was mostly intended to set up the code base. If all tasks take about the same amount of time, you can give each process a task, and then wait on them all to finish. A first way to do this is with non-blocking sends.

Exercise 37.11. Code a solution where you give a task to all worker processes using non-blocking sends and receives, and then wait for these tasks with MPI_Waitall to finish before you give a new round of data to all workers. Make a trace of the execution of this and report on the total time.
You can do this by writing a new class that inherits from queue, and that provides its own addtask method:

```
// mandel_bulk.cxx
class bulkqueue : public queue {
public :
  bulkqueue(MPI_Comm queue_comm,circle *workcircle)
    : queue(queue_comm,workcircle) {
```

You will also have to override the complete method: when the circle object indicates that all coordinates have been generated, not all workers will be busy, so you need to supply the proper MPI_Waitall call.

Figure 37.3: Trace of a bulk Mandelbrot calculation

37.3.4 Collective task scheduling

Another implementation of the bulk scheduling of the previous section would be through using collectives.

Exercise 37.12. Code a solution which uses scatter to distribute data to the worker tasks, and gather to collect the results. Is this solution more or less efficient than the previous?

37.3.5 Asynchronous task scheduling

At the start of section 37.3.3 we said that bulk scheduling mostly makes sense if all tasks take similar time to complete. In the Mandelbrot case this is clearly not the case.

Exercise 37.13. Code a fully dynamic solution that uses `MPI_Probe` or `MPI_Waitany`. Make an execution trace and report on the total running time.

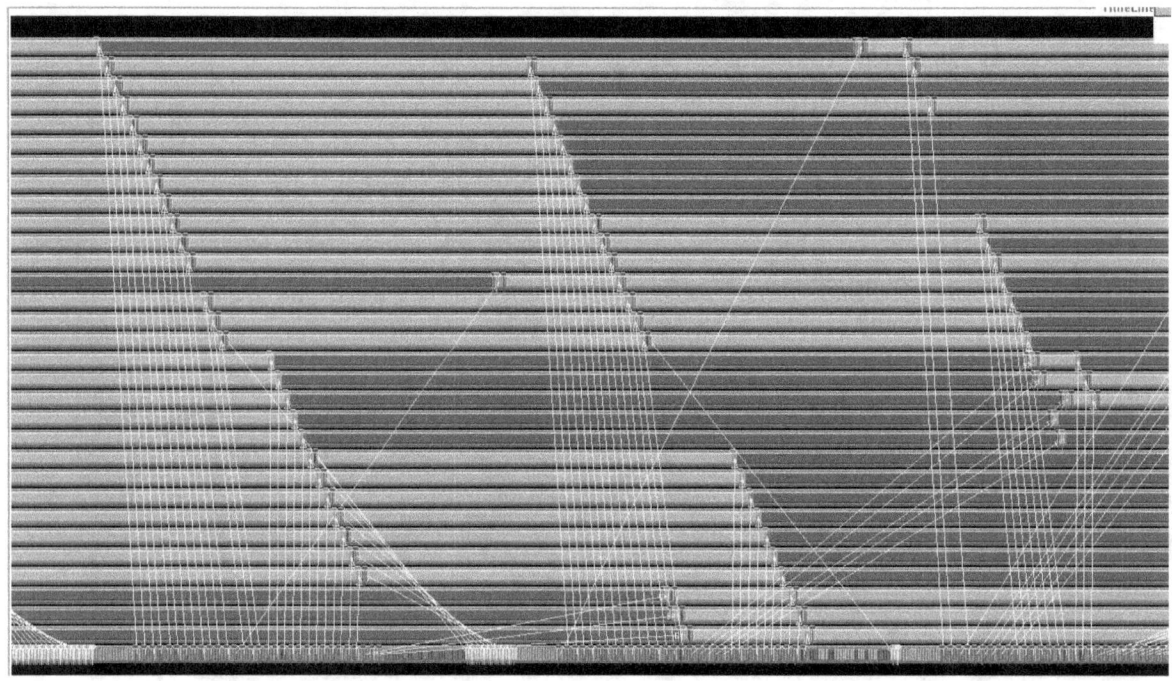

Figure 37.4: Trace of an asynchronous Mandelbrot calculation

37.3.6 One-sided solution

Let us reason about whether it is possible (or advisable) to code a one-sided solution to computing the Mandelbrot set. With active target synchronization you could have an exposure window on the host to which the worker tasks would write. To prevent conflicts you would allocate an array and have each worker write to a separate location in it. The problem here is that the workers may not be sufficiently synchronized because of the differing time for computation.

Consider then passive target synchronization. Now the worker tasks could write to the window on the master whenever they have something to report; by locking the window they prevent other tasks from interfering. After a worker writes a result, it can get new data from an array of all coordinates on the master.

It is hard to get results into the image as they become available. For this, the master would continuously have to scan the results array. Therefore, constructing the image is easiest done when all tasks are concluded.

Figure 37.5: A grid divided over processors, with the 'ghost' region indicated

37.4 Data parallel grids

In this section we will gradually build a semi-realistic example program. To get you started some pieces have already been written: as a starting point look at `code/mpi/c/grid.cxx`.

37.4.1 Description of the problem

With this example you will investigate several strategies for implementing a simple iterative method. Let's say you have a two-dimensional grid of datapoints $G = \{g_{ij} : 0 \leq i < n_i, 0 \leq j < n_j\}$ and you want to compute G' where

$$g'_{ij} = 1/4 \cdot (g_{i+1,j} + g_{i-1,j} + g_{i,j+1} + g_{i,j-1}). \tag{37.1}$$

This is easy enough to implement sequentially, but in parallel this requires some care.

Let's divide the grid G and divide it over a two-dimension grid of $p_i \times p_j$ processors. (Other strategies exist, but this one scales best; see section HPSC-6.5.) Formally, we define two sequences of points

$$0 = i_0 < \cdots < i_{p_i} < i_{p_i+1} = n_i, \quad 0 < j_0 < \cdots < j_{p_j} < i_{p_j+1} = n_j$$

and we say that processor (p, q) computes g_{ij} for

$$i_p \leq i < i_{p+1}, \quad j_q \leq j < j_{q+1}.$$

From formula (37.1) you see that the processor then needs one row of points on each side surrounding its part of the grid. A picture makes this clear; see figure 37.5. These elements surrounding the processor's own part are called the *halo* or *ghost region* of that processor.

The problem is now that the elements in the halo are stored on a different processor, so communication is needed to gather them. In the upcoming exercises you will have to use different strategies for doing so.

37.4.2 Code basics

The program needs to read the values of the grid size and the processor grid size from the commandline, as well as the number of iterations. This routine does some error checking: if the number of processors does not add up to the size of MPI_COMM_WORLD, a nonzero error code is returned.

```
ierr = parameters_from_commandline
    (argc,argv,comm,&ni,&nj,&pi,&pj,&nit);
if (ierr) return MPI_Abort(comm,1);
```

From the processor parameters we make a processor grid object:

```
processor_grid *pgrid = new processor_grid(comm,pi,pj);
```

and from the numerical parameters we make a number grid:

```
number_grid *grid = new number_grid(pgrid,ni,nj);
```

Number grids have a number of methods defined. To set the value of all the elements belonging to a processor to that processor's number:

```
grid->set_test_values();
```

To set random values:

```
grid->set_random_values();
```

If you want to visualize the whole grid, the following call gathers all values on processor zero and prints them:

```
grid->gather_and_print();
```

Next we need to look at some data structure details.

The definition of the number_grid object starts as follows:

```
class number_grid {
public:
  processor_grid *pgrid;
  double *values,*shadow;
```

where values contains the elements owned by the processor, and shadow is intended to contain the values plus the ghost region. So how does shadow receive those values? Well, the call looks like

```
grid->build_shadow();
```

and you will need to supply the implementation of that. Once you've done so, there is a routine that prints out the shadow array of each processor

```
grid->print_shadow();
```

This routine does the sequenced printing that you implemented in exercise **??**.

In the file `code/mpi/c/grid_impl.cxx` you can see several uses of the macro `INDEX`. This translates from a two-dimensional coordinate system to one-dimensional. Its main use is letting you use (i, j) coordinates for indexing the processor grid and the number grid: for processors you need the translation to the linear rank, and for the grid you need the translation to the linear array that holds the values.

A good example of the use of `INDEX` is in the `number_grid::relax` routine: this takes points from the `shadow` array and averages them into a point of the `values` array. (To understand the reason for this particular averaging, see HPSC-4.2.3 and HPSC-5.5.3.) Note how the `INDEX` macro is used to index in a `ilength` × `jlength` target array `values`, while reading from a $(ilength + 2) \times (jlength + 2)$ source array `shadow`.

```
for (i=0; i<ilength; i++) {
  for (j=0; j<jlength; j++) {
    int c=0;
    double new_value=0.;
    for (c=0; c<5; c++) {
int ioff=i+1+ioffsets[c],joff=j+1+joffsets[c];
new_value += coefficients[c] *
  shadow[ INDEX(ioff,joff,ilength+2,jlength+2) ];
    }
    values[ INDEX(i,j,ilength,jlength) ] = new_value/8.;
  }
}
```

37.5 N-body problems

N-body problems describe the motion of particles under the influence of forces such as gravity. There are many approaches to this problem, some exact, some approximate. Here we will explore a number of them.

For background reading see HPSC-10.

37.5.1 Solution methods

It is not in the scope of this course to give a systematic treatment of all methods for solving the N-body problem, whether exactly or approximately, so we will just consider a representative selection.

1. Full N^2 methods. These compute all interactions, which is the most accurate strategy, but also the most computationally demanding.
2. Cutoff-based methods. These use the basic idea of the N^2 interactions, but reduce the complexity by imposing a cutoff on the interaction distance.
3. Tree-based methods. These apply a coarsening scheme to distant interactions to lower the computational complexity.

37.5.2 Shared memory approaches

37.5.3 Distributed memory approaches

Chapter 38

Bibliography, index, and list of acronyms

38.1 Bibliography

[1] Ernie Chan, Marcel Heimlich, Avi Purkayastha, and Robert van de Geijn. Collective communication: theory, practice, and experience. *Concurrency and Computation: Practice and Experience*, 19:1749–1783, 2007.

[2] Eijkhout, Victor with Robert van de Geijn and Edmond Chow. *Introduction to High Performance Scientific Computing*. lulu.com, 2011. `http://www.tacc.utexas.edu/~eijkhout/istc/istc.html`.

[3] Brice Goglin. Managing the Topology of Heterogeneous Cluster Nodes with Hardware Locality (hwloc). In *International Conference on High Performance Computing & Simulation (HPCS 2014)*, Bologna, Italy, July 2014. IEEE.

[4] W. Gropp, E. Lusk, and A. Skjellum. *Using MPI*. The MIT Press, 1994.

[5] Torsten Hoefler, Prabhanjan Kambadur, Richard L. Graham, Galen Shipman, and Andrew Lumsdaine. A case for standard non-blocking collective operations. In *Proceedings, Euro PVM/MPI*, Paris, France, October 2007.

[6] Torsten Hoefler, Christian Siebert, and Andrew Lumsdaine. Scalable communication protocols for dynamic sparse data exchange. *SIGPLAN Not.*, 45(5):159–168, January 2010.

[7] L. V. Kale and S. Krishnan. Charm++: Parallel programming with message-driven objects. In *Parallel Programming using C++, G. V. Wilson and P. Lu, editors*, pages 175–213. MIT Press, 1996.

[8] Zhenying Liu, Barbara Chapman, Tien-Hsiung Weng, and Oscar Hernandez. Improving the performance of openmp by array privatization. In *Proceedings of the OpenMP Applications and Tools 2003 International Conference on OpenMP Shared Memory Parallel Programming*, WOMPAT'03, pages 244–259, Berlin, Heidelberg, 2003. Springer-Verlag.

[9] R. Thakur, W. Gropp, and B. Toonen. Optimizing the synchronization operations in MPI one-sided communication. *Int'l Journal of High Performance Computing Applications*, 19:119–128, 2005.

38.2   List of acronyms

AVX Advanced Vector Extensions
BSP Bulk Synchronous Parallel
CAF Co-array Fortran
CUDA Compute-Unified Device Architecture
DAG Directed Acyclic Graph
DSP Digital Signal Processing
FPU Floating Point Unit
FFT Fast Fourier Transform
FSA Finite State Automaton
GPU Graphics Processing Unit
HPC High-Performance Computing
HPF High Performance Fortran
ICV Internal Control Variable
MIC Many Integrated Cores
MIMD Multiple Instruction Multiple Data
MPI Message Passing Interface
MTA Multi-Threaded Architecture
NUMA Non-Uniform Memory Access
OS Operating System
PGAS Partitioned Global Address Space

PDE Partial Diffential Equation
PRAM Parallel Random Access Machine
RDMA Remote Direct Memory Access
RMA Remote Memory Access
SAN Storage Area Network
SaaS Software as-a Service
SFC Space-Filling Curve
SIMD Single Instruction Multiple Data
SIMT Single Instruction Multiple Thread
SM Streaming Multiprocessor
SMP Symmetric Multi Processing
SOR Successive Over-Relaxation
SP Streaming Processor
SPMD Single Program Multiple Data
SPD symmetric positive definite
SSE SIMD Streaming Extensions
TLB Translation Look-aside Buffer
UMA Uniform Memory Access
UPC Unified Parallel C
WAN Wide Area Network

38.3 Index

Bold reference: defining passage; italic reference: illustration.

ISBN 978-1-387-40028-7